Career Jungle Gym
It's not a ladder

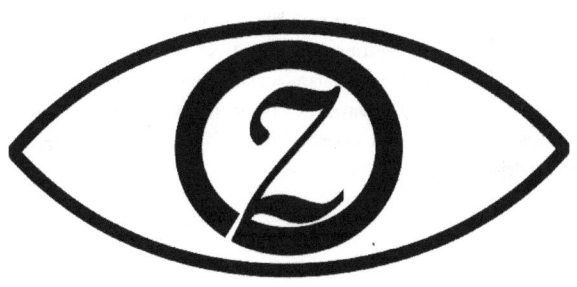

Dr. Ignatius B. Nowitall
Mental Gymnastics Coach

Copyright © 2025 W&N Edutainment Press

All rights reserved.

ISBN: 979-8-218-73707-8

For information about permission to reproduce selections from this book, send a postcard or letter to Dr. I.B. Nowitall, W&N Edutainment Press, P.O. Box 767, Williamsburg, VA 23187-0767.

I.B. Nowitall can be found on all the aethers @IBNowitall in case you want to follow him on various social media or send him gmail.

Citations and/or links to webpages have been included for convenience and to give credit for quoted material. All of the URLs were accurate at the time of writing. Neither the author nor W&N Edutainment Press is responsible for URLs that may have expired or changed since this manuscript was prepared. Having used email since the mid-80s and been an on-and-off webmaster since the mid-90's, the author is well aware of how links can go dead when some administrator thinks it's some kind of directory tree structure and not the world-wide web.

Disclaimer

It's not a career ladder, it's a jungle gym. If you think it's a ladder, you'll soon find your way blocked by those above. You'll often have to make daring leaps sideways in order to continue moving up in your career. Most people will very tightly hang on "their" rungs and complain that it's not an express escalator ride to the top. There's no right path upwards on the jungle gym, and so this book isn't some sort of recipe or template for you to follow. Instead, it's a selection of essays that you can read in any particular order, offering advice and anecdotes and observations about the modern workplace and issues faced by grown-ass, mid-career adults who are thoughtfully considering what they want to come next in their careers. Nothing in this book should be construed as legal or medical advice, because that sort of advice can only be offered by appropriately licensed professionals. Also, please be advised that Dr. I.B. Nowitall is not an actual person who you can blame if your career doesn't pan out the way you had hoped. That's on you.

CONTENTS

	Acknowledgments	i
1	WHATEVER MAKES YOU HAPPY.	1
2	WHAT IS YOUR EXIT STRATEGY?	4
3	DON'T LET THEM GASLIGHT YOU.	8
4	MID-CAREER MINUET.	12
5	HOBBY VS. SIDE-HUSTLE VS. ENTREPRENEUR.	16
6	IT'S ON THE GENERAL'S DESK.	21
7	HEY, THAT WAS MY IDEA!	24
8	SANDWICH GENERATION.	28
9	TOGETHER WE CAN DO SO MUCH.	32
10	RHYMES WITH WITCH.	36
11	SHE'S SAD ALL THE WAY TO THE BANK.	42
12	MEETING THAT SHOULD HAVE BEEN AN EMAIL.	46
13	STOP TRYING TO MAKE FETCH HAPPEN.	50
14	YOU'VE GOT TO DANCE LITTLE LIAR.	54
15	SAVING FOR RETIREMENT, OR NOT.	58
16	THE 'GENDER PAY GAP' IS A MYTH.	64
17	UPPITY WOMEN UNITE.	68
18	JUST BECAUSE YOU'RE PARANOID.	71
19	INCOMPETENT FAIL-UPWARDS BRUNCHLORDS.	76
20	SIGMUND FREUD WAS A PRETTY WEIRD GUY.	81

21	YANKEE DOODLE DANDY.	85
22	WE'RE ALL BEING PAID TO SOLVE PROBLEMS.	89
23	WHERE SO MANY PEOPLE WOULD DIE TO WORK.	93
24	YES, MISTER SIR.	97
25	UNLIMITED VACATION IS AN ACCOUNTING GIMMICK.	101
26	LEOPARD PRINT SPANX WITH THOSE WHITE PANTS.	105
27	FROM THE SKY WILL COME A GREAT KING OF TERROR.	109
28	EVERYBODY LEARN TO USE SCHEDULED SEND.	112
29	THE SKY IS FALLING.	116
30	EXTRA COLLEGE IS OPTIONAL.	120
31	OUT OF AN OVER-ABUNDANCE OF CAUTION.	124
32	THE RENT IS TOO DAMN HIGH.	128
33	DOES ANYBODY REALLY KNOW WHAT TIME IT IS?	132
34	TALENT, PREPARATION, HARD WORK AND LUCK.	135
35	YOU EXPECT ME TO PAY TO PARK?	139
36	OLD BRIDESMAID DRESSES.	143
37	FOREVER IN DEBT TO YOUR PRICELESS ADVICE.	147
38	I HAVE NOTHING TO HIDE.	154
39	YOU GO GIRL!	158
40	THE ELUSIVE GOAL OF THE CIVIL RIGHTS MOVEMENT.	166
41	WE WILL ADORE WHOEVER YOU BRING HOME.	169
42	DOCTOR, IT HURTS WHEN I DO THAT.	173
43	THE PRINCE OF CRANKS.	177

44	I WISH I HAD A MILLION DOLLARS.	181
45	HIGHLY MAGNIFIED AND THOROUGHLY EDUCATED.	185
46	IT TAKES QUITE A LONG TIME TO BUILD A LEGACY.	188
47	AGENT COOKIE BAKER REPORTING FOR DUTY.	191
48	WHY YA WALKING SO FUNNY, CARTMAN?	194
49	AREN'T YOU, LIKE, WORRIED?	197
50	LRH WHO MUST NOT BE NAMED.	201
51	REMEMBER WHEN MYSPACE WAS COOL?	204
52	TWEETS AND MEMES ARE ACTS OF WAR.	207
53	IF JOHN GALT HAD TWITTER, HE'D GET CANCELLED.	210
54	EVERYBODY GETTIN' CRUNK, CRUNK.	214
55	DR. JOHN MILLINGTON: G.O.A.T. OR GOAT?	218
56	CONFESSIO AUGUSTANA.	221
57	GET OFF MY LAWN.	226
	Denouement	232
	About the author	236

ACKNOWLEDGMENTS

A heartfelt thank you to the generations that have come before me.

1 Whatever makes you happy.

I always tell young people that one of the secrets to happiness is earning slightly more money than you need, because then you never have to worry about money and it's easy to be generous. I also tell them that it's worth it to work hard while you're young so that for most of the rest of your seventy-year working lifetime you can do work that you enjoy. The goal isn't to avoid work, the goal is to get paid embarrassingly large amounts of money to do things you'd almost do for free. What you're seeking, grasshopper, is work that pays you well and gives you joy. It's pretty rare outside of performers and professional athletes. Buddhist monks presumably achieve the desired Zen state by wanting fewer and fewer things until they already have everything they want. I'm not actually Buddhist, but I do say "Sorry Buddha." whenever I squish a bug. I am trying to have less stuff, though.

In Maslow's hierarchy of needs, the bottom two levels in the pyramid are covered by earning slightly more money than you need. These are the hedonic needs for 1) food, water, shelter, reproduction, etc. and 2) safety, employment, health, property, etc. The next three levels are the eudemonic needs, including 3) friendship, intimacy, family, sense of connection, etc. 4) respect, self-esteem, status, recognition, etc. 5) the Zen state of self-actualization where you feel that you are achieving your full potential, including creative activities. Some might add one more level to the very top of the pyramid, which is having tall, multi-talented grandbabies that you get to dote on and want to spend time with you. I'm more or less at level 5) but am starting to get a little salty about how long it's taking for 6).

Most empty nesters, whose kids are successfully adulting, take some time to take stock. They also usually redecorate a bit or even renovate a lot. Kids have come first for long enough that it's helpful to introspect about what might come next. There's going to be time to fill and there will be a new-found freedom to operate, professionally speaking. Ideally, you and your co-parent life-partner will find that you're each a solid Maslowian three or maybe even four. In most cases, one of you will have put their career aspirations in the third row of the minivan. It may have been a deliberate choice that you don't regret one bit, or it may have been a sequence of small accommodations that have now left you feeling like you're a mid-pyramid three as you respond to your cue to step out on to the stage for act three.

Let's resist the temptation to try to jump ahead to level five. If you've done your job as a parent properly, it's going to be quite a while before you have any grandbabies, so your goal is to stand happily in level four on the career jungle gym. That means: respect, self-esteem, status, recognition, etc.

Much like the third row of a minivan, the job you settled for, so that you'd be available to drive carpool and whatnot, has a very sticky floor. You've always known you're overqualified, but it worked OK for a while. Now your goal is to on-ramp. You're almost certainly going to have to make a leap to some other part of the jungle gym where people don't see you primarily as a parent to young children even if that's still a core part of your self-identity. You're probably going to want to go back to school for a bit and get some fresh certifications and perhaps even a master's degree. It's been a minute since you were in college, of course, so it will be pretty scary. Somebody else can do the housework while you're doing your homework. You've got this.

It seems like just a blink of an eye ago when you were doing all the college tours with your youngest, sweating SAT scores and AP classes and resume-building extracurriculars. You'll want to put some fraction of that mental effort into choosing what you do next, educationally speaking. Your singular goal is to use this to get a solid foothold in level four.

Let me remind you that the first characteristic of level four is R-E-S-P-E-C-T so you need to find out what that means to thee. (I assumed you were singing along, so I tried to rhyme. Sock it to 'em.) What academic credential will bring you the professional respect that you need? I hope it's not law school, because there are so many lawyers and the legal profession is ripe for disruption by AI chatbots, but take some time and make this choice thoughtfully. Just like you were (perhaps annoyingly) proud to put that "proud parent" bumper sticker on your car, think about which license plate frame you want to put on your post-carpool non-minivan where nobody is ever going to spill a Slurpee in the back seat.

The second characteristic of level four is self-esteem. Completing your chosen certificate/degree program will help with that. I suggest casually slipping into conversation, "Back when I was in graduate school…" even if that was just a few months ago. It may be only your significant other and/or kids who think that's funny, but you need to internalize how proud they are of you even if they never say that out loud. As your own kids finish up college and get on with their lives, feel free to have your mantra be, "I'm really proud of us."

Most people derive some significant portion of their level-four self-esteem from their work. Your immediate goal isn't to get the job of your dreams, your professional on-ramp will almost certainly be a sequence of jobs. Remember, it's a career jungle gym, not a ladder. In the modern world, changing jobs is normal and expected. Loyalty between employer and employee isn't a two-way street. It's a cul-de-sac. Pull in for a while. Do excellent work for fair pay. Move on to the next one, leaving the place you just left better for having been there. You and your twenty-something college-graduate children can talk about this quite a lot. It's really fun having adult-adult relationships with your kids. Everybody is just trying to figure life out as they go along, after all.

If you find that you're not respected at work, nope the hell out of there. You're never going to be happy in a job where you feel disrespected. You are an accomplished adult. You have accomplished some serious shit, so if you're surrounded by entitled little shits whose parents have snowplowed them into a position they didn't earn, leap to a different rung nearby. Let them clean up their own shit. They'll be totes jelly of your subsequent LinkedIn updates.

Status and recognition are the next two parts of level four. Status is going to be tied to professional accomplishments, which could be a job title or a corner office or a salary threshold. Different people care about different things. Don't pretend that you don't care about such things, but do try to think through which status markers actually matter to you because those are the ones that will contribute to your level-four happiness. Similarly, recognition might be formal awards and whatnot, or you might not care much about plaques on the wall and instead actually want to accumulate the private recognition of people you've helped along the way. Decide for yourself what matters to you and set yourself some goals. You didn't get to where you are in the world without the ability to achieve goals you've set for yourself.

Since kids these days wait oh-so-very-long before getting married and starting families, grandbabies are probably still a ways off. Along the way, you may find yourself reaching the elusive goal of self-actualization where you feel that you're reaching your true potential. Good for you, but don't get all down on yourself if you aren't feeling all Zen all the time. Level five is elusive. Time spent there may be transitory. That's OK. You may need to work your way around to some other face of the jungle gym for a while. Lifequakes will likely happen along the way that knock you down a rung or three, but that's just life as a grown-ass adult. Grit seems to be underappreciated by kids these days. They'll find out soon enough. Keep plugging away. You can take up pickleball when you've got some grandbabies to team up with.

2 What is your exit strategy?

There will be times when you're about to make a daring leap from one part of the jungle gym to another when it will feel more like a dismount. That's how your former co-workers will see it. They're all hanging on tightly to their rungs because they can't imagine doing what you're about to do. They may even have convinced themselves that they're on some sort of career escalator that's just about to start back up again.

How you leave things at your previous job can be important. Generally speaking, you'll want to stay on good terms with as many of your former colleagues as possible. Your future self will congratulate you for being the bigger person and biting your tongue rather than telling certain people exactly what you think of them. Their daily work-a-day drama is about to be unimportant to you. It may seem like your office would make good reality TV, but don't go there.

Framing the narrative is part of your exit strategy. You don't really owe anybody an explanation about why you make bold moves to advance your career, but you should have a coherent story to tell nevertheless. Sometimes the story arc of your career only makes obvious sense in retrospect, so don't try to explain to others your long-term goals and aspirations. You don't have to justify to others what you're about to do, except your significant other, of course.

Sometimes career moves are obvious. My great aunt Dorothy was a school teacher during the Depression. When the Tea, South Dakota school system couldn't meet payroll at Christmas, she and another teacher got a ride out to the western part of the state where they found jobs teaching in rural schools. She married a local heavy-equipment mechanic from the area mines and they lived in a one-room teacherage attached to the one-room school. When the mine closed her husband was unemployed, and the banks started discounting her paycheck because the school system had no money. They moved back to

Sioux Falls and opened a grocery store. She mostly ran the store, but also did some teaching. Her husband helped run the store, but also worked as a mechanic. An obvious reason to nope out of a job is any failure to meet payroll on time and in full.

When my daughter first got her driver's license I added her to one of my credit cards. I explained that this was for emergencies, which can include pizza and shoes on occasion. She still carries that card even though she's been out of college for several years. I've told her that I never want her to feel like she has to stay in a bad relationship or harmful situation when access to money could get her out of it. I've also encouraged her to develop her own FU savings so that she has a cushion that gives her confidence to get out of a bad job or living situation or relationship. When the time comes she can use that for her down payment on a house. One of the primary benefits of living slightly beneath your means is that you can put aside an emergency FU fund. That should be a part of your exit strategy. Along the way my daughter seems to have negotiated that her Hulu+ subscription can be charged to the credit card that I pay. I've told her that I'm cutting her off hard when she's 50, because that's about the time when I plan to retire.

I always find it quite strange when people seem to think that working is somehow optional, especially if our finances are fully co-mingled. This idea has gained popularity now that Obamacare has somewhat decoupled health insurance from having a job. Health insurance as a standard employee benefit dates mostly to WWII. Wartime price and wage controls led employers to use benefits as a way to attract employees. Wartime medical advances meant that there were more things that doctors could actually treat, and as health insurance became more common there was a financial incentive to treat more things. For most of my working lifetime, having health insurance was a part of having a job. For two decades or so I was the primary bread winner and it was my job's health insurance that covered us.

The other significant change in the employer-employee relationship is a systematic change-over from defined-benefit pensions to defined-contribution retirement plans. I'm just old enough to have had a choice, and I chose the latter. My parents had some of each. You may or may not have ever had a choice in the matter, or even know about traditional pension plans. The basic idea is that when you retire you get a monthly check that's some fraction of your final salary rate. You get that check each month until you die, maybe even with some cost-of-living adjustments. Government employees, including military, public safety and public education, are about the only holdovers. For everybody else, your employer makes a monthly contribution to a 401(k) type of stocks-and-bonds investment account, and when you retire you have that investment account to draw upon. You have to decide for yourself how much of a nest egg you think you're going to need in retirement in order to know when you should retire. You might want to do some genealogy to see if there are any super-longevity genes in your family, because the fear for everybody is outliving their money and ending up decrepit and destitute.

Defined-contribution retirement schemes can cause people to work much longer than they want to (or should) and thus cause rungs above you on the jungle gym to be blocked. It's not a good career strategy to wait for your boss to drop dead at his desk at the start of a long holiday weekend, even though it would be nice to get no emails while you're trying to rest and recharge. With traditional pensions some people hang on so long that it effectively costs them money to come to work in the morning. Part of the reason I chose a defined-contribution retirement plan thirty years ago is that I have always planned to work a long time. Mandatory retirement ages for university faculty were outlawed in 1994 and I've been saying ever since that I plan to keep my job for fifty years. I'm a full professor with lifetime tenure. Of course I could be smited at any moment and would have to agree that I deserved that, but I eat a healthy diet and exercise moderately and look both ways before I pick up a lucky penny in the crosswalk.

Since your employer's 401(k) and health insurance benefits don't tie you to that job so very tightly anymore, you have much more freedom to make a leap than people used to. Another obvious point to make is that your contact info—personal phone and email and on-line presence—aren't tied to your employer either. It used to be that a key part of getting ready to quit your job was to "take your rolodex home" so that you would maintain access to those professional contacts. Of course your office phone and company email and intranet access will terminate, perhaps a hot minute after you give your notice, but that won't really matter. Part of your exit strategy must be keeping lines of contact open with professional contacts. LinkedIn has been the best way for some years now. That's how I keep track of where long-time colleagues and former students are these days. I still have my old rolodex, but haven't bothered with it for many years. Your exit strategy should include all appropriate social media. You might even have enough followers to make it worthwhile posting a short video, although don't TikTok yourself being fired over Zoom. As I've said, framing the narrative is part of your exit strategy but you have to think enough steps ahead and not post something you'll later regret. Be diplomatic. I mean that. Even without social media, the world is very small.

When you do give two-week's notice to your boss that you're resigning to take a position elsewhere, you should expect to be sent packing right away. You might be escorted off the premises without even being allowed to stop by your now former office and box up your personal items. You should have already taken home those things, because it might take some time for the company to sort through them and decide which of them to send you. Ideally, your boss will blurt out something along the lines of, "What are we going to do without you?" in which case a key part of your exit strategy should be a sketch of a plan to move forward that you can hand to your boss. That might include the contact info or resume of someone you have already talked to who could be hired to backfill some of your key duties.

3 Don't let Them gaslight you.

I recently watched the movie Gaslight. The basic plot is that a man is secretly searching through an attic for some hidden jewels. He doesn't want the woman to know what he's up to, so he pretends to go out to work each evening. The attic door has been locked for some years, so he goes out and around to the alley where he can go up through an adjacent building and climb in through an attic window. When the woman mentions that she's been hearing noises up in the attic, the man tells her that she's imagining that. The attic has been locked for years, after all. The title of the movie refers to a once-common characteristic of houses lit by city gas. When a new gas lamp is lit somewhere in the house, the ones that are already lit will flicker and perhaps dim just a bit. When the man sneaks into the attic and lights a gas lamp there, the already lit lamps downstairs flicker and dim just a bit. When the woman cites this as evidence to reinforce having heard something up in the attic, the man tells her that she's imagining that too. The movie is a little hard to watch, because the man is systematically trying to convince the woman that she's imagining things, i.e. that she's going crazy. It's a not-uncommon form of domestic abuse.

In the workplace you may find that your co-workers, supervisors, etc. often gaslight you. Tearing others down is a deliberate strategy to get ahead yourself. Getting people to doubt themselves is a way to keep them grasping tightly to their current rung on the jungle gym, which neatly leaves the next rung above open for someone else to grab onto. In some cases, the aim of gaslighting a co-worker is to try to get them to relax their grip and climb down the jungle gym a rung or two, which conveniently leaves those rungs available for someone else to make a lateral and then an upward move. It's the workplace version of domestic abuse. It's not uncommon. Don't let this happen to you.

Gaslighting is often a gendered phenomenon. The Dunning Kruger effect, often known as confident dumb people, describes how people who know a little about something wildly overestimate their knowledge of it. True experts are often much more circumspect because they understand the limits of their own knowledge of that thing. Confident dumb people don't know enough to know how little they know. Experts often appreciate how little is known by anyone, even the world's leading experts, about things. They will even know when something is unknowable. The Dunning Kruger effect often seems to be a gendered phenomenon. It would be wrong to say that boys are stupid, but it would be equally wrong to say that men are smarter than women. Confident dumb people are mostly immune to being gaslit, though.

When you're making your way up and across the career jungle gym, there will be times when you feel like you have to fake it until you make it. This is expected in Silicon Valley, of course. Having an idea for an app or whatever and getting funding to develop it is only the first step or two towards making the app work and having it be widely adopted. Your pitch deck will have to downplay some of the difficulties to be overcome along the way. There may also be some exaggerations in your hockey-stick revenue projections. It's a silly game in many ways. Confident dumb people often excel at this game, as long as they're confident enough but not too dumb and have developers working extra hard hoping their options will vest.

Imposter syndrome is when you're uncomfortable about the whole fake it until you make it shtick. It even affects people who earned their current roost on the jungle gym through talent, preparation, hard work, and a bit of luck. Women are more likely to suffer from imposter syndrome than men. Men are also much less likely to wonder about whether these pants make their butt look big. Choosing an outfit for casual Friday is never what makes men a bit late for work. When you suffer inevitable periodic bouts of impostor syndrome you will be open to being gaslit.

First of all, you look awesome in that outfit, but you knew that already. You've had decades of being judged by other women (and perhaps your teenage daughter) about your fashion choices. You can afford to eschew fast fashion and invest in classic styles that can be worn for multiple seasons. You know how to wield an irrationally expensive handbag. Your shoe game is strong. Remind yourself of these unassailable facts when you leave the house in the morning. Men have mostly learned to never comment on such things, even if they happen to have noticed.

Second of all, you have some amazing accomplishments under your belt. You are outstanding. You know deep truths that many of your co-workers simply can't appreciate. "When we are young, we believe ourselves to be outstanding. But very few of us actually are; the rest of us are mostly delusional." Raina Raskin via @tinychalice on being a new mother and realizing there's nothing more important than being a mom to her new baby.

You don't need daily affirmations from your co-workers. The occasional thanks for assistance or verbal/written acknowledgement of a job well done are to be expected, though. Especially from whoever it is that determines your total compensation package. What you want to be watching for is co-workers (or supervisors) who seem to be always talking people down rather than talking people up. You may be more likely to notice when they're gaslighting others than when they're trying to gaslight you because they're often very practiced at this and subtle about it. They'll pick up on any chinks in your armor and that's where they'll aim their insults. Sometimes you'll see co-workers making it too easy for them by volunteering weaknesses and shortcomings, which the gaslighting fuckers will simply agree with. They'll then exploit that weakness by looking for any and all minor or imagined adjacent shortcomings. Try to avoid getting upset on behalf of your unfairly maligned co-worker(s). If you can, mentally take a step back and observe.

"Dian Fossey was an American primatologist and conservationist known for undertaking an extensive study of mountain gorilla groups from 1966 until her murder in 1985. She studied them daily in the mountain forests of Rwanda, initially encouraged to work there by paleoanthropologist Louis Leakey." Geez, Wikipedia, I didn't realize that Dian Fossey was murdered. "Although Fossey's American research assistant was convicted in absentia, there is no consensus as to who killed her."

OK, so keep an eye on your research assistant while you're studying the gorillas you work with. My point is that once you've identified their behaviors you'll be in a better position to defend yourself when they pull that shit on you. Fosse found that "mimicking their actions and making grunting sounds assured them" and that helped her to get closer and study the gorillas, but I'm not suggesting that you do that. Watch, listen, learn. You're an anthropologist, not a gorilla.

The thing that you'll find most alien is the steadfast refusal of your gorilla co-workers to admit fault. Whenever they screw up they will try to pin the blame on somebody else. They like to work on teams so that they can dump the real work onto their team members and also have somebody to deflect blame onto if the project crashes and burns. You've done innumerable group projects with monkeys like this your whole life. If you think about it for a minute, you know that the key is to make sure that none of your tasks in a group project depend on some monkey getting their task(s) done first. They have learned that people like you will do their work for them so that you can do your own work. You know they know they look good in a monkey suit and can deliver a polished presentation even if they didn't put one whit of effort into helping prepare the slide deck.

If the thing that's giving you impostor syndrome is you're uncomfortable giving a presentation you can fix that. "It's all about communication excellence, and for 100 years and counting, Toastmasters have been expressing themselves better, practicing, and evaluating in a fun club environment, shining all around the world." If Toastmasters isn't your thing, you could take an Improv class or something, but in either case the idea is to be able to project confidence that you may or may not feel at the moment. Back to the gendered nature of gaslighting for a moment. Gender-based workplace harassment is prohibited by law, and letting it go on opens the organization up to significant legal liability. Don't let those fuckers gaslight you or anyone else.

4 Mid-career Minuet.

The minuet is a slow graceful dance in triple time characterized by forward balancing, bowing, and toe pointing. The modern term for forward balancing is leaning in, so here's a Sheryl Sandberg quote, "There is no perfect fit when you're looking for the next big thing to do. You have to take opportunities and make an opportunity fit for you, rather than the other way around. The ability to learn is the most important quality a leader can have."

The clearest sign of a broken bureaucracy is that most mid-career folks feel stuck. Now that defined-benefit pensions have almost entirely been replaced by defined-contribution 401(k) plans, retirement isn't a set age. Depending on your life expectancy and how your investments are doing and your expected burn rate in retirement, you might be working rather a lot longer than you originally expected. I'm not saying you're going to work until you're 80; I'm not saying you're not going to be working until you're 80. How much longer can you keep doing the same-old, same-old, though? A healthy bureaucracy will insist that you, and everybody else, shuffle around to new positions every so often, so that talented mid-career employees develop the broad range of experience and expertise that gets them ready to be effective leaders.

Methodist clergy typically serve any particular congregation for about five years. Every year, at the Annual Conference, the bishop lets everyone know who's going to be assigned where going forward. Presumably there's some prayerful consideration involved, but the bishop decides and that's that. The clergy come back and announce to their congregations who is staying and who is going. There may be muttering from the pews and sometimes a quiet amen, but that's that. Pretty much the same thing happens in the military with chaplains, of course, but with everybody else in uniform as well. The logic is that as service members move up through the ranks, they need a broad range of experience in order to be effective leaders. Indeed, after a couple-three promotions based primarily on time in grade, the funnel begins to narrow more and more sharply: up or out. This is all the exact opposite of the way it works at the post office.

Without some sort of regular do-si-do, talented employees will come to feel stuck. They will have had their fill of the bowing and toe pointing parts of the minuet, and will go dance somewhere else. The organization will be forced to hire primarily from outside or all that will be left will be clumsy oafs with two left feet. There are innumerable variations on the Virginia Reel, of course, but the point is that there has to be a formal set of dance steps where staff are shuffled around to broaden their experience base. In one variation, when the head couple reach the foot of the set, they stop, join both hands to form an arch while the couples behind them join hands and go under the arch and up the center toward the head position. This leaves the original head couple at the foot and the second couple now becomes the head couple. Also, for you 90s kids, that song you danced to in middle school is about a girl named Macarena who cheats on her boyfriend with two friends while he's being drafted into the army. I always do half the Macarena when I get up from a deep couch sit to make sure I haven't lost my keys or whatever.

The side benefit of a regular do-si-do for staff is that malingerers can each be shunted off into a dead-end job where their damage to the organization is minimized. Pervasive ineptness can sometimes be overcome with pockets of excellence, but I think we can all agree that the goal is pervasive excellence with isolated pockets of ineptness. In very large organizations it's normal for employees to be transferred across the country or even to be expected to do tours of duty at company locations around the world. Such transfers can be highly disruptive, especially if you've got a spouse and kids or even just deep roots in a community. Your choice is to take the transfer or go find a job elsewhere.

Frank Bruni is a professor of journalism and public policy at Duke University, the author of the book The Age of Grievance[1] where he says, "We live in an era defined and overwhelmed by grievance — by too many Americans' obsession with how they've been wronged and their insistence on wallowing in ire. This anger reflects a pessimism that previous generations didn't feel. The ascent of identity politics and the influence of social media, it turned out, were better at inflaming us than uniting us. They promote a self-obsession at odds with community, civility, comity and compromise. It's a problem of humility." John Cleese of Monty Python and expert in silly walks says, "I don't think we should organize a society around the sensibilities of the most easily upset people because then you have a very neurotic society."

University of Florida President Ben Sasse, a former Republican senator

---

[1] https://www.nytimes.com/2024/04/20/opinion/students-humility-american-politics.html

from Nebraska, said[2] "What you see happening on so many campuses across the country is, instead of drawing the line at speech and action, a lot of universities bizarrely give the most attention and most voice to the smallest, angriest group. And it's just not what we're going to do here." Well before Israel's war in Gaza and the U.S. campus protests of it, "this is harmful and it makes me unsafe" was a familiar claim on college campuses. In the shadow of actual violence, the merely ideologically offensive pales, and the suggestion that even challenging ideas are inherently "unsafe" seems laughable.[3]

Meanwhile, a software company of some sort just had a round of layoffs, which isn't unusual. It's pretty normal to periodically cull the herd. Logistically and emotionally it's pretty simple if the "account executives" you're letting go for not having closed any deals this quarter are all work-from-home GenZers who haven't really developed any relationships in the company. All it takes is a sequence of carefully scripted, 15-minute Zoom calls. The only thing notable is that one of the now former junior account executives filmed herself being let go and that nine-minute video stayed on the front page of reddit for a couple of days. We couldn't see her Zoom screen because her phone was pointed at her, but we could clearly hear what she was saying and appreciate how good of a job HR was doing staying on script. Her point was that she had only been with the company for four months, with the first three being ramping up and the fourth being mostly holidays, and so she shouldn't be fired for performance issues because she worked really hard and almost closed two deals. HR didn't take the bait and argue that she actually closed zero deals, but simply acknowledged how she was feeling.

It always strikes me as odd that it's so easy for malingering employees to file grievances which then absorb months and months of time before they are resolved.[4] Nobody ever seems to have the guts to respond, "LOL, no." followed by "Everybody get back to work."

In broken organizations social media will tell employees who are about to be fired for poor performance to pre-empt the process by filing some sort of grievance. There are all sorts of accusations you can make to gum up the works and position yourself for a modest settlement down the road. Timing matters, of course, because your immediate goal is to frame any sort of change

---

2

https://www.politico.com/news/2024/05/05/ben-sasse-florida-protests-00156168

3

https://slate.com/news-and-politics/2024/05/college-protests-ucla-columbia-arrests-antisemitism.html

4

https://www.techdirt.com/2024/04/19/apparel-company-gives-perfect-response-to-lapds-nonsense-ip-threat-letter-over-fuck-the-lapd-shirt/

in your circumstances as retaliation for you having filed said grievance. Done properly, you can find that you'll even get cost-of-living pay raises instead of a 15-minute Zoom termination meeting. Anything your boss says or does can be used against them. Anytime anybody else gets any commendation or award or promotion or even just a pat on the back, that can be framed as exacerbating the hostile work environment you've been suffering under. Once you're ready to move on to some other job and wait out the honeymoon period there before pulling the grievance ripcord again, your boss will be so happy to see you go and so afraid to say anything bad about you that you'll dance out the door with a positive, if not glowing, recommendation.

Minuets and the like are formulaic. More so than even square dances, because the latter has a caller who is improvising within a structure that everybody learns sitting on hay bales waiting to be old enough to dance with the grownups. For an organization that's going to shuffle around employees in order to build experience among high performers and shunt low performers to dead ends, the primary choice is who, if anyone, calls the dance steps. My advice is to do it via a deep-learning AI system, because any actual person who makes the assignments will get grieved. Good luck filing a grievance against an LLM Chatbot which has been trained to never use language that is actionable. There isn't even an underlying algorithm to dispute in a deep neural network. Chatbots can even be trained to feign the sort of empathy that HR professionals learn to mimic when they tell you during your 15-minute Zoom that they understand how you are feeling before clicking over to the next 15-minute Zoom.

When I was getting ready to graduate from college and be commissioned into the Air Force, I filled out a form which we called "the dream sheet" wherein I told the Air Force which job I might like them to assign me to. I had looked up potential assignments via microfilm and wrote something sensible. Some cadets took this very seriously, with flow charts with if/then options and such. A friend of mine, then at Cornell, wrote simply, "Please send me someplace warm." He spent the first two years of his career in Hawaii, and luckily bought a condo just as the real estate market rocketed up. After two years he cleared $90k profit, and so he could deal with the weather for his next assignment in New England. I decided not to make a career in the Air Force because the job that I lucked into for my first assignment was considered a career-broadening job. Had I stayed on active duty, the chances of ever using my then newly-minted engineering PhD for teaching and research was miniscule. I know because I asked the chief-of-staff about exactly that.

5 Hobby vs. Side-Hustle vs. Entrepreneur.

After all those years of driving carpool you're obviously qualified to drive Uber. Not Uber Black, of course, because there are some stains in the back of the minivan that are never coming out. Some of your hobbies and/or volunteer activities might make even better side hustles, though. But now that you're done with carpool, PTA, etc. you should think seriously about various entrepreneurial opportunities. It's far too late to turn your scrapbooking hobby into the next social media empire, but it's perfectly fine to imagine how you would have done Instagram or Pinterest differently. You should also think about what you'd want to do next if you had actually come up with that next wildly popular social media concept and then sold it to Zuckerberg for a bazillion dollars. It's the standard mental exercise of what would you do with the rest of your life if money was no object. You've certainly done this when you've bought the occasional Powerball tickets.

Hobbies cost you money. Post-tax money. It's often money well spent, of course, because you're doing something you enjoy. Hobbies you don't enjoy are called chores. Woodworking or gardening are excellent hobbies. Plumbing not so much. I regret having learned to do plumbing. I don't regret having learned to tune pianos. These days I prefer to hire both plumbers and piano tuners when needed. I should tune that harpsichord I built when I was in high school, though.

Turning your hobby into a business has rather significant tax advantages. In simple terms, associated expenses are now tax deductible. Paying someone to do your taxes is tax deductible. Suddenly you are an entrepreneur. Actually, the title you're looking for is Founder. Starting a company turns out to be simple enough that I'll explain it in just a couple of paragraphs. You can also go to the bookstore and buy a workbook with downloadable forms that will walk you through the process. What I'm going to describe is a Limited Liability Company (LLC) rather than traditional Corporations (Inc) of various types. There are two flavors of LLCs, which are taxed differently.

One flavor of LLC is taxed as a corporation, and so the financial aspects are probably what you imagine a company to be. That's probably not what you're after at this point. The second flavor of LLC is called "pass-through" and it's taxed as a part of your personal return. That means that any profit the pass-through LLC earns is a part of your personal income, whether you draw salary from it or not. It also means that any loss from the pass-through LLC reduces your personal income and hence your tax obligation. The key point is that the LLC is taxed in whatever tax bracket you happen to be in. It's probably not going to matter all that much at first, but if the LLC starts making too much money, you can always convert to another corporate form.

Whatever you spend on a hobby comes out of money you have left over after you have paid your taxes. Whatever you spend on a pass-through LLC business comes out of money you have before you calculate how much you have to pay in taxes. I'm trying to say this in enough different ways that you'll fully appreciate this point. The pass-through LLC is expected to lose money, at least for a while. Indeed, if there's some danger of it turning a profit you're going to want to get some custom swag made up in order to prevent that. Paying a graphic artist to come up with a logo for swag is a legit business expense. Giving out custom T-shirts or hats or pens or water bottles is advertising. Have at it.

Step Zero is to come up with a name for your company and a simple paragraph that describes what it does. Of course it doesn't do anything yet, but think through what you "contemplate" it doing. Don't try to write a fancy mission statement, just put down a few descriptive sentences. Don't overthink this.

What you do need to think through is whether you're going to have a co-Founder for your LLC. The formal term is Member. You and any other members are the co-owners of the business, and pass-through LLCs tie the members' personal finances together in ways that can be awkward. You're probably better off being the sole Member for now.

Step one is to get yourself an email for the company, as well as a physical mailing address and phone number. You can set up a company gmail for free and while you're at it snag relevant social media handles. Your existing cell number can be used for company business and your residential mailing address works fine since you have that home-office already anyway where you did PTA and/or scrapbooking and maybe even compiled the neighborhood and/or church newsletters. You may want to get a post-office box or a mailbox with a street address via one of the commercial services. Hold off for just a minute on refurbishing your home office, because you want those to be business expenses.

Step two is to find the web page for your State Corporation Commission (SSC) or something similar. Two things which seem scary at this stage, but aren't, are the Articles of Organization and the Operating Agreement. The first of these gets generated automatically when you go to the SCC web page and click through things. The second is something you, or better yet a lawyer you pay, writes. I do recommend having a professional write the Operating Agreement for you. It will cost a few hundred dollars, but it's obviously a business expense. It's new and a little scary for you; it's routine for them. There may be specific wording related to particular state laws that matter, but mostly it gets you into the habit of seeking out professional guidance for company matters. This isn't just a hobby anymore.

Step three is to get a company Entity Identification Number (EIN) with the IRS. This is like the social security number for your new LLC. Once you've got your Articles of Organization, Operating Agreement and EIN, you're ready to get a company checking account. You're almost certainly going to have to prime the pump by making the first deposit from whatever money you've put aside to start your new company. The CPA you pay to do your taxes henceforth can give you guidance on how these "loans" you're making to the company affect things. In the early stages it might matter whether the minimum account balance to avoid fees is $2k or $5k. You'll quite like having a fancy company checkbook, though. You probably don't need a company credit card right away. The company can reimburse you by check for things you buy with your personal credit card(s).

Step four is to get yourself some business cards and some basic advertising materials. You've got a company name already, but now you're going to need logos. You probably did this part already, but now you need to begin to establish your trademark. You don't need to go through the expensive process of registering a trademark, you simply need to reduce it to practice and begin using it. What I do is to get custom postcards printed up at one of the many on-line sites which have my custom logo on one side and the company name & address on the other. Sending out postcards and handing out business cards is advertising. Using your new logo(s) in social media and even your gmail signature block also count as reducing to practice for the purpose of beginning to establish your mark(s).

Step five is to get your company a business license. This is a local process, i.e. city or county. There will be a nominal fee each year, of course. There will also be some business property taxes, but your CPA will help you deal with depreciation and such. Your city or town or county may even have local government resources that help you to navigate this bureaucracy. It will be a little daunting at first, but you'll figure it out. Step five-and-a-half is to get your company insurance. One of the key advantages of having an LLC is that should the worst happen and the company gets sued, you don't lose your house. The worst case scenario is that the LLC goes bust. Small business insurance protects what you're building if something unfortunate, but not catastrophic, happens. It's well worth the modest expense.

Your company is now real. Go ahead and update your LinkedIn profile. You may want to secure a domain name and put up a webpage. What else you do next depends on what you contemplated back in Step Zero. Maybe your next step is setting up an Etsy store. Maybe it's to publish books via Kindle Direct Publishing (Amazon). Maybe you'll be entering into contracts with the local school division to provide in-service training for teachers. The point is that you can now do business.

You may or may not want to do business with the Federal government. If you do contemplate that, you're going to have to register with the Small Business Administration at SBA.gov where the webpage purports to be a treasure trove of helpful information. What might catch your eye first is the section, "Learn how to find and win small business government contracts." The regulations associated with government contracting are substantial and may or may not make any logical sense to you, but there's essentially infinite money involved so it may be worth going to Login.gov and getting into the system. Be sure to block out a few hours....

Once you get your business license, you have to hang it prominently in your home office. You can also have a little frame there where you put the first dollar your company earns. Be sure to leave space on the wall for the required state and federal labor law poster. Several cities & counties have additional labor law posting requirements due to differences in local labor laws such as minimum wage. These posters are mandatory and required to be posted by all businesses with employees in addition to the State and Federal labor law poster. The sites that sell these annually-updated laminated posters recommend posting labor law posters in Spanish and English if more than 10% of your workplace speaks Spanish as a primary language. In the following states, it is a mandatory requirement: AZ, CA, FL, GA, NM, NY, and TX. I have such a poster in my home office even though I technically don't have any employees and I don't speak Spanish. You probably won't either right away.

It's a big step for any business to hire an employee. Starting with contractors or gig workers could be a smart step to help your business grow without taking on the responsibility of full-time employees, but you really do need to know the legal distinctions to avoid misclassifying employees. Contractors are self-employed workers selling you a service, while employees work for the benefit of and under the rule of your business. A 1099-NEC is an IRS form that states how much you paid a non-employee as an independent contractor. It lists compensations you paid a worker in a given tax year, plus any federal, state and local taxes withheld (likely none). You'll file a 1099 for workers who you paid at least $600 for services but didn't withhold taxes under an employment arrangement.

So now your hobby is an official side-hustle and you're an entrepreneur. All of the above can (and should) be done without quitting your day job, but at some point you presumably contemplate quitting your day job. I didn't list it as one of the steps on the previous pages, but I hope you had enough sense to check your current employee handbook or employment contract about what outside activities are discouraged or prohibited. If you're under some sort of non-compete agreement that will have limitations to it, of course, or it wouldn't be enforceable. Go back and double check. In the early stages, your position is that you've merely formalized your long-standing hobby as an LLC for the obvious tax benefits. The company had no issue with you winning the elementary school charity baking contest every year, so now you're just making your baked goods more widely available. Maybe your company wants to have you provide some for the company picnic. You might even give them the friends-and-family rate. Quitting your day job to pursue the entrepreneurial lifestyle full time is a big leap off the jungle gym. It takes some suspension of disbelief because it always takes rather a lot longer than every entrepreneur imagines. I'm not saying don't make that leap, though.

6 It's on the general's desk.

I've never had a secretary to type for me and answer my phone and keep my appointments. My wife has always kept our joint social calendar, though, and I make some effort to be a good sport about wearing what I'm told and being her purse boy and/or arm candy. I've even learned to pick up on when she's too hangry to be able to pick out a restaurant.

I happen to believe that purse boy is an honorable occupation. I fully understand that the function of an irrationally expensive handbag is to signal power and influence, and that if you're powerful and influential enough you rate a strapping young man to carry your purse and control access to you and your busy schedule. It's not really a gendered thing, though, except that the staffer who totes the man-purse of powerful male executives is called a body man rather than a man-purse boy. In the military the gender-nonspecific job nomenclature is "general's aide."

Being a general's aide seems like it would be good for your career. You're in on all the important goings-on and then can presumably depend on the general's influence to help you advance through the ranks. The problem is that if you're too good at what you do the general will want to hang on to you until the last moment. By that I mean when the general finally retires, you'll spend moving day at the general's house making sure everything gets packed properly, despite the fact that there are movers at your own house that very same day because you're not retiring and so you've got orders to your next duty station. Also, if the general has to hit the head before a speech and gets his zipper stuck, you will be there in the men's room on your knees trying to fix his zipper hoping that nobody walks in. If you can't fix the general's zipper promptly, you'll be giving the general your pants to wear. Those are both actual stories from a former aide, BTW.

A general's aide does have a very specific source of immense power, though. The aide arranges the folders on the general's desk each morning, and the general attacks each of them in that order. There are always more folders than the general can get to in any given day, so if you piss off the general's aide the folder containing your issue will always get reshuffled to the bottom of the pile in the morning. When you inquire about the status of your issue the general's aide will respond sincerely that, "It's on the general's desk. The general will get to it in turn."

The bureaucratic jujitsu I've just described is called negative timing. Once you get to a level of seniority where you can decide which of the many and various requests for your time and attention you respond to in which order, negative timing is your friend. The first place most people learn to do this is with emails, because in modern office environments it's the 24/7-365 flood of emails that seems to make healthy work-life balance impossible. Triaging 5am email vomit can make you sick. Checking your inbox first thing to see what flame wars erupted while you slept fitfully for a few hours is not healthy. Can't anyone else figure out how to use schedule send?

Out of pure self-preservation you've almost certainly developed certain habits whereby you quickly decide which emails to ignore and which to save for later and which to respond to as soon as you've had some coffee or checked that file at the office or whatever. You need to think through a more complete strategy on this. The asynchronous nature of email is what you're going to exploit. Many problems will sort themselves out if you simply wait a hot minute before responding.

"All our circuits are busy at the moment. Please wait for the next available representative." How long you make people wait before responding is the key issue, because it's a single-service queue that goes through you and like everyone else you have finite bandwidth. It wouldn't make sense for you to use up a chunk of that bandwidth by estimating for everyone how long it might take for you to respond to each of their requests. Of course everybody wants to jump the queue and have you deal with their issue right now, but that's simply not the way the world works. Urgent requests have to come from pretty high up in the organization to make it sensible for you to drop everything and attend to them.

The key philosophy behind negative timing is that you're not actually telling people no, at least not at first. There will always be people who want their issue(s) dealt with immediately, particularly when they've neglected to do something until the last possible second like they always seem to do. The only way such people can ever be expected to change is by having to deal with the consequences of not planning ahead. Don't let them jump the queue; reshuffle them to the back of the queue. You can even use an email feature like schedule send to time your response and minimize your own cognitive load. You're being responsive to their issue, just not on the timeline they wanted. You have finite bandwidth, after all.

The best thing about gmail isn't the excellent spam filters, it's that gmail sorts bacon for me. While my social tab seems to be empty for some reason, things are well sorted into primary, promotions, updates, etc. It learns which things are important to me and there are various ways that I can file or star threads so I'm less likely to lose track of something somebody thinks is oh-so-very important. I can also click the button to "mark all as read" within a tab, which is surprisingly satisfying. Equally satisfying is to declare with a simple click someone's annoying emails to be spam. Later you can feign surprise at finding all their requests in your spam folder.

The bane of your existence might not be your overflowing inbox, though. The calendar system your organization uses may allow just about anyone to see vacancies in your schedule and unilaterally fill them. Often what they want is to come and hector you about why you haven't responded to their email yet. You probably have no choice about giving calendar access to your peers and superiors, of course, but don't be an idiot about letting just anybody grab chunks of your time. In addition to arranging files on the general's desk, the other primary function of the general's aide is to control the general's calendar. If you wanted to get in to see the general, you'd have to go through the general's aide in order to make an appointment. You couldn't just show up and expect to get time with the general. That's not how it works.

Professors have always handled this issue via office hours, telling their classes that they will be available at certain days/times for questions, concerns, etc. The problem with office hours is that students almost never show up for them, except for the occasional students who think getting in some face time with their professor will translate into a better grade or letter of recommendation or whatever. Usually, you sit there for that hour waiting and nobody shows up. Students prefer to email after you've gone to bed expecting their question to be answered by the time they wake up.

Rather than office hours, get in the habit of walking around in ways that are predictable. You can swing past the workstations of your staff and chat about the weather or sports (but not politics or religion) and since they know kind of when to expect you they can be ready to ask about their email request. You can assure them that you got their message and will get to it as soon as your finite bandwidth allows, which will be somewhat reassuring to them. Rather than getting sucked into a conversation about their issue then and there, your exit is something along the lines of needing to get back at it. One final pro tip: don't let your staff see you reading email on your phone while at work. Deal with email only from your office computer where you have all the ancillary materials you'll need to respond promptly.

7 Hey, that was my idea!

You may have done many group projects in college. You may even have thought that everybody in college was smarter than you, except for the three dumbasses in your group project. I hope you weren't the one who did all the others' work because you were all being graded together. If so, I hope you've found some way to break out of that pattern. Go read Ayn Rand's Atlas Shrugged if you sometimes fantasize about ghosting on a group project and letting those dumbasses get the grades they deserve.

When I was a young assistant professor I had a new project funded, which was done in partnership with a small company. It was a two-phase project where Phase I was a relatively small amount of money for six months, but if that went well then Phase II was a great deal of funding lasting two years. The scientist I was working with at the small company took a job at Johnson & Johnson just as the project was about to start, so I was left to work with people I didn't know at his old company. They didn't know how to do his part of the project, so I had to do that part of the work in order for Phase I to be a success and we could advance to Phase II. Young assistant professors have to have a certain number of successful projects before they can get tenure.

Since my collaborators didn't contribute much of anything to Phase I, they didn't realize that when I wrote the Phase II workplan I made sure that none of my tasks depended on them. If any did, I knew that they would slow-walk things hoping I'd do their work this time too. My first two tasks were relatively straightforward, but the third task was very difficult and would take most of the available budget in my subcontract. They were the prime contractor to the Navy, which is how these things are structured. When my subcontract showed up, they had only sent $144k instead of $201k. WTF? They had in mind that I would apply for some matching funds to get more money for the overall project and this would be an underhanded way for us to split that extra funding. I said: No. Fucking. Way. Send all the money you promised and then we'll talk. For $144k I'll only do my first two tasks.

They also tried to stiff one of my former colleagues who had agreed to consult for the project. His other funding had dried up while we were waiting for the Phase II project to start and he went off to teach high school. Some extra consulting income would have mattered a lot to him. I made sure my graduate students never answered any of the questions they were supposed to pay him to address.

My two easy tasks went really well and we didn't do the third task because we had been shorted on the subcontract. I happened to have lunch at a conference with the Navy program officer, who I knew quite well because one of my other PhD students worked in his branch. I explained to him about the $144k vs. $201k and whatnot. A short time later the Navy happened to send a letter to the small company explaining that their technology was no longer of interest to the Navy and they were withholding the last $50k of funding. I was presenting our results at another conference a few months later and my colleague from the small company was on the project just after me. I knew he wouldn't have any actual results to show and would fill up his talk with background material and simulations. I had lots of actual results to show, but used some of my slides to do a comprehensive background and then talked a bit about how useless simulations were compared to the actual data I was showing. The Navy put out a new solicitation for continuation of the work and I responded to it with a joint proposal with a different company. It was funded and we continued the work for several more years.

Remember a few years ago when some guy in China ate a bat and the whole world had to shut down for a year? Some people thought it might have been a fuckup in the Wuhan Institute of Virology instead, but they were pretty much all shouted down. Lab leak vs. zoonotic transmission became a political issue. Dr. Fauci may have fibbed a bit about what NIH was or wasn't funding.

I find it ironic that Chairman Mao insisted on being treated by doctors who had trained at the best medical schools in Europe. He realized that there weren't enough medical doctors to go around, so he required that everybody pretend that there was a thing called Traditional Chinese Medicine. And that it was just as good as Western medicine. Oh, and in China, they were going to integrate the two schools of thought which would be better. It was a stop-gap measure intended to save face while enough actual doctors were trained, but even newly-invented traditions die out slowly. We all thought Viagra would save the endangered white rhino population. Alas.

This was a serious problem for the rest of the world in 2019, because TCM doesn't acknowledge viral causes of disease. Hence, when some laboratory technician fucked up and loosed a novel coronavirus on the world, people who didn't believe in viruses didn't feel the need to take sensible measures. Even with a significant head start on the rest of the world, the Chinese vaccines didn't work much at all. Mixing in some acupuncture didn't help, because that's merely a theatrical placebo.

We now have the smoking gun which proves the lab leak hypothesis.[5] In March 2018 a team of American and Chinese virologists applied to the Pentagon's Defense Advanced Research Projects Agency, seeking a $14 million grant to manipulate viruses related to SARS-CoV-1, the bat virus that caused a minor epidemic in 2002. Their goal was to identify bat viruses in Asia with the highest potential for jumping to people and to immunize bats so they wouldn't infect soldiers in the region. The proposal for Project DEFUSE specified that the viruses' infectivity would be enhanced by inserting into them a genetic element known as a furin cleavage site. Emily Kopp of U.S. Right to Know obtained the proposal documents through a Freedom of Information Act request from the Interior Department, having noticed that a researcher at the U.S. Geological Survey was a member of the DEFUSE team.

The authors of the proposal were a team led by Peter Daszak of the EcoHealth Alliance[6] of New York, Shi Zhengli of the Wuhan Institute of Virology and Ralph Baric of the University of North Carolina. Although Mr. Baric is the leading expert on the technology, Mr. Daszak intended for much or most of the work to be done in Ms. Shi's laboratory, despite giving a different impression to DARPA. He writes in the recently discovered documents that "I do want to stress the US side of this proposal so that DARPA are comfortable with our team. Once we get the funds, we can then allocate who does what exact work, and I believe that a lot of these assays can be done in Wuhan."

After DARPA turned down the DEFUSE proposal in February 2019, the researchers in Wuhan got Chinese government funding and went ahead by themselves. Viruses made according to the DEFUSE protocol would thus have been available by the time COVID-19 broke out, sometime between August and November 2019. This would account for the otherwise unexplained timing of the pandemic along with its place of origin.

That all tracks with the way science actually works. Some proposals are funded. Some aren't. Sometimes people are on the team to do some minor part of the work because they have the necessary facilities, but aren't leading the project. Everybody on the team has a full copy of the proposal and sometimes one of them goes rogue. This is stealing, BTW. Using somebody else's ideas to go get funding without them is a grave sin. Doing work you're unqualified to do and kicking off a global pandemic that kills millions of

---

[5] Next bit from:

https://www.wsj.com/articles/where-did-covid-come-from-new-evidence-lab-leak-hypothesis-78be1c39

[6]

https://hotair.com/david-strom/2024/05/15/breaking-ecohealth-alliance-grants-suspended-and-formal-debarment-procedures-begun-n3788438 people is a mortal sin.

I have a rule of never collaborating with people who are desperate for funding. They will steal your clever idea and pretend they were the ones who came up with it. I tell my students that their primary career goal is to get to the stage where they are in charge of their own projects. The measure of success isn't how much funding they have, but it's being able to choose who to work with and who to avoid as collaborators. Science is a never-ending search for reliable partners who will do what they say they're going to do and share credit where credit is due.

I wonder if after four years the Wuhan Institute of Virology dumbasses thought they had gotten away with it. The CCP has long since destroyed all the evidence, including scientists who seemed inclined to talk about COVID origins. But the proposal planning documents of a US government scientist are FOIA-able. That gun was still smoking four years after some guy ate a bat and we all were locked down for more than a year.

8 Sandwich generation.

Kids these days seem to be taking forever to settle down and start raising a family. I'm starting to think that we should bring back arranged marriages. I fully admit to having no understanding for on-line dating. My wife and I are high school sweethearts and have been together since 24 October 1981. We eloped on Leap Year Day, 1988. In 2024 we celebrated our 9th anniversary, and by celebrated I mean we went out for lunch. Yes, I did just have to count up on my hands which anniversary that was. We've been empty nesters for more than a decade, so in principle we could go on some lavish anniversary trip. We did something of that sort for our 8th anniversary, having the kids both fly into Boston for the weekend and revisiting all our old haunts from the 80s. It was the start of the COVID-19 pandemic and there was, in fact, a super-spreader event happening at another hotel in town, but when I expressed worry about going to our favorite Dim Sum place I was told in no uncertain terms to STFU. Knowing when to STFU may be the secret to a happy marriage.

Sandwich generation is when you've got both child-care and elder-care responsibilities at the same time. I think it should be called panini generation because the heat and pressure involved is intense and you can't really avoid ending up with grill marks. Something has to give, and that usually means somebody's career aspirations have to take a back seat. I assume you're nodding along with me. You may even be sharing a sofa right now with someone who thinks paninis are delicious but can't ever seem to figure out how to plug the panini press in and/or wipe it down with a damp paper towel after using it.

The hard part about being in the panini generation is aging parents. Sooner or later they're going to need your help. They may stubbornly resist asking for help, or they may feel reluctant to ask you for help because they know how much you've already got on your plate and they don't want to be a burden. If their needing help looks like it's going to be later rather than sooner, I have a strategy for making the transition seamless. This strategy depends on proximity, so whichever children live closest to mom and dad are on the hook. My parents retired here when the kids were little and bought a house in our same neighborhood. When the kids were growing up, Granny and Gramps were always there. It's so unusual for children and grandparents to be so close these days, and for them to be so very close. So, whenever my parents would go off for a little golfing trip or an Elderhostel or whatever, my daughter and I would stop by their house and do a little project. We had been watching the home renovation show, While You Were Out. One time we got new hand towels and a rug for the hall bath. Another time we installed an under counter water filter in the kitchen. One time we put a "tree face" on the tree next to the driveway. It was always fun to see how long it took for them to notice what we had done. They got used to the idea of us doing things and so it was natural when they asked for help with something.

Proximity also makes it easy to keep track of how they're doing. I developed a routine where I would stop by just to chat at two or three specific times each week. Knowing that I'd be stopping by and that I was happy to be able to help, it was easy for them to have a chore or two queued up for me. Sometimes my father would ask my opinion about some change to investments. Once my parents wanted to ask me about a list of seemingly minor symptoms that might have indicated Parkinson's, which it was. The day before my father died from a bowel blockage due to Parkinson's, he asked me to help my mother with managing investments because that had been his hobby. Because I had been routinely helping more and more as they needed more and more routine help, it was natural for me to step up when my mother had to transition to managing the household affairs on her own.

During the COVID-19 lockdowns my mother was still living in the big house on the cul-de-sac, with a little Yorkie for company, but otherwise alone and isolated. I made a point of stopping by once or twice or thrice daily, including first thing on my morning jog. At the height of the lockdowns I was sometimes the only in-person person she saw for a couple-three days. I was never all that afraid of getting COVID myself, but I was quite fearful of passing it on to her. After the worst of COVID she decided to sell the house and move to a nearby "continuum care" country-club style oldster neighborhood. She had thought it through and made the decision to downsize herself, but she and I did the sorting through of things together. It took us ten weeks of steady effort to decide what to keep and what to toss and what to donate and what would go to my house. I was a little surprised when the ten-year-old Yorkie got re-homed to me in the process. Dogs are allowed at the new place and she has a lovely garden apartment, but she's too busy to have a dog now. My wife may have googled Yorkie life expectancy (13) but the two of them are becoming buddies. I'm the dog's favorite, although that might have something to do with feeding her soft food from a can three times a day and taking her on walks to smell all the smelly smells and contribute to the neighborhood smell story.

My mother could have stayed in her house if she had wanted to, but the cul-de-sac is quiet and empty most of the time and she has to get in the car to go anywhere and she has never really liked driving. She also has been over having to cook for some years. Her new apartment is in the main building of the neighborhood, where there are lots of activities, and all of her meals are provided in either the formal dining room or the casual grill or by takeout if she prefers. She has a compact, but complete kitchen for when she feels like just making something herself. She thinks it's kind of silly that so many people there choose to live in detached houses because they have to get in the car to drive over to her building for meals. She still has her little red car for whenever she needs it, but she and I typically do an "errand hang" to the grocery store when she needs things because carrying the groceries in from the car is getting hard for her.

Continuum care community means that residents start out in good health and are living independently in either a house or an apartment. Meals are provided as a part of the monthly fee as are health club/spa access, concerts, parties, daytrips, etc. Rides to medical appointments or even across the complex to play bridge are included. Utilities, tech support, maintenance, gardening, bi-weekly cleaning, etc. are also all included in the standard fee. Two weeks of post-hospitalization rehab (per year) are also included because sooner or later everybody needs that. There is also an assisted living complex for when that's needed. When you think of a nursing home that's more or less what you're thinking, although the term of art seems to be "skilled nursing" and I think there's an upcharge for that. There is also a memory care unit and I know there's a significant upcharge for that, but the point of a continuum care community is that when and if such services are needed they are there within that same community.

But what does this lavish oldster lifestyle cost? Excellent question. You and your parents/in-laws may or may not have the sort of relationships where you can talk openly about finances. My parents are of that slice of a generation where they have quite generous pensions, and they both invested sensibly and deliberately lived beneath their means. They paid for most of my children's college with money invested after my mother's father died and she sold off his rental properties. The family strategy exploited the loophole that grandparents' 529 college savings plans are invisible to the FAFSA when expected family contribution is calculated. My kids graduated college with no debt and I didn't have to take out a second mortgage for their tuition.

Enough stalling, here's what it costs. There is a six-figure, up-front, cash buy-in that keeps the riff raff out. That, along with really invasive financial and medical disclosures combined with a cognitive test that some applicants have to study for, selects for a healthy, affluent population. Most people sell their house in order to write that $200k check. After that, the monthly all-inclusive fee is in the $4k range. Some places don't have the six-figure, up-front, cash buy-in, but then the monthly fee might be in the $8k range instead. Everybody's fear is outliving their savings, so putting up the up-front money and then having the monthly cost be less eases that fear somewhat. My mother's monthly income from investments, pensions, etc. is enough more than $4k that she doesn't have to worry about outliving her money. I also don't have to worry about having to backstop that monthly, which is nice. My mother's biggest worry these days seems to be whether she is going to "eat up" all of her food allowance. It's a bit of a game for everybody there to get that down as close to zero as possible and sometimes we're asked to come and help eat extra when the end of the quarter is approaching. There is usually a panini on the menu.

9 "Alone we can do so little; together we can do so much." – Helen Keller.

I may have just googled group project quotes. You're likely at the stage in your career where an ongoing source of frustration is how to get the group of young people who work for you to all work together. Some days it may feel a bit like the blind leading the blind. I hope your young charges aren't also deaf and dumb. You'll need to have them take out their airpods while at work and actually use words to communicate with their co-workers. They likely picked up lots of bad habits doing group projects in college. I hope you're not the sort who picked up the slack for the slackers on your group projects because everybody was getting the same grade on it.

When I scope out a new project I have two primary goals. The first goal is making sure that the parts my graduate students are working on for their dissertations are sufficiently challenging, but can be accomplished in a reasonable amount of time. They want to graduate and I want them to graduate. They can't graduate until they've "made a novel contribution" to the field, so they have to be breaking some new ground, scientifically.

My secondary goal is to make sure that they aren't going to be sitting around waiting for somebody else on the team to do something that feeds into their work. That's much trickier because our group projects typically involve collaborators at other organizations, some academic, some government labs and some small or large research companies. It's common for more senior collaborators to try to manipulate other people's graduate students into doing their work for them, typically by dragging their feet on something those students need to get their own tasks accomplished hoping the students will get impatient and just do those tasks too. By now I'm very practiced at writing project plans to prevent this.

Your first challenge is to get an accurate sense of what your team members are best at, and what you think they each could realistically accomplish if everything went well and they were working full out. You'll have to extrapolate a bit from smaller scale project tasks before you can do this on more important efforts. You'll have to talk to them about what things they wish they were better at or thought they could be really good at if they had a chance to show it. Don't forget to talk to them about what things they're kind of (or a lot) afraid to try. Some of those things might turn out to be their jam. There are probably opportunities for training to build skills.

Your second challenge is to assign your team members to teams in various combinations and see who works well together. You'll have to mix and match to get a sense of who brings necessary flexibility. There will be combinations that simply don't go together. There may be someone who poisons every team interaction. There may be someone who makes everybody else better. You need a mechanism to get confidential feedback on the internal dynamics of teams. It doesn't have to be complicated, but it must be confidential in the sense that people can give you their honest opinions without having to say words in an open meeting. You need to know who said what, though.

Here's a scheme that my department uses for faculty members to rate each other once a year. We evaluate each other's contributions in teaching, research and governance. We each provide a listing of accomplishments and a 100-word summary paragraph, and then our colleagues grade us on a 6-6-3 scale for the three categories. In order to encourage collegiality, our merit review score includes a self-score which is the mean of what we gave everyone else. That prevents someone from giving everybody else low scores so theirs would be higher by comparison. Mean tends to amplify the effects of outliers, so giving someone you hate a zero will drive your self-score down. So then, the department chair takes the median of the set of scores (including self-scores) for each faculty member and those are the numbers that go forward to the Deans. Median downplays the effects of outliers because it's the middle number in a list of ordered numbers. I sometimes confuse median and mode. Some people confuse median and mean. It's mathy.

You'll have to decide on what categories of things you want people to rate each other on in group project dynamics. That's the third challenge. The key point is that you'll use this information to provide feedback to both the group and each member of your team. When I was department chair I always gave everybody both their ratings and the histogram of scores for the department so they could see where they stood. The histogram was unlabeled, but they could usually figure out who was who because they had just rated everybody else. My colleagues all rated me, BTW, even though I was the chair. I think that's just fair because we were all peers. You almost certainly don't want your young charges to rate you. You're their coach, not a player.

Part of the reason his time at the Lakers doesn't seem to be working out quite the way LeBron James wanted, is that he's trying to be coach/manager in addition to star player. Bill Russell won nine NBA championships for the Boston Celtics as a player before winning two more as a player-coach. Baseball hall-of-famers Ty Cobb and Frank Robinson played while coaching. NFL great Tom Landry played defensive back while defensive coordinator for the NY Giants. Coaches see the big picture. They call the plays. They decide which players play and who rides the bench. They deal with upper management after a loss. They don't throw and catch and run and block and pitch and hit. They used to, and might remember fondly those simpler days. Now they delegate.

Delegating is hard. You'll have to practice delegating and then not micromanaging. Sometimes you'll do your best coaching and will still have to own a loss. You're playing a long game here. Especially with rookies, it will take longer for you to explain to them what to do than to just do it yourself. You'll find yourself weighing that balance pretty often, but they're never going to learn unless you put them into the game. Coach them, but don't grab the ball out of their hands every time you think they might fumble it. Bench them if you have to, but that means you sub someone else in their spot. You're not Bill Russell.

One of the joys of my job is to watch students master new skills and gain the confidence that comes from solving hard problems. I sometimes view my job as a coach or personal trainer, but a better analogy might be helping a child learn to ride a bike. They start out with training wheels on the sidewalk. Eventually they can ride around the cul-de-sac and then comes the day when the training wheels come off. They're excited, but scared. You make sure the chin strap is tight on their helmet. You hold the bike seat to steady them as they get going and then run along next to them, hoping to catch them before they wobble over or dent a parked car. In short order they get steady enough that you can launch them and then sit down on the curb while they pedal around the cul de sac until it's time for dinner. A minute later they can do it all, all by themselves and you're relegated to reminding them to tighten their chin strap. Then off they go on a four-block solo ride to Granny's house, with you watching out for traffic from the corner: "Call us as soon as you get there."

Actually, my son was quite reluctant to learn how to ride a bike for some reason. All of his friends learned before him, and my wife said to him, "You're embarrassing us. We're going over to Granny and Gramps." My father was a former PE teacher, referee and coach of every youth sport known to man. His driveway had just enough of a slope to it, that he simply nudged my son and down the driveway he went. He was zooming around their cul de sac minutes later.

Figuring out what roles the members of your team should play is what you do as their coach. They'll be proud that you're proud of them. Make sure they know the plays you're going to call and what their position is. Check that they've got their chin straps tight. Maybe give them a pep talk before they take the field. Then it's game on. Go team!

10 Rhymes with Witch.

There are an amazing number of strong, independent women in my children's family tree. I've recently compiled a ten-generation genealogy, complete with stories and pictures, for my eventual grandbabies. "It's going to be a while, Dad." say both of my children for the hundredth time. "Would you like me to tell you about the DC dating scene?" says my late-twenties daughter. I typically respond with something about maybe it's time to think about bringing back arranged marriages because I still have no grandbabies and I'm starting to get a little salty about it.

One of my mother's ancestors is the original Southern Belle, who is said to have introduced the concept of flirting to Virginia. She came to Jamestowne Colony in 1610 as a ten-year-old girl. She was about 23 and pregnant when she was widowed for the second time, leaving her with a five-year-old from her first marriage and a two-year-old from her second. She was also responsible for a thousand-acre plantation, newly crowded with refugees from the 1622 massacre that had wiped out fully a third of the English colonists. Subsequent disease had killed at least that many, including her second husband. The creeper minister who had buried her husband three days before proposed marriage and then heard yes when she said no I'm not marrying anybody until after I have this child and besides I'd rather marry William Farrar who's helping me run the plantation. The minister sued her for breach of promise and may have said some unchristian things about her that rhyme with witch. It was the first breach of promise suit in America. Cicely eventually prevailed and was able to marry, but it was a bit of a scandal because they were cohabitating. Farrar was one of those refugees from the massacre, but he wasn't after Cicely for her money as evidenced by his own 2,000-acre headright for bringing over 40 indentured servants. There's still a law on the books making it illegal to be engaged to two different men at the same time.

Cicely's granddaughter, Mary Browne, shows up in the court records as someone who "possessed a peppery temper as well as a spirit for the administration of worldly affairs." Mary Browne, the daughter of John Browne and Temperance (Bailey) Browne, was born about 1631 in Charles Cittie, where her mother Temperance Bailey Browne held property. Temperance had inherited 300 acres and Ancient Planter status when she was three and her father died. Mary was very young when her mother remarried and Richard Cocke became her step-father. This sort of thing was common. Men died and women were left to carry on. It was easiest to remarry right away because widows with large property holdings were somehow suspect.

Mary Browne married Joseph Tanner, who was quite wealthy, but he of course died leaving her with property and four kids to take care of. Her second husband, Gilbert Platt, was born in England about 1620 and came to Henrico, Virginia "in an exceedingly humble capacity" as an indentured servant in 1635, "and concerning the first forty years of his stay in the Colony no record exists." He struck it rich when he married the well-to-do widow of Joseph Tanner and became the legal guardian of her four children during their immaturity. It is said that this marriage "seems to have been productive of considerable disturbance" with several episodes recorded for all posterity in the records of the Henrico court. Platt was quite evidently only a tenant by courtesy on the Tanner property and "appears always to have been a person of small means" which would have been a problem for him in those days because it was unusual for women to own property on their own, and he probably wanted to mansplain obvious things to them. But keep in mind it's the maternal lineage we're talking about here. Mary's mother was Temperance Bailey and so that means her grandmother was Cicely Reynolds Bailey Jordan Farrar who came to Jamestown at age 10 in 1610, and was besties with Pocahontas. Temperance's honorary grandfather was the Chief of the Powhatan Confederation, and she grew up on some of the largest plantations of that day which, from the perspective of English colonists, had been carved out of the primeval wilderness. Hence, Mary would have heard lots of stories about the women of the family carrying the load as a never-ending sequence of husbands, fathers and step-fathers made brief appearances on the scene before dying young and leaving orphans to be cared for. It is said that Joseph Tanner, the younger, seems to have taken after his mother.

A deposition by John Seawood describes an episode that began with Joseph Tanner splitting kindling wood somewhere near the door of the house. Joseph was apparently upset that his stepfather had "slandered him at a certain Mrs. Farrar's" presumably his grandmother, Cicely. The tossing of lightwood sticks by the step-son at the step-father one evening as the latter was returning home elicited a complaint from Mr. Platt to his wife relative to the treatment he had received from Master Joseph Tanner. "And for his pains he was promptly called a liar, since, as Mrs. Platt explained, she had reared her children so carefully that in common reason none of them would ever have been guilty of such outrageous conduct." And then the storm broke as young Joseph, going into the room, accused Mr. Platt of having slandered him on certain occasion and recourse was had to a "tobacco stick" whose blow seems to have knocked out Mr. Platt. Again the courts were sought and the upshot of the matter was that Gilbert Platt no longer troubled his wife and her children with his presence…. He may have used a word which rhymes with witch. Gilbert Platt spent the last years of his life in very ill health, with his son-in-law, Edward Osborne of Henrico. He died in the spring of 1692. In his will he bequeathed to his wife, Mary Platt, "precisely one shilling." Mary was rich AF, BTW.

Puritans weren't welcome in Virginia. They were considered nonconformists disloyal to the Church of England. Puritan William Durand wrote that God has condemned "many poore soules in Virginia" for their ungodly conduct, "if ever the lord had cause to consume the citys of Sodom and Gomorrah he might justly and more severely execute his wrath upon Virginia." Governor Berkeley and the Virginia General Assembly agreed to legislation ordering "all nonconformists… be compelled to depart the colony with all convenience." In May 1644, one month after the second Indian massacre, a boatload of Puritan refugees fleeing Virginia arrived at Boston. However, the Puritans were not fleeing the Indians. They were driven out by the intolerance of Church of England loyalists.

In New England, as in Virginia, the peoples who had been living there for uncounted generations made repeated attempts to repel the invaders. It ultimately didn't work, of course, because the colonists had guns, germs and steel on their side. They also had an inexhaustible supply of eager reinforcements. America is the land of opportunity, after all. Except that it was already full when Columbus sailed the ocean blue in 1492.

In September 1691 two Indian raids hit the town of Dunstable, Massachusetts. While the residents of nearby Billerica paid little attention to the squabbles in Salem Village, they cringed at news of English colonists to the north being killed or sold into captivity. The raids on Dunstable were too close to home, so the Billerica town militia began to fervently guard its borders. One of the ingredients necessary for mass hysteria to overtake a community is fear of outsiders.

As usually happens, the first accusations of witchcraft in Salem implicated misfits and social outcasts, but then the second wave were against the opposing factions or often based on grudges, jealousy or revenge. The third wave of accusations targeted anyone who opposed the witch trials and dared speak out about them. In Salem, John Procter called the "afflicted" girls frauds and liars, so he was the first man to be accused. The Salem mass hysteria soon spread to two dozen other nearby towns including Billerica.

Many citizens of Billerica, which was about 20 miles west of Salem Village, found themselves accused. Sarah Carrier accused her uncle and aunt, Roger and Mary Allen Toothaker. John Durrant and Rebecca Chamberlain, both of Billerica, were thrown into prison on accusations of witchcraft. On 16 June 1692 Roger Toothaker of Billerica died in prison after a few weeks of incarceration. In Aug. 1692 Indians stunned the village of Billerica raiding two households killing two mothers and four children. On 26 Sep 1692 Rebecca Chamberlain, age 67, wife of William and mother of 13 children, died in Cambridge Prison. Apparently the conditions there weren't great.

Mary Toothaker had confessed to practicing witchcraft in 1692 and said she had been a witch for about two years. Mary told the court that she was terrified of Indians and had fought with them in her nightmares. Therefore, she said she had yielded to the Devil, and signed the Devil's book. For this, the Devil promised her that the Indians would not hurt her. Mary admitted attending a witches meeting where others were present including the leader, Reverend George Burroughs. She thereby implicated Burroughs and at least five others. The court set her free for her testimony. The Indians killed Mary Toothaker in the raid of August 1695, and took her youngest daughter captive.

In 1667 John Tillerson charged the wife of Matthew Griswold of Lyme, CT with being a witch and induced others to suspect her of witchcraft, for which Matthew caused him to be arrested and arraigned before the court. John stated the cause of his suspicions and jealousies. The court decided that she was not a witch and that he had no cause to be jealous of her; that he had greatly sinned in harboring such jealousy against so good a neighbor who had done him so many favors. To clear Mrs. Griswold of all suspicion of the offense the Court ordered that its opinion should be published by the constables at Saybrook and Lyme at some public meeting. To recompense her for the wrong, and because Tillerson was poor, he was ordered to pay 7 shillings for the express warrant and 5 shillings for the constable.

The first Mudge in America was Jarvis. Born in England, he came to this country about 1638. He was in Boston that year, in Hartford in 1640, in Wethersfield in 1644, and removed to Pequot, now New London, in 1649, where he died in the early part of 1653. He had married the widow Rebecca (Steele) Elsen, of Wethersfield, in 1649. She is assumed to be the child of George Steele, a founder of Hartford, because he included Micah Mudge and his brother Moses in his will and they are assumed to be his grandchildren. That she married at least 3 men is undisputed. Jarvis Mudge was the second husband and died as her first husband did after a few years of marriage. Her third husband was Nathaniel Greensmith.

Rebecca was accused of being a "lewd, ignorant and considerably aged woman" by her minister. I think that's minister-speak for a word that rhymes with witch. This triple combination of personal qualities soon elicited the criticism and animosity of the community, and Rebecca fell under the most fatal of all suspicions of that day, that of being possessed by the evil one. After

Nathaniel sued his wife's accuser for slander, Nathaniel himself was accused of witchcraft. Both Greensmiths were indicted in 1662 as having familiarity with Satan, found guilty and hung on Gallows Hill in Hartford. They were exonerated by a joint resolution of the Connecticut legislature in 2023, following nearly two decades of lobbying by the CT Witch Trial Exoneration Project.

Witch hunts still happen hundreds of years later, of course. During the Cold War people were looking everywhere for Communists, and people who were accused of communist sympathies were professionally black listed. When my daughter was in her first job after college it was the start of the #MeToo movement, which had the noble goal of purging society of creepers who used their professional power and standing to sexually abuse young co-workers. In practice, men could be accused without any evidence and the mantra "believe all women" led some women to make accusations simply to destroy the careers of people they didn't like or settle unrelated scores. It scared everybody, and caused good and upright family men to pull back from mentoring women in the workplace because someone might accuse them of doing something untoward and their careers would be over. The middle-aged family men who were supposed to be mentoring my daughter were too afraid to take her along on meetings with potential clients so she could make the connections necessary to succeed at selling Mutual of Omaha group-benefits packages to insurance brokers in Houston, Texas. We were all quite happy when she moved back to DC after a little more than a year.

Back to Hartford, the colony, not the insurance company. The origins of the Hartford[7] outbreak are obscure, but the trouble apparently began in the spring of 1662, with the possession and subsequent death of eight-year-old Elizabeth Kelly, who in her fits had cried out on her neighbor, Goodwife Ayres. Convinced that their child had died from bewitchment, her parents demanded an investigation. Ayres was probably the first person named, but two other people, Mary and Andrew Sanford, were brought up for examination not long after. Ayres's husband, who would eventually come under suspicion himself, accused Rebecca Greensmith, who in turn supported accusations against her own husband and implicated several other Hartford residents. And so it went. The community was caught in the grip of a witchcraft fear that would eventually result in accusations against at least thirteen people, and that would take the lives of four of them.

At some point during the early period of the Hartford outbreak, Ann Cole, who minister Increase Mather described as a "person of real Piety and Integrity," succumbed to possession. She was, he said, "taken with very strange fits, wherein her Tongue was improved by a Daemon to express things

---

[7] I'm quoting from: THE WITCHCRAFT DELUSION IN COLONIAL CONNECTICUT (1899 by John M. Taylor)

which she herself knew nothing of." In the presence of several local ministers, the demons said "that such and such persons... (who were then named and who included some of the people already accused) were consulting how they might carry on mischievous designs against her and several others..." Statements made by Cole that a number of witches were at work in the area seem to have intensified the community's desire to ferret them out. One of the women mentioned by Cole was her next-door neighbor, Rebecca Greensmith, who was already in prison awaiting trial. When Greensmith was confronted by the ministers and magistrates, she fully admitted her "familiarity with the Devil." She denied making "an express Covenant with him," but said that "at Christmas they would have a merry Meeting" and seal their bargain. She also acknowledged that "the Devil had frequently the carnal knowledge of her Body," and that she and the other accused witches "had Meetings at a place not far from her House." Nathaniel Greensmith steadfastly denied his own guilt, but according to Mather, Ann Cole was "restored to health" after the executions and that would have been taken at proof.

I happen to have resting bitch face. Generally speaking I'm not mad at you, this is just my face. I never liked wearing a mask during the pandemic because my glasses would always fog up. I also didn't like that it was very hard to read other people's facial expressions. Lecturing to a class of socially-distanced, masked-up students meant I couldn't tell whether they were laughing at my jokes so I simply assumed they thought most of what I mumbled through my own mask was hilarious. Once people stopped wearing masks I was often quite surprised by their appearance, but stopped myself from saying out loud, "That's what your face looks like!?!" Some people still wear masks and I'm OK with that. I assume that they have spinach in their teeth, or they didn't get around to shaving and/or putting on makeup this morning. They might also have health concerns that are none of my damn business. Or they might just have resting bitch face and are sick of people telling them they should smile more.

11 SHE'S SAD ALL THE WAY TO THE BANK.

A chief scientist at NASA who thinks there are aliens was once trying to tell a group of aerospace engineering department chairs that their universities should somehow want to teach NASA personnel for free. I am still famous for saying, "It takes money to buy whiskey and everybody's thirsty. If you don't have any money there's a water fountain in the hallway." In case you've ever wondered about the economics of going to graduate school in engineering, students get paid a modest salary, which they can kind of live on, plus health insurance and tuition. First-year students typically earn their keep as teaching assistants, but then they usually transition to research assistants where the money to support them comes from research grants their professors have gotten from places like NASA. It would be absurd for the aerospace engineering schools to teach NASA personnel for free when the way it actually works is NASA pays the professors and their students to do research that is of interest to NASA. Sometimes we'll take on students who are NASA employees, but that's just a way to have former students who are then in a position to fund the next generation of students in our labs.

Engineering professors at top universities are paid quite well, but it's not just about the money. Most could make more money doing something else, but have chosen to do what they do because they enjoy it. One of the ways I know I'm in the right line of work is that I get a little bummed at the end of each semester, but then very excited when the next one is about to start. I don't really like it when the students are gone and the campus is too quiet. I've been a tenured full professor for quite a long time already, and since there's no promotion beyond full professor it wouldn't be wrong to say that I'm in a dead-end job with no hopes of promotion. Also, mandatory retirement ages for faculty were outlawed in 1994 so I get to keep doing what I love for perhaps two more decades. I understand how unusual this is.

You may someday find yourself in the more common, but still rare, position of getting paid quite a lot of money but not really liking what you do. My mother started out as a first-grade teacher and ended up a college professor. She took early retirement rather than moving up from department chair to dean because she knew that she would not enjoy being a dean. That sort of job is mostly personnel and budget mixed up together in angry ways all day long. With grandbabies to dote on and investments/pensions to easily sustain a comfortable retirement, my parents both pulled the early-retirement rip cord. My wife is currently an associate dean, which she thought was going to be the job of her dreams but turns out to be no fun at all. She gets paid so well that I don't technically have to work anymore, but I like what I do quite a lot. I'm a little afraid to make too much extra money from consulting and research grants, because my wife might do the obvious math and conclude that I get paid so well that she technically doesn't have to work anymore. Meanwhile, she's figuratively sad all the way to the bank on the first and sixteenth of each month.

I've always said that part of being a grown-up with people who depend on you is that you face the prospect of getting up every day and going to a job you hate. My millennial son thinks this is bullshit. Of course, he is unmarried and has neither kids nor pets. He still thinks that his work should both give him joy and pay him enough to live comfortably. Since he's an actor, I suppose that he is always just one lucky break away from affluence, ease and acclaim. That whole industry shut down hard for a couple-three years recently, though. There was a pandemic and then some strikes and some issues related to compensating talent for streaming residuals.

Some might argue that money can't buy you happiness, but I'd then have to say that lack of money can make you and the people who depend on you unhappy in various ways. My point is merely that you may find yourself in the situation where you're paid quite a lot of money but not happy about it. People who are unhappy because they have no money are pretty unlikely to want to hear you complain about getting paid a lot of money but being so very unhappy. They might suggest that you giving them some of your extra money will make both of you happy.

Some other rung on the career jungle gym might make you much happier. You might even be in a position to make a lateral move that will make you happier on the way to the bank. There's two bits of math you should do, along with a fair amount of introspection. The first bit of math has to do with where your retirement nest egg stands and where you want it to be when you actually do pull the retirement rip cord. The second bit of math has to do with your current standard of living which is enabled by your present salary. You may conclude that stepping up contributions to your investments will get you to retirement a bit sooner than you thought, and you can suck it up for a while at your current place on the jungle gym. You may conclude that you could get along just fine with a bit less each month (for a while) and you'd be a lot happier. If you think about it, you might find that you've been spending quite a lot of money on travel/recreation as a way to get a break from the job stressors that are making you hate your so-called life. You probably worked very hard to get to your current job title and salary, and think you'd somehow be failing yourself to take a deliberate reduction in salary and responsibility. What if you had a lot less job stress and a little less money? Your Instagram story could be much more interesting if you volunteered locally rather than traveled to exotic locales.

The best field trip I ever went on was to a coal mine in Big Stone Gap, VA. It was high coal so we could walk around comfortably, and my engineer and I were there to get a reality check for a new coal-mine safety concept we were proposing. We went with my colleague, who was the State Geologist, along with the mine superintendent and two state mine inspectors. We got to see everything up close and talk with the miners in order to better ensure our system would make their jobs better (and safer). We figured out how to make it work, but never implemented it because there was no money for improving coal mine safety. The operators refused to admit that they needed any safety improvements, and the government zeroed out all coal mine research money because they didn't want to have any coal mines anymore. My colleague had thought he could do lots of good things as State Geologist, but that job turned out to be no fun at all, so he demoted himself back to his prior position at the University where he worked happily until he retired.

If you could retire early, what would you do? Golf? Pickleball? Travel? Volunteer? Maybe you could do some of those things now, at least on the weekends and holidays. There aren't all that many jobs that get a sabbatical every seven years. It's probably too late for you to go back to school and become an aerospace engineering professor, but maybe tutoring or coaching or something would be fun for you. Dads with kids get to skip out of the office early on game nights. Think of all the times they expected you to cover for them. Your turn, even if you skipped out early sometimes back in the day for your kids' games or concerts or recitals. I'm just spitballing here because I have no idea what extracurricular activities you should consider. I just know that you need some socialization to get away from job stress for a least a little while each week.

Part of what's driving you nuts about your job is that you get emails/txts all the damn time. I don't carry a smartphone and my coworkers don't know my cell phone number, so they have to email me and wait for me to step into my home office and check my desktop computer there. They can't bother me when I'm on the sofa downstairs watching a game on Sunday or out on my back deck reading a book. You may not be able to get away with that, but I'd suggest taking up water sports where you can't have your phone with you. Sailing is lovely and your phone has to stay dry in the car. Swimming is excellent exercise. There might even be a rowing club nearby that isn't too hardcore. Pick something.

12 I SURVIVED YET ANOTHER MEETING THAT SHOULD HAVE BEEN AN EMAIL.

For some people meetings are their work. For other people meetings distract them from getting their work done. At least with Zoom you can get some work done on your other screen(s) while the useless meeting drones on. I hate meetings. I generally loathe Zoom, although there are a few things for which it works pretty well. It has to be a small group of people with well-prescribed roles and regular talking turns. I'm fine with a tight Zoom meeting if it substitutes for me having to travel to some other city for a meeting that probably could have been an email. I'm also fine if people want to travel here from some other city for an in-person meeting in the little conference room just down the hall from my office. As they're headed back to the airport I always tell them that I hope their flight is boring.

I've been a faculty member for more than three decades, so I know from meetings. When I was department chair, I called only a couple of meetings a semester because most issues could be resolved better by walking around and asking my colleagues what they thought about them. I got some exercise and their time wasn't wasted. On the rare occasions when we had to record a formal vote, we'd have a department meeting and do our business. Since I had the responsibility of attending many meetings around campus on behalf of my department, I would compile a page of "gossip and speculation" about what was going on around campus and print that on the backside of the meeting agenda. Those are all filed with the official meeting agendas/minutes in case anybody wants to go back and see how good I was doing at predicting our future.

I don't go to the monthly college-wide faculty meetings unless I have to. I'll sometimes open up the Zoom link and listen while I'm doing something else, but I find that I can skim the minutes of the meeting very quickly and know exactly what's going on. I can even hear my colleagues talking in their own voices while I read the minutes, and then pat myself on the back for not having wasted 90-minutes attending. Generally speaking, the only useful part of such meetings is the update that the Dean gives about the issues she's been dealing with. She also puts out an email every Friday evening with that info, so there's that.

In 1944 the predecessor to the CIA put out a "Simple Sabotage Field Manual" which was distributed to workers in foreign countries who were interested in quietly upending efforts against the allies during World War II. In the guide, they hypothesized that productivity and morale could be subverted with "purposeful" stupidity. If you're bored during some meeting, you can find the whole thing online. Look up from it periodically to see if any of your co-workers seem to be purposefully stupid. Here are some bits of that advice about sabotaging meetings:

- Insist on doing everything through "channels." Never permit short-cuts to be taken in order to expedite decisions.
- Make "speeches." Talk as frequently as possible and at great length. Illustrate your "points" by long anecdotes and accounts of personal experiences.
- When possible, refer all matters to committees, for "further study and consideration." Attempt to make the committee as large as possible — never less than five.
- Bring up irrelevant issues as frequently as possible.
- Haggle over precise wordings of communications, minutes, resolutions.
- Refer back to matters decided upon at the last meeting and attempt to re-open the question of the advisability of that decision.
- Advocate "caution." Be "reasonable" and urge your fellow-conferees to be "reasonable" and avoid haste which might result in embarrassments or difficulties later on.

I've just concluded that all my colleagues are engaging in purposeful stupidity. Here's the all-time winner, though. We were having a department meeting to discuss the outcome of the PhD Qualifying Exams. It's a three-day, closed-book test that graduate students take after they've finished their coursework and are about to embark on a multi-year research project leading to a doctoral dissertation. The questions can cover anything the students have learned, or should have learned, or might-could have learned. It takes about ten weeks of more-or-less full-time preparation on their part. They have to pass their Quals in order to advance to research graduate status. If they don't pass, they can try one more time in six months, but if they don't pass then they are sent down with a master's degree (and shame).

The advisor's opinion on pass/fail is most important, because their judgement about whether their own graduate student is ready for research is most relevant. In a borderline case we will simply ask them what they want to happen and then we'll all vote for that. My colleague, who had previously been a Senate staffer and knew all about *Robert's Rules of Order* and pre-meeting meetings and whipping the votes and whatnot, had a borderline case with whom we were discussing. We asked what he wanted to do and he told us. We called the question and we all voted that way. He then said, "I didn't vote. I want the record to state that I abstained." Abstaining after the fact is a running joke now.

Part of the reason I hate Zoom is that it's too easy to have too many meetings. Scheduling a Zoom meeting for something that could get answered by a quick phone call is especially annoying for me. I'm in my office all the time. Calling me on my desk phone doesn't disrupt my workflow. Neither does poking your head in my office and asking your question. Ricocheting emails around the aether is a good way to get me to ignore you, though. Email is asynchronous, so I might not read yours until later. I might even wait to see if you resolve your issue on your own without me spending my bandwidth on it.

I also loathe MS Teams. I use it now and then because some of my sponsors prefer that. Each time I do an MS Teams meeting it deletes the Zoom shortcut from my desktop, which amuses me somehow. I've been making a deliberate effort to forget how to set up a Zoom meeting, which isn't a problem because everybody else knows how to do that. I put my foot down with the Calls feature on Teams, though. The unhelpful dumbasses in our IT department convinced somebody that it would be a good idea to yank all the desk phones and have everybody use Calls instead. They forgot to order headsets. Since IT never came to set my computer up for that, when someone calls my former landline, their vmail gets converted to text and emailed to my spam folder where I find it eventually. That seems to be working fine.

I think it's safe to say that Zoom et al. are here to stay and you must master them. Here's some basic guidance for you:

- Make sure your camera is at or just above your eye level. Put your laptop on a pile of old phone books if you have to. Maybe get a good USB camera/light.
- Put the presenter window close to your camera, so when you're looking at the presenter it looks to them like you're looking at them. Ignore your phone.
- Learn to share your screen: you want Reading View in PowerPoint and need a cursor that people can see if you're using it as a

pointer. No shadow puppets.
- If you have to use notes, print them out and hold them because we can see your eyes moving if you're reading them from your laptop.
- Pay close attention to room lighting and how a light ring reflects in eyeglasses.
- Use a thoughtful physical background with interesting things for others to look at when they're bored. Have things that could be conversational openers.

One more bit of advice that goes for both in-person and Zoom meetings. Show up a bit early to the meeting and chit chat with the boss. There always seems to be somebody who's late for the meeting or having trouble connecting or whatever. Use that otherwise dead time to get some face time. Your thoughtful background might catch the eye and stick in the memory of someone you want to notice and remember you. The same goes for in-person meetings, where I hope you've thought through how the various stickers you have on your water bottle and laptop might start a conversation. If you haven't thought that through, go do that right away and get yourself some new stickers. Be ready with some anecdotes when your impromptu talking turn comes along. A meeting that would otherwise have been a complete waste of your time could become the moment your big break happened, unless you spend most of the meeting being purposefully stupid.

13 Gretchen, stop trying to make fetch happen. It's not going to happen!

Recent research into corporate psychopaths, and how they operate in their high-achieving roles in the workplace, seems to indicate that female psychopaths are five times as common as we thought. They are almost as common as among men, but female psychopaths are more manipulative than males. They use different techniques to create a good impression, and use deceit and sexually seductive behavior to gain social and financial advantage more than male psychopaths do.

> People generally attribute psychopathic characteristics to males rather than to females. So even when females display some of the key traits associated with psychopathy – such as being insincere, deceitful, antagonistic, unempathetic and lacking in emotional depth – because these are seen as male characteristics they may not be labelled as such, even when they should be. Also, female psychopaths tend to use words, rather than violence, to achieve their aims, differing from how male psychopaths tend to operate. If female psychopathy expresses differently, the measures designed to capture and identify male, criminal, psychopaths may be inadequate at identifying female non-criminal, psychopaths.

That's from Dr. Clive Boddy, who has been researching the effects of having psychopaths in the workplace since 2005 and has published more on corporate psychopaths than any other academic. If you lived through "middle school girl world" you probably aren't surprised by Dr. Boddy's findings. It may still shock you some days how much of corporate life is exactly like middle school, though.

I had a dean recently who constructed for herself a classic mean girls cult. Her vice deans were stereotypical wannabes to her queen bee. They all lived in fear of falling out of favor by wearing the wrong color scrunchie or whatever. They would then not be allowed to sit at the dean's table at lunch and would have to go back to actually teaching. The Dean was a French surrealist, so she obviously spoke French. The vice dean who nominally advocated on behalf of our department freaked out when we hired two women who were native French speakers. They could carry on whole conversations with the Queen Bee that the Wannabe Deanlet couldn't follow a word of. There was panic.

The Queen Bee Dean hated the Vice Provost for Research. According to the organizational chart they were peers, both reporting to the Provost. They were supposed to be working together on getting a new engineering program started. I have a copy of the memo where the Provost told them in no uncertain terms to play nicely together. They refused to even talk to each other, which is so fetch. Or maybe un-fetch. I forget what Gretchen meant by fetch.

The deanlet (wannabe) asked me to do the detailed curriculum planning for the new program. She refused to appoint either of my two French-speaking colleagues to the committee because they would get facetime with her Queen Bee. Mapping out the curriculum was straightforward, and since it was the VPR who had been advocating for a few years for this program, I vetted my assumptions and preliminary conclusions with him. He and I had started a department decades before so we were comfortable working together. Of course, since I was friends with her enemy I got to be the enemy of the Queen Bee and she had to send her underlings out to savage me. It was unpleasant, but I had read the literature about the middle school girl world in order to help my daughter navigate that fraught time, so I didn't take it personally.

In case you don't already know it, bullying in "girl world" is psychological and largely consists of granting and then withholding membership in the in crowd. It doesn't work for people like me who don't care at all about such things. I'll wear whatever scrunchie I feel like, and don't care who I happen to sit with at lunch in the cafeteria. I finished the curriculum and sent the detailed plans and required budget forward. The Dean pretended to be surprised that it would cost money, but I had run the numbers past members of the Board of Visitors (as well as the VPR) and the cost was what such things cost. The Queen Bee didn't want to do it because it was the idea of her enemy the VPR. She was only going along with it because the President insisted that such a program get on the books before he retired. It wasn't some sort of bottom-up, faculty-led, grass-roots effort. It was a top-down directive, and so the faculty said if you want us to implement such a program here's what it will take.

I refused to be bullied. In particular, I refused to pretend that such a program could be implemented without new resources. I've been around the block enough times to make sure that I structured the academic program such that my department wouldn't be on the hook to deliver it without additional resources. Since the Queen Bee didn't understand that I saw right through her modus operandi, she thought she could get back at me by having the Provost appoint someone malleable to the implementation committee which took up the effort where my planning committee left off. It was very fetch. I happily went back to my actual work, and watched with some satisfaction while my colleagues across campus tried to get the program going without any new resources. My department contributes as we have availability and interest, but are under no obligation to do so.

I freely admit that dealing with middle-management psychopaths in the workplace is much easier when you're a tenured full professor. I can tell a dean, "I'm not going to do that and you can't make me." I can insist on doing what's in the best interest of the students and the university. If a psycho dean wants to try to come after me, she has to come after my whole department. She tried that. It didn't work. She's gone now, because deans only last a few (or at most several) years and then there's a new one. Same for Provosts and university presidents. I've been through ten deans in the last thirty years. The last one only lasted a bit more than a year. She butted heads with her boss, the new Provost, and then failed to get the Provost's new academic initiative approved. The Provost then refused to talk to her Dean all summer. It was very fetch. In this particular instance, the Dean, Provost and President all happened to be women, and of course there can only be one Queen Bee, so when the new Dean acted like she was all Fetch and dis-invited her boss from attending the Zoom faculty meetings that didn't exactly get her off on the right foot. I was muted on that Zoom so my audible gasp didn't show up in the meeting minutes.

I should point out that I'm not a clinician, but I do have access to the internet and can cut-and-paste from Psychology Today: "Clinicians generally don't expect females to be psychopaths, so they might miss key signs. It is important to note that professional ethics enjoin experts from diagnosing someone they have not personally evaluated, but some do offer opinions when solid biographical information shows a person's behavior to be consistent with psychopathy. In such cases, details of the person's life must be observable enough to data collectors for an evaluation. Since more data is available for killers and con artists than for 'mean girls' who merely defy social conventions, they are disproportionately represented in case studies of female psychopathy." You might wonder whether they are just born this way. More from PT, "The development of psychopathy is a complex interaction of biology, culture, and environment. Genetic factors influence predispositions and temperament. Researchers have posited that there are two subtypes of psychopath: The primary type shows distinct neurological deficits and a blunting of emotions, while the secondary type exhibits more anxiety, substance abuse, and other mental health problems." It's very fetch.

14 You've got to dance little liar.

The liar takes a lot less time to decide on his saunter. Just like those fibs that pop and fizz, you'll be forced to take that awful quiz. You're bound to trip and she'll detect the fiction on your lips and dig a contradiction up. Have you got itchy bones, and in all your time alone can you hack your mind being riddled with the wrong memories? The clean coming will hurt, and you can never get it spotless when there's dirt between the dirt. I heard the truth was built to bend, a mechanism to suspend the guilt is what you will require, but still you've got to dance little liar. (Drum solo.)

The above lyrics are adapted from Arctic Monkey's 2009 Humbug album, but I think they apply to an increasingly common frustration among managers in all types of industries. Malingering employees are pretending to have itchy bones and other sorts of invisible maladies that could get them ADA accommodations to work from home whenever they don't feel like showing up for work. If you google "itchy bones" like I just did, you might reasonably conclude that there's no such medical condition. I'm not an osteopath, so I'm not qualified to make an itchy bones diagnosis. I am, however, cynical enough to think that there's some quack out there on the internet who would be willing, for a fee, to write a doctor's note attesting to someone's intermittently-debilitating case of itchy bones.

Go ahead and read through the employee handbook and even fire off an email to HR, but I think you'll find that there's technically no prohibition against claiming a medical condition that doesn't actually exist. There are people who think their health is adversely affected by electrosmog. There are people who think the inaudible infrasound from wind turbines causes ghosts to manifest in their basements. There are people who think vaccines cause autism when it's obvious that the causality goes the other direction. There are people who think Real Housewives personality conflicts are real, despite the actors routinely breaking kayfabe.

I suppose technically it's not a lie if you believe it, but it seems to me that there needs to be some sort of objective medical test that can be performed in order to establish a condition that is then eligible for an ADA accommodation. I have another song for you: "Last night I saw upon the stair, a little man who wasn't there. He wasn't there again today. Oh, how I wish he'd go away." Actually, that's from a poem "Antigonish" written by William Hughes Mearns in 1899, but if you've heard of it, it was probably the 1939 Glenn Miller recording with Tex Beneke doing the vocals. It shows up lots of other places in popular culture, of course. Everybody loves a good ghost story. Some people are opposed to wind turbines for no apparent reason.

But what if you have a borderline-incompetent employee who can't show up for work on time because that little man who wasn't there wasn't there again today and that causes itchy bones? You might suggest that your malingerer use some sick leave or PTO and go to urgent care. You cannot sign a falsified timesheet, so if sick leave and PTO are all used up it's going to have to count as unpaid leave. Your itchy-boned malingerer will briefly get over their irrational fear of electrosmog and use the company WiFi to search the interwebs for advice on what to do next. The answer will come back on how to file a grievance against you for creating a hostile work environment, which exacerbates itchy-bone syndrome (IBS) and also makes your tummy hurt (also IBS).

Fear is the simplest way to control populations, because it short-circuits the rational part of people's brains which might cause them to question what they're being told to do or not do, say or not say, think or not think. If there isn't something already out there to be afraid of, it's a pretty simple matter to invent something or someone ominous that everybody is supposed to be afraid of. When you're dealing with a malingering employee who claims IBS, you will be afraid of what HR might do.

It's important to understand that HR will be useless, even though this sort of issue is what they are there for. They will tell you to document, document, document. But when you detect the fiction on your malingerer's lips and dig a contradiction up, they will always let that slide. How can one be expected to keep their story straight when their bones are all itchy? Mearns could write a whole other poem about HR being not there again today.

The rational answer is for the person who claims IBS to go see the company doctor. In the Army if your tummy hurts and you don't want to crawl around in the mud or whatever, you show up at the base clinic for sick call. If you get your bell rung during an NFL game you go into that little blue tent on the sidelines and an independent neurologist determines whether you can go back into the game. There are no licensed medical professionals in your HR department, so they aren't qualified to diagnose itchy bones. They aren't even qualified to call bullshit on that internet-degreed naturopath who wrote your malingering employee a doctor's note. It would be irrational, though, to expect your organization to handle this rationally. The organization is quite fearful of not granting proper ADA accommodations to someone who might then sue.

While it's true that the liar takes a lot less time to decide on his saunter, you can take your time on this one. There's no reason to try to apply reason and logic. Fight fire with fire. You should be able to find a witch doctor of some sort who has a ready remedy for itchy bone syndrome. Since there is no medical test to establish the existence of IBS there is no way to disprove your assertion that you have the magic cure for IBS.

The placebo effect is quite real. If you think something will make you feel better, it will. Conversely, the nocebo effect is when you think something will make you feel worse and it does. Your malingering employee is probably lying about all of this, but you can't prove that. It's been well established that expensive placebos work better than cheaper ones. The most effective placebos are theatrical. That's why witch doctors wear funny costumes and do incantations and burn incense or whatever. It's also why actual doctors wear white coats and have those examination rooms with their diplomas on the walls and that ridiculous paper on the padded bench you're supposed to sit on while you're waiting for them to finish the Wordle and then come in and mispronounce your name.

In the process of documenting every damn thing like HR told you to do, you've presumably compiled a list of symptoms that are claimed to contribute to IBS flare-ups. You may even have detected some obvious patterns related to weather forecasts or holiday weekends or important deadlines at work. The witch doctor you find on the internet can incorporate all of this into a customized treatment plan. You probably should pretend that it's AI-driven for good measure. You'll want to make sure that there is a nutritional component, of course, with severe dietary restrictions on triggers like sugar, gluten, etc. There is no way to disprove a claimed link between donuts and itchy bones. A food diary will need to be submitted along with each time sheet, but after six months of abstinence from all things delicious the IBS will clear up on its own.

If the IBS persists in causing your employee's work performance to suffer, that means that there's been some cheating on their diet and their food diary has been falsified. If they've lied about that, what else have they falsified at work? HR needs to be tasked with looking into that, because you would never have thought to question what your employee reported as their hours worked or what they ate for lunch. You care about your employees' well-being so you'd, of course, be willing to have the witch doctor come to the office again this weekend and burn some more incense, cast some more spells, etc. in order to cleanse the entire workspace of bad juju.

Itchy bone syndrome can be exacerbated by working on a laptop from your sofa while you're streaming Real Housewives. It's that invisible electrosmog again. The answer to that is simple. Have IT replace your IBS-afflicted employee's laptop with a hardwired TEMPEST desktop computer in their cubicle at work. The TEMPEST specification means they are shielded so that they don't emit electromagnetic radiation in a manner that can be used to reconstruct intelligible data. The NSA identifies this as a concern in situations where classified information may be accessible and must be protected from outside agents, but the shielding also protects IBS-sensitive employees from electrosmog.

15 SAVING FOR RETIREMENT, OR NOT.

Professor Ronold Wyeth Percival King, mentor to 100 doctoral students in the Harvard University Division of Engineering and Applied Sciences, died peacefully in his home on April 10, 2006 at the age of 100. In 1938, he joined Harvard University as an instructor, became an assistant professor in 1939, an associate professor in 1942, and in 1946 became the Gordon McKay Professor of Applied Physics. In 1972, he became professor emeritus which didn't mean that he actually retired. In those days there was a mandatory retirement age for university faculty and so, by rule, when a professor reached that age the Harvard president would personally come to his office and both congratulate him for his service and announce that he was now Professor Emeritus. There weren't many women professors in those days, but presumably a Harvard president would know enough Latin to say Professor Emerita. Here's a fun fact. Way back in the day it was common to pay your Harvard tuition with agricultural goods, especially turnips. I recently calculated the current cost of Harvard in turnips. It's a lot of cabbage.

Professor King's dedication to his doctoral and master's students was profound, and they showed their appreciation by sharing many happy occasions with him. The very first event was a testimonial on the occasion of King's involuntary transition to professor emeritus. On April 15, 1972, students, spouses, and guests toasted King at the Harvard Club of Boston. One of the highlights of that evening was the announcement that his students planned to establish the Professor R.W.P. King Education Fund. In 2005, at a celebration of his 100th birthday, King was in good spirits, happy to see his former students and colleagues, and a good time was had by all 80 attendees. He published his last of 12 books at age 97 and published more than 300 journal articles with his last at age 98.

Mandatory retirement for university faculty was outlawed in the early 1990s, so as to head off a looming shortage that would have been caused by all those Sputnik-era professors hitting retirement age. That shortage was about as real as the Cold War missile gap, but the result is that I never have to retire. I have no expectation of living (or working) until I'm 100, but I think an even 100 semesters in my current job is doable. I hope to be a sprightly 79-year-old when I hit that mark, and I think the occasion should be marked with the award of a sword and the title Centurion Professor. I've had enough doctoral and master's students who have gone on to highly-successful careers that I think they could get together and endow such a thing.

My parents both took early retirement at about age 60 so they could move close to their grandchildren and dote on them. It was an unusual situation facilitated by a combination of defined-benefit and defined-contribution retirement plans, as well as wise real-estate investments by my mother's father. The booming stock market didn't hurt things either. We still have zero grandbabies, but my wife would very much like to pull the retirement ripcord as soon as one comes along. Both of our kids say it's going to be a while yet. I have enough flexibility in my work that I think I could both keep professoring and dote on grandchildren. My wife is a senior university administrator, but that turns out to be no fun at all so she really would like to dote full time. She was out of the workforce for fifteen years while raising kids, so I'm a little worried that she hasn't got enough of a retirement nest egg despite making quite a lot of money these days. The issue is that she carries the super-longevity gene.

Ora Empress Newell's father was the oldest man alive in 1954 at age 108. Wayland Merle Newell was born in Oswego, New York, USA on 15 September 1846. He was nearly a century old before antibiotics came into use, which means he must have been careful to wash any cut or scrape because those could get infected and be fatal. I'm kind of a germaphobe, so that might be the part that impresses me the most.

Wayland Merle Newell married Esther Caroline E. Treat on 15 May 1874 in Rock, Wisconsin. In 1880 they are living in Des Moines, Iowa, where Wayland works as an accountant. Their daughters Ora and Ada are 3 and 1 years old, respectively. Ora died fairly young and her sister Ada moved in to help take care of her kids and then married Ora's widow and they had three kids of their own, one of which is my wife's ancestor. I should clarify that Ora died due to complications from childbirth while in Burma where her husband was an agricultural/teaching missionary.

In 1900 the Newells are still living in Des Moines, IA where Wayland is working as a Clerk in a drug store. Ora and Ada are living at home, but both are working as teachers of music and drawing, respectively. They have a 13-year-old sister Mabel and a 7-year-old brother Roy who are in school. I wonder if they had Ora and Ada as teachers. Ten years later, Wayland is working as a Bookkeeper for the Des Moines city railway while Ada and Mabel are art and music teachers in the public school and Roy is 17 and a janitor at a church.

Ora Empress Newell married Ambrose Clark Rice on 28 Oct 1903 in Des Moines. They had a son named Wayland Revillo Rice in 1904 and a daughter Esther Clark Rice in 1906 while they were living in Burma, but Ora died in 1909. In 1910, the widowed Ambrose Rice and his children, aged 3 and 5, are all living with his mother, Frances Rice, in Fremont, IA which isn't too far from Des Moines. In 1920 Wayland Newell is 73 years old and recently widowed. He's living with Mabel and her family, in Des Moines. Wayland is still working as a bookkeeper in Real Estate and Banking. It's important to keep mentally active as you get older, and in those days there were no calculators or computers or anything, so being a bookkeeper/accountant required a keen mind and keen eyesight. They're all still the same, except five years older, in the 1925 Iowa state census. In 1930, Wayland is working as a bookkeeper for a Coal Co. where his son-in-law is a manager. He's 83.

Ten years on, in 1940, Wayland was 93 and still living with Mabel and her family, but he seems to have finally retired. When the 1950 census came out I was able to look up Wayland. He was living in a retirement home in Omaha, NE and his next-door neighbor was his daughter Ada. Ambrose Clarke Rice had died in 1965. Two of their children lived to be centenarians, though. Margaret, who got the nickname Bumps for breaking her collar bone repeatedly as a child, died in 2023 at almost 102. William lived to 103, despite having also spent several years in Burma, where he helped re-establish the agricultural school in Pyinmana, before settling down as a Professor in 1959. Following a lengthy career at U. Mass Amherst, Bill signed on with the U.S. Aid for International Development to set up a seed testing lab and experiment station in Zimbabwe.

The current life expectancy for the U.S. in 2024 is 79.25 years, up from 68.90 years in 1954 when Wayland Merle Newell died. The current life expectancy for Myanmar (née Burma) in 2024 is 67.96 years, way up from 37.28 years in 1954. Zimbabwe is now at 62.41 years, up not so much from 50.12 years in 1954. But of course those numbers are badly skewed by infant mortality numbers because they are averages which are distorted by outliers like Wayland living to 108 and his daughter Ora's daughter Janet, who died as a toddler.

What matters to those who are actually looking forward to a long retirement is the remaining life expectancy for those who have already survived to adulthood. It turns out that the Social Security Administration has an on-line tool to calculate this. I'm sixty-ish. My "Estimated Total Years" is 83.2 which seems kind of low given what I know about my ancestors. My wife, who carries the super-longevity gene(s), has an "Estimated Total Years" of 86.1 which I think we can all agree is a rather poor estimate. Also, her normal (or full) retirement age is 67, so she's apparently expected to collect Social Security for only about 20 years. That's assuming that the whole system doesn't collapse by then.

Senator Strom Thurmond's eldest child, Essie Mae Williams, was born to Carrie Butler, a 16-year-old African-American girl who worked as a domestic servant for Thurmond's parents, and Thurmond, then 22 and unmarried. Williams grew up in the family of one of her mother's sisters, not learning of her biological parents until 1938 when her mother came for a visit and informed Essie Mae she was her mother. She graduated from college, earned a master's degree, married, raised a family, and had a 30-year teaching career in the Los Angeles public schools, retiring in 1997. She did not reveal her biological father's identity until she was almost 78 years old, after Thurmond's death at the age of 100 in 2003. He had little or nothing to do with her upbringing, although he paid for her college education and took some interest in her and her family all his life. She died at age 87 in 2013.

Strom Thurmond was a South Carolina Senator for 48 years. Despite his record-breaking filibuster of 24 hours and 18 minutes against the civil rights bill of 1957, Thurmond wasn't a racist. (Insert some sort of states-rights BS here, or if you prefer blame Communists for trying to end segregation.) According to his obit in the NY Times, "Until his last years, Mr. Thurmond was a man of uncommon energy and legendary fitness. He neither smoked nor drank, did more pushups and sit-ups than many men decades younger and fathered children into his mid-70's. He was also known for fondling women in Senate elevators, including a woman who turned out to be a fellow senator, much to his surprise." The Times also tells us that in preparation for that record-breaking filibuster, he had taken steam baths to dehydrate himself so he would not have to yield the floor to go to the restroom. The Times doesn't say whether he was wearing a diaper late in his Senate career when he was too hard of hearing to follow business on the Senate floor and his aides had to prompt him loudly when and how to vote.

Senator Dianne Feinstein's final years in office were similarly marred by concerns about her health and mental competency. She died in office in September 2023, at the age of 90. By the time of her death, Feinstein was the oldest sitting U.S. senator and member of Congress. She was also the longest serving U.S. senator from California and the longest-tenured female senator in history. As San Francisco mayor, Feinstein angered the city's large gay community in 1982 by vetoing legislation which would have extended city-employee benefits to domestic partners, but she was the lead Senate sponsor of the Respect for Marriage Act, which required the federal government and all state governments to recognize same-sex and interracial marriages.

The Senate's median age is 65.3 years, up from 64.8 in the 117th Congress, 63.6 in the 116th and 62.4 in the 115th. Chuck Grassley and Bernie Sanders were born in 1933 and 1941, respectively. I just counted sixteen other Senators who were born in the 1940s and forty-one who were born in the 1950s. We could be stuck with most of these geezers for two or three more decades. Although many of them may be already wearing adult diapers, there's no longer any need for them to stand in the well of the Senate for hours on end to filibuster term-limits legislation. There is no way that some sort of mandatory retirement age is going to get a two-thirds majority when two-thirds of the Senate would then be forced to retire.

In the 2024 Presidential election there has been a steady drumbeat of calls for tests of cognitive decline. We can't really believe video anymore, since it's now fairly simple to edit video clips to make candidates look better or worse than they are in person. Video is also simple to fake these days. We simply can't believe what we see with our own eyes anymore, but voters have a right to know before they vote who may or may not be pulling the strings behind the scenes. The fundamental problem with tests of cognitive ability is that somebody just off camera might be holding up a giant cue card with the answers. Reading from a teleprompter is a core skill of all politicos.

So here's my answer. Everybody take a lap. Before you can be sworn in to your next term as Senator Old-AF, get your butt down to the Lincoln Memorial and back here to the Senate chambers. Take as long as you want. There's benches to rest on all along the Mall. Ride your trusty old Rascal scooter if you want. There's plenty of ramps and elevators. You're going to be timed, though. It's not technically a race, but it is going to be live-streamed. Your aides are not allowed to steer for you though. If you head off towards the Jefferson Memorial and end up wandering by the Cherry Blossoms, you're not going to be allowed to take the oath of office.

If Senators' constituents agree to keep sending them back to Washington decade after decade that's their choice. I do think after a certain number of terms a Senator's seniority should fall off sharply. It's the rules that allow them to bring home the bacon, whether they are effectively contributing to governance or not, that is the root of the problem. I was unsurprised just now to see that more than 50 buildings built with funds from US taxpayers directed to West Virginia are named for either Senator Robert Byrd or his wife. There's even a system of highways to nowhere. And so on. Without that pork made possible by seniority rules, I can't quite see why he would have been re-elected so many times. Byrd was a Senator for over 51 years until his death in office at age 92 in 2010. He had first entered the political arena by organizing and leading a local chapter of the Ku Klux Klan in the 1940s.

Senators have old-school pensions, BTW. Defined-benefit retirement plans can encourage employees to retire because eventually it more-or-less costs them money to come to work. Dropping dead at work means you miss out on your pension. Defined-contribution retirement plans discourage employees from retiring because that investment nest-egg represents a finite amount of money that has to last you and yours for the rest of your lives. The fear among even affluent elderly retirees is that they'll outlive their money. The fear of their children isn't that they'll miss out on an inheritance, it's that Mom and/or Dad will be destitute and will have to come live with them. The flip side for defined-contribution retirement plans is that any money still in that nest egg when you die gets passed down to whomever you specify in your will, even if they are only related to you biologically and not quite legally.

So, when you're calculating your own life expectancy, using the IRS web tool or whatever, you have to judge for yourself when it is going to be the right time to retire. Don't wait too long if you've got things you want to do or see in retirement. Depending on your genetic background and long-established pattern of exercise and diet, you may have many more or somewhat fewer years than the IRS thinks. You might love your work and want to keep doing it as long as you can. Good for you. You may or may not be concerned that you're blocking somebody else's path up the jungle gym.

Pay attention to your more senior colleague's plans for retirement, noting especially HR rules about mandatory retirement policies and federal rules about age discrimination. It's probably some sort of violation to ask colleagues when they are finally planning to retire, but you can certainly take an interest in their grandchildren. I always talk about how my parents retired early and were able to be actively involved in the lives of their grandchildren from toddlers on up and how unusual it is for children and grandchildren to be so close. When my youngest went off to college, it wasn't clear who would miss her the most, me or my mother. She's in her late 20s now and still has a standing phone appointment with Granny at 7pm each Sunday. She calls me on Tuesday on the way home from work.

You may be able to tell when an oldster who never plans to retire is blocking your career progression. They might even be willing to assist you in a sideways leap on the career jungle gym. They're unlikely to be like my father, who realized he was blocking the progression of a protégé he had trained. He deliberately took a phased retirement to clear that rung.

16 THE 'GENDER PAY GAP' IS A MYTH THAT WON'T GO AWAY.

My daughter makes quite a lot more money than her older brother. She's a business development manager for a mid-level accounting consultant firm in Washington, DC. He's an actor in Chicago, except that the entire theatre ecosystem collapsed during the pandemic. The income disparity has nothing to do with gender. It's entirely due to choices they each have made. They both tell me that, "It's going to be a while, Dad." when I mention that I still have zero grandbabies and I'm starting to get a little salty about that. Choices that they and their significant others make when navigating co-parenting will affect their income trajectories. My daughter and I agree that her brother will make an excellent room mom. He could be the parent helper that organizes the school plays. He starred in Pirates of Penzance when he was in 5th grade, after all.

March 9 is "equal pay day," which accounts for the additional days that women would need to work, on average, to earn the same amount as men earned in the previous year. The day keeps moving earlier as the earnings gap has grown smaller, BTW, which some people try to ignore by fixing the date as March 12. It used to be that men and women were paid quite differently because men were assumed to be breadwinners while women were just working a while until they married a breadwinner. Airline stewardesses had to quit if they got married or reached age 32 still a spinster. School teachers had to quit as soon as a baby bump started to show. That changed in the 1970s, though. By the 1990s, pay differentials based strictly on gender had mostly equalized.

These days any gender pay gap is the natural economic result of choices men and women make, including how much or how little to work and which occupations to enter. The conclusion that women earn 84-cents on the dollar compared to men is arrived at by dividing the average annual pay for women who work full-time all year by the average annual pay of men working full-time all year. That comparison is misleading because full-time, year-round work is defined so broadly. Full time is defined as working more than 35 hours per week. For those working less than 35 hours a week, women's earnings are, on average, 105% of men's pay.

My parents both started out professional life as school teachers. My father was a PE teacher, and he had both bachelor's and master's degrees in PE. He went on to become a prison warden. My mother started teaching first grade once she had earned an associate's degree, stepping back from the workforce while she had preschool children. She ended up a college professor, having earned bachelor's, master's and doctoral degrees while teaching full time and raising a family. School teachers and college professors are paid for the nine or ten months of the school year, but typically their salary is spread out over the full twelve months. Since many more women are teachers than men, this introduces an artificial gender pay gap. At the university level, professors are typically paid their academic year salaries over twelve months. Some teach summer school classes to augment their salary. At research universities, research grants typically include some summer salary for the PI along with stipend support for graduate students, postdocs, etc.

Before we had children, my wife and I both were getting started on highly-promising careers. She didn't go back to work as a retail executive after our son was born, because that job required quite a lot of travel to both her markets in New York and production facilities in China. We found that we could live reasonably well on my faculty salary, as long as I busted my butt and got enough research grants to pay my full summer salary and did some outside consulting. She didn't step back into full time paid work until our youngest got her driver's license. She now makes more money than I do unless I bust my butt and get enough research grants to pay my full summer salary and do some outside consulting. Our finances have been fully co-mingled for decades, but our relative lifetime earnings do show a gender pay gap.

It's still the case that men tend to choose higher-paying college majors and occupations. Only one of the 10 highest-earning college majors graduates more women than men, while nine of the 10 lowest-earning majors graduate more women than men. Physicians are the highest-paid occupation. Today more than half of students enrolled in medical school are women. More than three-fourths of doctorates in health and medical sciences are earned by women, as are more than half of the doctorate degrees in biological and life sciences.[8]

Men are more likely to choose occupations with greater financial risk, such as jobs that pay commissions on sales. They are also more likely than women

---

[8] I'm quoting from:
https://www.wsj.com/articles/the-gender-pay-gap-is-a-myth-that-wont-go-away-1f0e3841

to take jobs with physical risk, such as construction, whose pay is higher owing to the risk premium. But things are changing quite a lot. More and more women are choosing to enter highly paid occupations and there has been a significant shift in the relative roles of men and women in the home. As a part of her deliberate on-ramping strategy, and as a way of compensating when her baby boy grew up and ran away to college, my wife went back to graduate school. I was trying to be supportive and I'm kind of a smartass, so I said, "No housework until your homework is done." She said, "OK!" which is how I volunteered myself to be in charge of the housework. When my son went off to college my wife and my daughter had used their new super-majority voting powers to declare that yardwork and general maintenance was gender-specific male. Housework was declared to be gender-non-specific, but then I opened my mouth. Since I'm the world's OKest housekeeper, eventually professional cleaners started showing up twice a month. I still don't like it that people are touching my stuff, but I've learned to keep my mouth shut. When I occasionally complain about yard work my wife offers to make a phone call and get me a lawn service since we both make quite a lot of money and can easily afford that.

Back to Senator Gramm's op-ed in the Journal: The claim that the gender pay gap reflects discrimination assumes that employers would pass up the chance to hire a woman at 84% of what they pay a man with the same training, skills and experience to do the same job. Since labor costs make up a significant share of total business costs, not only would employers have a strong incentive to hire women but discriminators would have a hard time staying in business. Market forces penalize discrimination and reward inclusion.

The March of Dimes Syndrome[9] often leads us to ascribe increased public concern about a social problem which is inversely proportional to its actual incidence. The better that things get, the harder we look to find something bad. As we become richer, better educated, and longer-lived, we have more disposable income and free time to spend caring about curing humanity's woes, real or imagined. It can be harder and harder to get people's attention. This can lead to increasingly apocalyptic rhetoric about more and more nebulous future woes, particularly among young activists who have no idea how much things have already improved over their short lifetimes.

When my mother became department chair back in the 80s, she got a significant pay raise and a big chunk of back salary, because she was about to find out how much more her male colleagues had been paid all those years. When I was department chair back in the late 00s, I used salary inversion to get a somewhat more senior female colleague paid quite a bit more when we hired a junior male colleague at market-competitive rates. That was fun to do

---

[9] https://www.city-journal.org/article/the-march-of-dimes-syndrome

because it was during a time when there were no pay raises for anybody. As chair I knew exactly who was getting paid what, of course, but I also shared a public link with all of my colleagues that detailed all of the salaries at the public universities in the state. I managed to get several of my colleagues pay bumps during that three-year period when there were no pay raises for anybody. I had to use different strategies each time, and I always apologized that it had taken so long.

Adam Ruins Everything is an educational sketch comedy show that aims to teach people why their conceptions of the world are wrong. You should look up his episode[10] which dealt with sharing salary information, and how we should all be doing more of it. It's one way for employees to gain leverage in salary and raise negotiations and to make sure there's no gender pay gap where you work. A cool thing about this show is that they cite the sources they draw upon.

---

[10] https://www.trutv.com/shows/adam-ruins-everything/articles/adam-ruins-work

17 Uppity Women Unite.

One of the strangest things about climbing the career jungle gym is that it often turns out to be more or less pyramidal. There simply aren't all that many rungs up near the top. That makes good sense organizationally because if you have too many senior administrators you'll end up like Ivy League schools where they now have one administrator for every undergraduate. Administrative bloat still horrifies those of us who have been in academia for long enough to watch this all happen. There's no mystery about why college costs so much these days. Senior administrators make a fuckton of money. Professors not so much. Don't even get me started on football coaches. The English department faculty have no sneaker deals.

Universities aside, once you start to find yourself in the upper echelons of most organizations, it can start to get lonely. When you were first starting out, all eager and unjaded, you had this whole cohort to pal around with after work. If your kids were about the same ages you would get together for birthday parties and soccer games and school plays and maybe complain about your bosses a bit. It's been a minute since you've been to a happy hour, hasn't it?

You simply can't pal around with people you supervise. It would be awkward when they got a couple drinks into them and started ranting about their boss and how unfairly they're treated. I take that back, it would be hilarious waiting for them to realize one-by-one that you're sitting right there and taking mental notes. You'd probably buy the next round just to keep them rolling so you'd know what they actually think. I'm not saying you'd retaliate in any way, but having your direct reports tell you what they actually think of you could help you understand how to motivate them to do a better job at their actual jobs.

Back in the 80s, my mother and several of the other women faculty used to get together for breakfast on Wednesdays. For some reason that made their male colleagues very nervous. I don't think the women were ever threatened when the men went to Toastmasters or Kiwanis or the Elks. Some of them may have been annoyed that the golf course and the grill were off limits to women some days, but my mother never played golf. We weren't the country-club types anyway. My father and I played at the scruffy public course across the lake from where we had built a cabin with our own hands. My mother and I had terraformed an alfalfa field into a perennial garden. In Lake Wobegon all the men are strong, all the women are good looking, and all the children are above average, dontcha know.

We had no TV at the lake, so we all read a lot of books. I still read a lot, but I've never been to a book club. I'm a little suspicious that book club is a euphemism for day drinking and complaining about your significant other, but that doesn't make me nervous when my wife goes to book club. I understand that it's psychologically healthy to get together with peers and perhaps vent a bit. If everybody gets all real about their significant others, I might even come out well by comparison. Or not. It's not really my business.

My wife has a solid friend group that formed spontaneously thirty years ago when they all had two-year-olds in the same preschool. They were mostly professional women who had deliberately stepped back from high-powered careers to be stay-at-home moms. The kids are all grown now and some of them have kids of their own, but the moms are still in touch. They used to call themselves Mom's Night Out because they would go out together once a month or so, without the pretense of reading some book beforehand. Pretty much all of them eventually on-ramped back into professional careers once the kids were a little older. All of them, I suppose, if you count Pickleball Pied Piper as a profession. They have history and the common tie of being 90's moms, but they're all in different places career wise.

You may have been nodding along with some of that, whether you play Pickleball or not. I do hope that you recognize the deep human need for belonging and that because you spend so much of your waking life at work, you'd be a happier human if you had a friend-group of peers there. Some of this need can be satisfied by professional associations, of course, and you should take advantage of whatever professional development/networking opportunities your organization may offer. Sometimes it will be worth it in the long term to pay out of pocket for such memberships yourself. The power of weak ties is hard to over emphasize. Some person you know almost always knows someone who can help you advance up the next rung on your career jungle gym. What is it you think the men are doing at their Elks meetings? Yes, there are ridiculous costumes and silly little rituals, but the main point is networking. And getting out of the house one evening a month.

But at your work where you spend fifty or sixty hours most weeks (don't argue, you know you do) you need to cultivate a mutually supportive peer group. It doesn't have to be all women, of course, but your goal is not to replicate meetings where men are gobbling up all the talking turns and ideas as if they have some genetic right to both even though they've only ever been to three aisles in the supermarket and would straight-up starve to death without pre-made to-go meals. Grubhub and the like are anti-Darwinian.

I was curious and looked it up just now. In 1995, "The New York Civil Liberties Union and the Women's Rights Project of the American Civil Liberties Union today hailed the settlement of a lawsuit brought by a local woman who was denied admission to an Elks Lodge here solely because of her gender. Bonnie Orendorff has agreed to drop her lawsuit on the condition that the Benevolent and Protective Order Elks Lodge No.96 admit women members on the exact basis that they admit men." That's from an ACLU press release, which also says that the Grand Lodge of Elks national policy provides for no discrimination on the basis of gender. I hope you snorted just a bit when you read that last one.

Go ahead and join the Elks if you want, but my recommendation is to form your own little lodge. You can adopt some animal as your mascot if you like, but there's no need for initiation rituals or costumes. The point is for you and other uppity women to unite and support each other in reaching your professional goals. You could get together for breakfast on Wednesdays. You could go out for lunch every other Friday. Happy hour is probably off the table given your low tolerance for alcohol these days. Wine has a lot of empty calories in it anyway and that study claiming resveratrol had health benefits was faked. The point is to get together and just be together. If that makes your male co-workers too nervous, you could all join an after-work Pickleball league. Pick one where a large fraction of the players are retired senior executives, and get yourself some free career coaching to boot. You all have long since learned that the secret to manipulating men is to let them win at something meaningless like Pickleball. Your male colleagues will scoff because they play real sports like squash, which is just ivy league racquetball. It's almost too easy.

Back to the jungle gym before I start telling you how good I used to be at racquetball back in the day. You and your Pickleball Mafia (you should all get that on T-shirts) are going to leverage everybody's weak ties, including those of the oldsters you get to know out on the courts and sitting in the shade afterwards, to make some bold leaps in order to climb further up your respective jungle gyms. You're going to stick together. You're going to stay united when those squash assholes try to play you off against each other to their own advantage.

Even as you inevitably disperse to other organizations with available rungs up higher on their pyramids, you are going to remain united. You all share the same simple goal: retire at the top of your game on your own terms, and then take up Pickleball for real. Don't worry, by then you won't hear all that well anymore. The TOCK-TOCK won't bother you a bit.

18 Just because you're paranoid that doesn't mean they aren't out to get you.

I'm a big believer in management by walking around. I also understand that it's quite unhealthy to sit for too long, so getting up and walking around is good for me. You may have found that one of the problems with open-plan offices, though, is that co-workers who should be sitting at their cubicles getting some of their own work done seem to be forever swinging by to tell you about some new conspiracy theory they read about on social media.

I have a copy of a sign that I got from the rector of a local church, which he used to put outside his office when he had to be left alone to get his sermon finished. It reads, "Visitors not received with zesty jolliness at this moment." I tried putting that on my closed office door a couple of times when I had an urgent proposal deadline, but people got butthurt about my exceedingly rare un-availability. Now I just close the door and put up a Post-it note saying I'm on a Zoom call.

When someone knocks on my door at home to ask my political opinion or to try to sell me something, I open the door briefly and say, "I'm not available today." I shut it before they can object that it will only take a minute. I don't bother telling them that I won't be available tomorrow either, or that I never buy anything from someone who knocks on my front door. If it's a neighborhood kid selling Girl Scout cookies or something and my wife happens to be home I'll call her to the door, but if she's not home I explain that I'm not allowed to buy things and they'll have to come back when her blue CR/V is in the driveway. The only exception was when I took a moment to say, "Your position on Intelligent Design disqualifies you for service on the School Board." before shutting the door and going back to the chore I was in the middle of. LPT: If Jehovah's Witnesses start to think they can pester you by coming to your door, simply say that they shouldn't talk to you or they might get "disfellowshipped" and they will nope out of your yard in an ungodly hurry.

My personal strategies hinge on having a door that I can close. You may be just shy of the necessary seniority to get an actual office with an actual door, or you might be the sort of keystone in your organization where you need to be available for people to seek out your sage advice and you don't want to inhibit that by making people knock on your door all sorry to disturb you. You may have even learned to affect the appearance of having nothing better to do than to chat with a co-worker who has a work-related problem you can help them with.

The world is complicated and hard to make sense of. The world is uncaring because the dominant feature is billions of people making choices on their own for their own reasons, which manifests as apparent randomness in most things. There are so many people in the world that if you're a literal one-in-a-million there are several thousand people just like you. This is in sharp contradistinction with the Barney song:

'Cause you are special, special
Everyone is special
Everyone in his or her own way
Oh, you are special, special
Everyone is special
Everyone in his or her own way.

My mother is a retired professor of special education, so let's use the word special instead of the R-word that is now on the list of banned words. I assume you have one or more colleagues who want to think they're special but they act like they're special. They're always going on about some new conspiracy or other, which shouldn't be your problem.

Except that they take advantage of your open-door policy to swing by your office and regale you with their new insight about how the world actually works. They'll want to close your door because it's super-de-dooper secret, but I do insist that they keep the door open so as not to arouse suspicion. You're going to want to have a pretend Zoom meeting starting in a few minutes, though.

You probably don't quite get the appeal of conspiracy theories. It turns out to be uncomplicated. Being continually buffeted by the randomness of an uncaring world is hard. It means you're not special, despite what Barney told you. But, if there's a big secret and you're one of the few who are aware of it, that makes you special. You can feel even more special by selectively telling everybody the secrets that only you and a few others know about. Being the first to know is really special.

If you're special, the big scary world is especially scary. Things are happening all the time for no reason. But if there's a big, secret conspiracy controlling everything, that's simple to understand even for someone who is bluntly rather simple in a special sort of way. That's the second appeal of conspiracies.

The best reason to ascribe to super-secret conspiracies is that you can then lead yourself to believe that the nebulous "they" are out to get you somehow. They are thwarting your grand plans. They are keeping you from achieving greatness. If not for their nefarious activities, all would recognize how special you really are. You are, in fact, so special that this super-effective world-wide conspiracy that secretly controls the world has chosen, after suitable deliberation, that you warrant attention. What could be more special than that?

One of the best things about conspiracies is that they are non-falsifiable. That was kind of a big word, sorry. It means that you can't argue there's no evidence for the alleged conspiracy, because the conspiracy is so good at covering their tracks that there isn't any evidence, duh. Also, anybody who denies being a part of the conspiracy is only saying that because they're a part of the conspiracy. It's crazy-facebook-uncle 101 we're talking about here.

I tease my friends who work at NASA that if we're getting all our advanced aerospace technology by reverse-engineering crashed flying saucers, it follows logically that NASA is merely a front organization designed to deflect attention. They don't think that's very funny. It's a little funny.

The Air Force used to deny that Area 51 even existed. When people climbed up onto surrounding hills with telephoto lenses to take pictures of the hangers and airstrips there, the Air Force moved the fences back farther. They mean it when their signs say "no trespassing" and "use of deadly force authorized" if you try to sneak a peek at their sneakiness. Now that commercially-available satellite imagery allows anyone to peek at such things, the Air Force has stopped denying the place exists. You still don't have a need to know what goes on there, though. The US Government has conspired to keep certain things secret. Indeed, the Manhattan Project was so secret that Vice President Truman knew nothing about it. When he needed to know he was read into the program and then since the buck stopped with him, he had to decide if it was worth saving a million lives by vaporizing a couple of Japanese cities. It apparently wasn't a hard call.

The Pentagon just put out another report denying the existence of UFOs. I downloaded it and skimmed through it.[11] Meh. About the only thing new about it is the acronym Unidentified Anomalous Phenomena (UAP) which they're using instead of UFO. I didn't read it carefully enough to tell if there's

---

[11] Report on the Historical Record of U.S. Government Involvement with Unidentified Anomalous Phenomena (UAP) Volume I. THE DEPARTMENT OF DEFENSE ALL-DOMAIN ANOMALY RESOLUTION OFFICE, February 2024

anything different from the previous iteration, known as Project Blue Book. Project Blue Book was one of a series of systematic studies of unidentified flying objects (UFOs) conducted by the United States Air Force. It started in 1952, and it was the third study of its kind; the first two were projects Sign (1947) and Grudge (1949). A termination order was given for the study in December 1969, and all activity under its auspices ceased in January 1970.

The most common object reported as a UFO/UAP is the planet Venus. Even Jimmy Carter made that mistake, and he was a nuclear engineer with a photographic memory. Triangular UFOs/UAPs always turn out to be the landing lights of an airliner or an artifact of the iris of certain models of night-vision scopes. Most people aren't aware that weather balloons flatten out into flying-saucer shapes at high altitudes and that because the earth demonstrably is not flat, dammit, the balloon can be sunlit even though it's dark where you are. Now that drones with LED light kits are so common, it's a pretty simple matter to pwn UAP-spotters with one of those. Still no word on WTF was up with all those drones over New Jersey in December, 2024.[12]

You might be interested to know that the reason we think UFOs are flying saucer shaped is because a reporter mis-reported Kenneth Arnold's report. He said the objects he saw "moved like saucers skipping across the water" , not that the objects were shaped like saucers. Also, the Roswell crash was a Project Mogul balloon and since that project was top secret it was better to let the Ruskies think that it was space aliens than to have them know that we were spying on their nuclear testing program. Go ahead and download the Air Force report. It's 232 pages, approved for public release: distribution unlimited. You should be able to find it on the interwebs. You could also go to Roswell, NM on vacation. Tourism is their main business, of course, and there's no other reason on earth to visit there if not for aliens.

Here comes another big word: irreducible minimum. Most of the Project Blue Book[13] and subsequent compilations of UFO/UAP cases are explainable, but there will always be some that remain unexplained. You can safely assume that some special souls have combed through the thousands and thousands of sightings and collected together those that yet remain a mystery. In those cases there typically isn't enough evidence to say one way or the other. You would be within your rights to conclude that there's no there there and how about if we all just get back to work because the quarterly report is still due tomorrow.

Oh, sheeple, says your special co-worker. Don't you know that the reason there's no evidence is that all the good evidence is covered up? Even without a Men in Black style neuralyzer, it's easy to cover up this kind of evidence. All

---

[12] https://apnews.com/article/drones-new-jersey-buzz-6ef6cfdd5dd6508da22b3c3a1d2f6718

[13] https://archive.org/details/bluebook

the Government has to do is to make it classified Top Secret and then anybody who knows about it can't talk about it. You saw what they did to President Trump about the presidential documents he had at the Mara Lago office he used while he was President and could declassify anything just by saying so. It's not like he had boxes in his garage or something.

It can be an effective political strategy to say that there's a vast right-/left-wing conspiracy out to get you. It kind of worked for the Clintons and there was a lot of there there. I have to assume that they chuckle among themselves about how amateurish the Biden family is with their non-global, non-foundation, grift. Networks of LLCs, Geez.

I find that I can only listen (patiently) to people yammering on about conspiracies for so long, but I know that it's pointless to try to argue with them. It simply won't work to try to rebut their arguments point-by-point. They're not bound by logic. They cray-cray. Well, technically they're not crazy. They're special and they want to feel special. They want the world to be simpler than it actually is, and they're grasping for some explanation for why their life hasn't turned out the way they had hoped. It's decades too late for them to apply to the Air Force Academy and then become a top gun and then test-fly super-secret spy planes at Groom Lake and be the only one who has the skills and guts to take the pilot's seat in that newly-restored flying saucer and see what she can do before the aliens come back in force to finish the job. The quarterly report that's due tomorrow suddenly isn't going to matter when the fate of all mankind hangs in the balance.

Fortunately for you it's time to sign on to that pretend Zoom meeting. You'll have to close your door for it because nobody else in the office is cleared for several of the items on the agenda for today. You can neither confirm nor deny any of this, of course, because even the existence of the group which is meeting is strictly on a need-to-know basis. Your special co-worker will understand, of course. For all you know he's one of the other participants who never seems to turn his camera on and whose voice always sounds familiar, but distorted, when he offers off-the-wall opinions that nobody else in the group would ever think of. Catch the door, please. We'll talk more tomorrow, or not.

19 INCOMPETENT FAIL-UPWARDS BRUNCHLORDS.

Some industries are predominantly run by utterly incompetent individuals who fail upwards into positions of power. Cable news is over. Upstart new media operations include everything from streaming services to YouTube channels to newsletters to interview podcasts are now where younger, less traditionally TV-centric news consumers get their news.[14] Once solid companies are being run into the ground by a rotating crop of utterly incompetent trust fund failsons who create unrealistic, hype-fueled company valuations, hoover up exorbitant salaries, implement numerous incoherent strategy pivots, and set giant piles of money on fire on a rotating crop of increasingly stupid ideas. That's from the TechDirt.com actual journalist Karl Bode[15] who was lamenting the self-destruction of Vice Media. He calls bullshit on the idea that the collapse of Vice, like most mismanaged modern U.S. media companies, was somehow the unfortunate, unforeseen consequence of ambiguous externalities in the thankless job of informing the public about factual reality online.

In the first three months of 2024 alone, *The Messenger* shut down, *BuzzFeed* cut 16% of its remaining staff, and *Vice Media* laid off hundreds of employees as it ceased to publish on its website. *TIME* also laid off 15% of its unionized editorial staff and *The Los Angeles Times* cut over 20% of its newsroom staff. Meanwhile, at *Condé Nast*, staffers walked off the job, protesting layoffs, and staffers at *The New York Daily News* and *Forbes* staged a walkout. *Deadspin*, the irreverent sports and news site best known for its commentary and analysis, laid off all of its staff after the outlet was sold to a startup firm. Last

---

[14] https://reason.com/2024/11/21/cable-news-is-over/

[15] https://www.techdirt.com/2024/02/27/the-vice-media-collapse-was-entirely-the-fault-of-incompetent-fail-upward-brunchlords/

year, *Deadspin's* former parent company, *G/O Media*, sold *Jezebel* to *Paste Magazine* after briefly shutting down the publication and laying off its entire staff. Jim Spanfeller, the chief executive of *G/O Media*, said "The rationale behind the decision to sell included a variety of important factors that include the buyer's editorial plans for the brand, tough competition in the sports journalism sector, and a valuation that reflected a sizable premium from our original purchase price for the site." Fucking brunchlord.

The opposite of this sort of empty suit is termed an insecure overachiever: talented and hardworking, driven by their fears of inadequacy. Such employees can be a dream to manage. All their brunchlord boss has to do is point them in the right direction and watch them crush it. They are self-motivating and self-disciplining. Never finished proving themselves, these ambitious strivers look to their brunchlord bosses for affirmation. They take comfort in working for brand-name businesses, finding the prestige reassuring and corporate culture comforting. Brunchlords love their commitment, and understand that these anxious achievers will always come through because their self-worth is on the line.[16] Also, true brunchlords don't have brunch at 10:30 am. It's more of a 1:30 pm kind of thing.

A good boss dampens insecurities rather than heightening them. You've got enough on your plate without that shit. There's nothing wrong with working hard at things you find deeply meaningful, but it's no fun to always be worried that your extensive portfolio of amazing accomplishments don't count because that was yesterday and what are you going to do to prove yourself tomorrow. If your brunchlord boss can't extemporaneously crow about your accomplishments, that's on him not you. You're awesome and your boss should be telling you that a couple-three times per week. You should also feel awesome twice a month when your direct deposit hits. Compliments are nice, of course, but money is the only language that brunchlords actually understand. If you happen to be in the business of writing clever words for money, you're probably not going to be making a living at that for all that much longer. The writing game just leveled up and AI chatbots can string together words that brunchlords think are clever. And they're free.

Now that Chatbots have been out in the world for a couple-three years, we are beginning to understand how people are using them. The key point is that everyone already is, and those who have figured out these new tools are forty-percent more productive. Chatbots and the like are most helpful for chuckleheads because they take a poor writer (or coder or artist or whatever) and make them good enough for most purposes. People who were already quite skilled and talented and productive have to learn to exploit chatbots to

---

[16] https://www.bloomberg.com/opinion/articles/2024-02-29/are-you-an-insecure-overachiever-how-to-calm-down-about-work

get better and faster at what they do. The game has leveled up.

Because they're prone to bullshitting, Chatbots need to be fact checked so they don't get you into trouble. Hallucination, as this aspect of Chatbots is usually termed, is a feature to be exploited in creative tasks. Humans are inhibited during brainstorming sessions even if you stipulate that there are no stupid ideas. Chatbots will instantly generate as many ideas as you want, and then you can decide which few might be worth pursuing. Chatbots can summarize for you long reports (or email screeds) so you can focus your attention on the underlying nuggets of information that might be pertinent to you. They can do lots of other things pretty well also, and you should be insisting that your young employees learn to use them. You want them to crowdsource best practices for you and your organization. At least some of your competitors are doing that already. What I've been telling my students since early 2023 is, "If your meatbrain doesn't add value to what the AI can instantaneously do for free, why would anybody pay you?"

The Free Press (https://www.thefp.com) is a new media company built on the ideals that once were the bedrock of great journalism: honesty, doggedness, and fierce independence. They publish investigative stories and provocative commentary about the world as it actually is—with the quality once expected from the legacy press, but the fearlessness of the new. Bari Weiss is the founder and editor of The Free Press and host of the podcast *Honestly*. From 2017 to 2020 Weiss was an opinion writer and editor at *The New York Times*. Before that, she was an op-ed and book review editor at *The Wall Street Journal* and a senior editor at *Tablet Magazine*. Here are three paragraphs from her NY Times resignation letter[17]

> I joined the paper with gratitude and optimism three years ago. I was hired with the goal of bringing in voices that would not otherwise appear in your pages: first-time writers, centrists, conservatives and others who would not naturally think of The Times as their home. The reason for this effort was clear: The paper's failure to anticipate the outcome of the 2016 election meant that it didn't have a firm grasp of the country it covers. Dean Baquet and others have admitted as much on various occasions. The priority in Opinion was to help redress that critical shortcoming.
>
> My own forays into Wrongthink have made me the subject of constant bullying by colleagues who disagree with my views. They have called me a Nazi and a racist; I have learned to brush off comments about how I'm "writing about the Jews again." Several

---

[17] https://www.bariweiss.com/resignation-letter

colleagues perceived to be friendly with me were badgered by coworkers. My work and my character are openly demeaned on company-wide Slack channels where masthead editors regularly weigh in. There, some coworkers insist I need to be rooted out if this company is to be a truly "inclusive" one, while others post ax emojis next to my name. Still other New York Times employees publicly smear me as a liar and a bigot on Twitter with no fear that harassing me will be met with appropriate action. They never are.

What rules that remain at The Times are applied with extreme selectivity. If a person's ideology is in keeping with the new orthodoxy, they and their work remain unscrutinized. Everyone else lives in fear of the digital thunderdome. Online venom is excused so long as it is directed at the proper targets.

I've been reading a fair number of quite thoughtful pieces by Bari and her talented journalists. I've been buying books that they recommend. What I haven't done, though, is pay money to subscribe. I understand that they're trying to make quality on-line journalism pay the bills, but then I haven't subscribed to anything for many years. That's not quite true, I guess. I write an increasingly large check each month to the cable company which inflicts a large number of channels on me, a few of which I watch some of each day. I don't feel the need to donate money to PBS, though, because that's included in my cable bill. I watch something else during pledge week, and generally have my DVR set to record various series and sometimes movies that usually run past my bedtime. That way I can watch them at my convenience and fast-forward through the commercials. My wife subscribes to too many streaming services, which I'm OK with if our extended family can password-share. Fair warning to streaming brunchlords: cut that off and I'm not paying that monthly fee anymore. I hope that Bari Weiss can make high-quality on-line journalism work. I don't know what the right business model is going to be, but then who would have thought that 99-cents per song would have been the answer for music? Steve Jobs figured that out. I still have my daughter's iPod Nano with my CDs ripped to it. These days, though, artists get paid "homeopathic fractions of a penny for each stream" and making art is not an "economically rational" activity.[18]

Sallie Krawcheck points out that the glass cliff has been in the news lately and that we should stop hiring women as crisis managers.[19]

If you haven't heard of it, it's the irritating younger cousin to the

---

[18] https://pluralistic.net/2024/12/21/blockheads-r-us/#vocational-awe
[19] https://www.ellevest.com/magazine/disrupt-money/glass-cliff

glass ceiling; and it describes a tendency for businesses in crisis to put women and/or people of color in charge of turning the businesses around with the odds stacked against them.

Then when she's asked to do the impossible and fails — because it's ... well ... impossible — it can be seen as evidence that "women CEOs fail" (instead of evidence that a woman has been set up to fail, as researchers found).

When women are hired in times of crisis, their work is much more difficult and stressful — and scrutinized — than in times of success. They're judged solely by their ability to get the company out of that crisis (and one that's often quite literally man-made).

Let's all say it together, "Fucking Brunchlords!" As you contemplate dramatic leaps to some other part of your current, or even some other, jungle gym, it's important to not let yourself be set up for failure, but don't automatically reject such opportunities. Sallie K. again, "If it's your one and only shot at a C-suite title, you just might shoot it. The challenge, the opportunity, the energy, the money ... it can be enough to look beyond how damaged a business might be." The Harvard Business Review[20] concluded some years ago that "as people become more used to seeing women at the highest levels of management, female leaders won't be selected primarily for risky turnarounds—and will get more chances to run organizations that have good odds of continued success." I'm looking forward to that.

---

[20] https://hbr.org/2011/01/how-women-end-up-on-the-glass-cliff

20 Sigmund Freud was a pretty weird guy.

You may have noticed that young people are stressed out these days. You'd have to be pretty oblivious to not notice that because everybody seems to talk about how anxious they are. All. The. Time. I suppose that's better than never talking about your mental health challenges, but us mature grownups can get a little tired of hearing about it from people we don't really even know all that well. We've got work to do here, and some of us feel like just doing your damn job will make you less anxious about doing your job, Skippy. Also, I'm not your mother. Or your therapist.

Since everybody is worried about their own mental health issues these days, there is a rather severe shortage of trained, licensed mental health professionals. Maybe AI chatbots will be able to pick up some of the load eventually, but for now anxious young people can be left waiting far too long to even get a Zoom appointment with a qualified therapist.

Freud wanted to do medical research for a living, but there was a quota for Jews in that prestigious profession back in the day, so he sat around and thought about icky things. He also came up with a scheme that meant he was never wrong. His idea was that you are currently all messed up because of some early trauma that you have repressed. He will use symbolic interpretation of ink blots or dreams or whatever to uncover your hidden trauma and that will magically make you all better just after your insurance runs out or Buzzfeed goes bankrupt, whichever happens first. These repressed thoughts are in your unconscious, so you can't ever just remember them and deal with it all yourself and thus save on your co-pay. Nope. Only the expensive Freudian psychoanalyst can use symbolic-interpretation hocus pocus to peer into your subconscious and then interpret your engrams. Freud's brilliant insight was that whenever a patient tried to argue with his interpretation, he took that as further evidence of repression. That's the part that means he can never be wrong. It also makes Freud a quack. The scientific word for this is non-falsifiable, and that makes it not science.

So, no matter how anxious someone might be, they should never go to a Freudian psychoanalyst. They'll just end up running out the clock on their insurance and then be left with unresolved mommy and/or daddy issues. Freud makes things worse, not better. Freud can suck it.

Psychogenic illnesses are the body's natural response to being all stressed out all the time. We don't use the word hysteria anymore because that term is typically gendered. Some non-specific fear then triggers the nocebo effect, which is the opposite of the placebo effect. The placebo effect makes you feel better if you think something is supposed to make you feel better. The nocebo effect makes you feel bad if you think something is supposed to make you feel bad. The nocebo effect spreads in characteristic ways via social networks. It always has, but now things can blow up and be everywhere all at once because of social media. Fear works to drive engagement, and if everybody you're connected with is afraid of the same thing right now you aren't going to rationally question whether there's any there there.

Your hyper-connected, hyper-sensitive employees, who are stressed about their so-called lives as compared to everybody else's highly curated social media personas, will periodically need to burn some of their PTO and/or sick days due to psychogenic illnesses that are making the rounds. The Olds will be tempted to tell them to just man-up because it's all in their heads. That simply will not work, and since many psychogenic illnesses predominantly affect young women it could get them into real trouble with HR. The answer is rest and relaxation and placebo, along with reassurance that they aren't being poisoned or irradiated or whatever. There's no need to have the office fumigated, unless it actually does need to be fumigated of course. There's no need to get everybody tinfoil hats, unless Vistaprint is having a sale on some cool new swag. Nobody is immune to psychogenic illnesses, not even highly trained diplomats in our embassy in Cuba who misinterpreted the mating calls of crickets and cicadas as a malevolent sonic weapon which caused concussion-like symptoms that were actually all in their heads. It's very stressful being a diplomat in a place like Cuba where spies will sneak into your house while you're gone and alphabetize your bookshelf just to mess with you.

The educational establishment, from pre-K up through medical school, recognizes that their charges are anxious and wants to be helpful. But here's a scary thought. What if the things that schools are doing—at all levels—is making things worse rather than better? Aren't they supposed to be experts about such things?

True experts are frustratingly circumspect about things they know a lot about. They're always hemming and hawing when you just want them to tell you the answer(s) to your question(s) in plain language that you can understand. The reason for this is that experts understand both the limits of their own knowledge and the limits of all human knowledge, as long as you're talking about their specific area of expertise. They may know next to nothing about most other things, of course. Non-experts are often quite confident in their pronouncements, simply because they don't know enough to appreciate how little they know about the issue(s) under discussion. It's called the Dunning Kruger Effect, but I usually pronounce it as confident dumb people. A little knowledge can be a dangerous thing.

School teachers are not trained to give mental health advice, but they often care deeply about what their students are feeling. Again, they're utterly unqualified to give mental health advice. Therapists are never supposed to have relationships with patients outside of therapy. That includes math class, which makes many people anxious, of course.

In the vast majority of schools these days, therapists and non-therapists offer in-school counseling and mental health and wellness instruction.[21] We're talking 96 percent of public schools. They inadvertently exacerbate kids' worry, sadness, and feelings of incapacity. Trauma-informed education treats all kids as if they had experienced some debilitating trauma. Not everyone has experienced trauma. Indeed, my son recently complained that a lack of trauma growing up was holding him back in his acting career. His little sister said that she did her best at inflicting trauma.

You may have heard the term social-emotional learning (SEL) and assumed it was the new name for what they used to call character education: treat people kindly, disagree respectfully, don't be a jackass. Nope. SEL pushes kids toward a series of personal reflections, aimed at teaching them "self-awareness," "social awareness," "relationship skills," "self-management," and "responsible decision-making." Instead of the Pledge of Allegiance, today's teachers are more likely to inaugurate the school day with an emotions check-in. The problem is that this unceasing attention to feelings is likely to make kids more dysregulated, which is a word Freud wishes he had come up with.

What kids need to be told is to worry less, ruminate less, verbalize your feelings less, self-monitor less, be less mindful. Kids are more likely to meet a challenge if they focus on the task ahead, rather than their own emotional state. This is especially true if kids are doing something hard and they might fail, which is scary. School is a place to safely learn new things, like scary new math concepts, and to develop increasing confidence that you can meet any challenge because of the feeling of mastering all kinds of mathy things that were at first a little scary. Einstein said that most people "hold a secret grudge against arithmetic" by which he meant that math scares most people and they resent things that make them feel scared. I resent corn dogs for that reason.

Advocates of social-emotional learning claim that nearly all kids today have suffered serious traumatic experiences that leave them unable to learn. They also insist that having an educator host a class-wide trauma swap before lunch will help such kids heal. Neither claim is well-founded. It sounds like the kind of BS people come up with when they are stuck at home during a pandemic and spend far too much time on the internet. What we do know is that a horrifying percentage of children depend on public schools to get enough to eat. Delicious, healthy food is too tricky for school lunch programs, though, which is why they so often inflict corndog trauma on hungry children.

---

[21] Much of this is from Bad Therapy: Why the Kids Aren't Growing Up, by Abigail Shrier, Penguin Random House 2024.

Good therapists are trained specifically to avoid encouraging rumination, a thought process typified by dwelling on past pain and negative emotions. Rumination is a well-established risk factor for depression. But school staff who cosplay therapist rarely seem aware that they might be encouraging rumination during lunch and then after-lunch walk-and-talk, which everybody knows is a poor substitute for actual recess. Kids don't need some sort of pseudoscience AA meeting where they talk about their feelings instead of math class. They need to go out onto the playground and play so that they can sit still and concentrate during math class.

Your children may be regularly seeing a counselor or therapist in school and you don't have to be told about it. They think they know your children better than you, but they don't know what the hell they're doing.[22] When my son was in 2nd grade, my father and I yanked him out of school mid-afternoon every other Friday to go play a round of golf and then get ice cream. In school all they had going on during that time was some sort of SEL BS and then recess, and we can handle such things much better ourselves, thank you very much. Golf is an excellent venue for talking with caring adults about whatever might be bothering you. Don't ruminate. Not keeping score is the secret to enjoying golf.

---

[22] This Executive Order was intended to put a hard stop to such things. https://www.whitehouse.gov/presidential-actions/2025/01/ending-radical-indoctrination-in-k-12-schooling/

21 YANKEE DOODLE DANDY.

Nathaniel Carter's wife, Sarah Fair, was from England. She often teased her Yankee husband about his macaroni hat. He was born in Virginia in 1751 so he was a Yankee in the archaic usage of that term. The invention of baseball was still decades into the future when they were married in Prince William County, VA about 1771 or so. My wife often calls me honey, but our kids know that sometimes she means butthead and that the Yankees suck. I hope hundreds of years from now our descendants understand that honey was a term of endearment, even if there was some exasperation.

In the 1760s the term macaroni meant sophisticated, upper class, and worldly. Hence the insult of a rube from America who stuck a feather in his cap and called it macaroni. But then the meaning changed, according to *Atlas Obscura*[23]

> The new macaronis were characterized in a relatively singular way: most were gaunt men with tight pants, short coats, gaudy shoes, striped stockings, fancy walking sticks, and—most recognizably—extravagant wigs. Humorous depictions showed macaroni men wearing giant wigs topped off by comically small tricorn hats and attached to thick pigtails. Often these wigs were heavily powdered and were nearly half the size of the macaronis themselves.

English commentators variously referred to macaronis as "that doubtful gender," "hermaphrodites," and "amphibious creatures." Today we might say

---

[23] https://www.atlasobscura.com/articles/the-macaroni-in-yankee-doodle-is-not-what-you-think

gender-fluid or metrosexual. In 1770 The Oxford Magazine described the macaroni as not belonging to the gender binary: "There is indeed a kind of animal, neither male, nor female, a thing of neuter gender, lately started up among us. It is called a Macaroni. It talks without meaning, it smiles without pleasure, it eats without appetite, it rides without exercise, it wenches without passion."

My daughter recently bought me a copy of "Queer Eye for the Straight Guy: The Fab 5's Guide to Looking Better, Cooking Better, Dressing Better, Behaving Better, and Living Better" even though I already know quite a lot about fashion. My wife used to be the boss of fashion, by which I mean that she was a sportswear buyer for a chain of department stores. My wife and my daughter both have strong shoe games. I've read "The Primates of Park Avenue" so I understand the function of a very expensive handbag. At social events with my wife's macaroni colleagues back in the day, nobody wanted to talk about radar physics, so I learned to talk about fashion.

Perukes, e.g. powdered wigs, were adopted because of syphilis which was one of America's few microbial gifts to Europe. A small payback for smallpox. Late stage syphilis leads to hair loss and dementia, so anybody going bald could be snickered at. You could even suggest that they take a mental competency test. Hence, various balding kings and whatnot started wearing powdered wigs so then everybody had to. Except George Washington. He merely powdered his red hair so we wouldn't have to suffer the indignity of having a ginger for our first president.

If you take a look around your office, you may notice the occasional macaroni. I'm not talking about the later gender-fluid meaning of the word. I don't care one whit about such things. I've always been comfortable with the box that Dr. Frost checked on my birth certificate sixty-some years ago. I understand that that isn't the case for everybody and that must be hard. I try not to inadvertently do anything that would make that harder, but that's just having good manners. I simply don't spend any time wondering about the personal lives of my co-workers. I assume they all have them.

The macaronis I'm talking about are the Yankee Doodle sort who always want to stick a feather in their cap and call it macaroni. I assume you also find their behavior infuriating. Every little fucking thing they do they stick a feather in it and expect everyone to be impressed. It's a PowerPoint deck. We're not going to applaud you for that, unless you're in third grade then good job honey. Macaronis usually can't even get the aspect ratio correct or put the company logo in the right place. Also, that's the old logo you rube. The new one has no feathers in it because that was culturally insensitive. IT sent us all the new company template months ago. You forgot the land acknowledgement statement.

Macaronis never suffer from imposter syndrome, but maybe they should. Confidence is good most of the time. Overconfidence, not so much.

According to the Cleveland Clinic[24] imposter syndrome "isn't a diagnosis or a medical problem, but a pattern of thinking that can lead to self-doubt, negative self-talk and missed opportunities." Apparently, it's hard-working high-achievers and perfectionists who are most likely to suffer. Here's how it manifests at work: "People with an imposter mindset often attribute their success to luck rather than their own abilities and work ethic, which could hold them back from asking for a raise or applying for a promotion. They might also feel like they have to overwork themselves to achieve the impossibly high standards they've set."

The most important thing to keep in mind about imposter syndrome, whenever you start to feel like you're some sort of fraud, is that true imposters don't ever have this feeling. The macaronis you work with actually think they look good in that peruke with a small tricorn hat perched way up high and with a ridiculous feather on top.

While the second meaning of macaroni is gender-fluid, imposter syndrome is strongly gendered. If there are some men in the world who suffer from imposter syndrome they must all be keeping those feelings to themselves. It's apparently unmanly to admit such things. They say that true bravery is doing something scary even though you're scared. Fear is often a useful tool to stay alive in a dangerous situation, though. Powerpointing us all to death with your unformatted, mis-logoed, overly-detailed yet egregiously-vague slide deck should have been career death, you macaroni. All of us actual over-achievers whose afternoon you just wasted now have to spend their evening cleaning up your mess.

I suppose you just have to come to terms with macaronis in the workplace, but that doesn't mean that you and your competent co-workers can't hum Yankee Doodle now and then. It could be especially fun at the 4th of July company-wide picnic that nobody wants to go to but somehow you got voluntold to organize. It wouldn't be passive-aggressive at all to assign all the macaronis to bring pasta salad. Most of them can't boil water, so they'll all swing by the supermarket on the way but then leave it in the car while they run a few last-minute errands and show up late. Don't let anybody you don't want to get food poisoning eat that. Being macaronis, they won't understand how deeply shameful it is to take a mostly full dish home after a potluck. Maybe you can arrange some sort of potluck contest where the winner gets priority parking and the losers can hoof it from the overflow lot. You know perfectly well that your pies are going to win. What could be more American than apple pie on the 4th of July?

One more thing. Be sure to make the 4th of July company-wide picnic a

---

24

https://health.clevelandclinic.org/a-psychologist-explains-how-to-deal-with-imposter-syndrome costume party, perhaps even with a Colonial Williamsburg theme. Back in the day, it was men who wore wigs with tricorn hats and high heels and, of course, stockings to show off their shapely calves. See how macaronis like having to wear pantyhose when it's 100 degrees.

22 WE'RE ALL BEING PAID TO SOLVE PROBLEMS, NOT TO PROBLEMATIZE NEW ONES.

I always find it strange when I say thank you to the young person manning the cash register at WaWa at the end of our brief transaction and they respond, "No problem." I understand that paying with cash seems as strange to some people as swiping your debit card for a cup of coffee seems to me. I assume it's a reflexive response rather than a statement by the clerk that they have no problem counting out change even though they were probably taught that via worksheets. The value of the different coins clicked for my son when I took him along to the university library to photocopy a few articles for a proposal I was writing. He grasped right away that you put a quarter in the slot and push the button. A piece of paper comes out the side and then a nickel and a dime dingle into the little tray. You could then put either a dime or two nickels into the slot and push the button to get another piece of paper out. In case you're wondering, we didn't photocopy our faces that day, although now I wish we had.

One of the most annoying things about young people these days is their tendency to endlessly problematize things. It's not just whining that things are hard, it's forever imagining new and more ridiculous ways to somehow be the victim in everything. You probably find yourself wanting to tell them to STFU and just start solving some real problems instead, but you know full well that they'd burst into tears and that would then be your problem. For those of us whose kids aren't toddlers anymore, it's a problem when our supposedly grown-up co-workers behave like toddlers who didn't get their nap today and now are pitching a fit because you cut the crust off their PB&J wrong.

My wife recently fussed at me about my profile picture on my webpage, "You need a new picture." I fully admit that my selfie game is weak. I don't like to have my picture taken, and I don't have a camera on my phone because

I sometimes go places where cameras are not allowed. It's actually rather difficult to get a phone without a camera these days. Everybody else has excellent cameras on their phones and so if there's someone or something that needs to be photographed, it's no problem. The webpage my wife was referring to isn't one that I maintain. I'm not really sure anybody does, but if I had a substitute picture it wouldn't be too much of a problem to sort that out and swap it out. My wife has an excellent camera on her new iPhone, and presumably has a fair number of photos of me on her camera roll. She could have sent me one of those and suggested it as a replacement profile picture, or she could have asked me to hold still for a moment and smile a little bit so she could snap a picture or twelve of me. If she liked one of those she could have sent it to me so I could forward it to a webmaster or something. Nope. All she did was fuss at me.

One of the things we seem to have to explain patiently to n00bs in the workplace is that you always want to present both the problem and the solution. The organization is paying us to solve problems, not just to whine about them. People who advance in their careers are the ones who solve more problems than they create. Nothing is more annoying than forever having to mop up other people's problems, except perhaps literally mopping up other people's problems. It would be better if you pooped on your own time, of course, but if you have to drop a log while on the clock and the toilet overflows don't come back to your cubicle and pretend that wasn't you. Figure out how to get a custodian or plumber or hazmat team here, stat. Then go wash your damn hands. Geez.

I often regret knowing how to do things like plumbing. Even the simplest plumbing chore seems to take at least three trips to the hardware store, and because I don't do plumbing all that often I'm never quite sure how tight the fitting needs to be. Also, now that I wear progressive lenses I find that seeing what I'm doing up under the sink is kind of a problem. Nobody wants to listen to me complain about any of that, though. They just want the water back on.

I wish I had some magic way for you to help twenty-four-year-olds unlearn their learned helplessness. The best I can come up with is not getting sucked into solving all their problems for them, because that will encourage them to forever keep coming up with new problems for you to solve. They'll quickly learn that their primary role in the workplace is to point out issues for you to deal with because you're so much better at fixing things than they are. You already know how to call a plumber so there's no point in them doing that, especially since Dad always does that at home where they still live. They maybe could text their Dad if you need a recommendation for a plumber or something.

The first lesson for entitled little shits in the workplace has to be that shit goes downhill. They don't assign you tasks. You assign them tasks. They don't come up with problems for you to solve. You give them appropriate challenges to figure out how to attack, and then gently but firmly correct them when they haven't tightened the fitting sufficiently and the water is still leaking. It's not even your job to tell them where to go to find a mop to clean up that spill before someone slips in the puddle and then there's a real problem.

I'm in the business of solving hard problems that require decades of high-level, hard-won, specialized expertise. There's usually quite a lot of math involved. And physics. And computers. The perfect sort of problem for us is one that's so hard nobody else can solve it, and so important that money is no object. If the problem is too easy, there are lots of other people who could solve it. If the problem isn't important enough, nobody would pay our fair, but high, rates to solve it. We don't sign up to solve impossible problems, of course, because that would be a waste of our time and our clients' money. We like novel problems because it gets boring to do the same thing over and over. I get nervous when a graduate student thinks they've solved a problem easily because that would mean that I've mis-judged the inherent level of difficulty. I've been doing this for decades, and so far it's always been that the graduate student has overlooked some aspect of the problem. I patiently explain that that's a good thing, because they can't graduate until they've solved a couple-three problems that are actually as challenging as I expected them to be.

In your business you're going to have to define appropriate challenges for your new hires, and then see if they can rise to those challenges. You have to resist the temptation of reaching down to their lowly rung on the jungle gym and pulling them up against their will. They will complain that you jerked them too hard and now their shoulder hurts. Some will insist on staying on that first rung while endlessly inventing problems that prevent them from climbing up. Some will figure out that they can actually solve problems and then will be eager to solve more and even harder problems. A few will develop a can-do attitude and will begin to make your job easier rather than harder.

People who grew up in the former Soviet Union learned to never be too happy about some success. It was a problem if things were going too well. One of my graduate students in the late 1990s was from Ukraine, and had learned to affect an Eeyore attitude about things. Of course he was solving hard problems because that's how you earn a doctorate. We developed an amusing routine where he would describe what he was working on as, "Big problem. Big problem." and I would tell him to do his best. The next day he would have solved that issue and his current challenge was a big problem. I encouraged him to periodically write down a description of the problems he was having, and so when he sat down to write his dissertation he found that about 80% of it was already done.

Endlessly problematizing is part of the prevailing culture which honors and rewards victimhood. There's this ridiculous idea that everybody is either an oppressor or oppressed, but once you've sorted all humans into one or the other there needs to be a way to determine who is the most oppressed and therefore the winner. The answer is to define innumerable axes of oppression and whoever has the most intersections is the champion victim. @fakegreekgrill identified the actual problem, "It seems like where 'intersectionality' went wrong was assuming that anyone with any claim to oppression must be part of one omnicause + global warming for some reason." The omnicause means that everything is one big problem which is therefore unsolvable and we are therefore all absolved from solving it. It's a non-problem. Global warming, though.

23 THIS PLACE, WHERE SO MANY PEOPLE WOULD DIE TO WORK, YOU ONLY DEIGN TO WORK.

The fact that AI can't do your job, but that your boss can be convinced to fire you and replace you with the AI that can't do your job, is the central fact of the 21st century labor market. AI has created a world of "algorithmic management" where humans are demoted to reverse centaurs, monitored and bossed about by an app. Automation theorists call a human augmented by a machine a "centaur" – a human head supported by a machine's tireless and strong body. A "reverse centaur" is a machine augmented by a human – like the Amazon delivery driver whose app goads them to make inhuman delivery quotas while punishing them for looking in the "wrong" direction or even singing along with the radio.[25]

In the movie, The Devil Wears Prada, new-college graduate and writer wanna-be Andy complains to Nigel that she's trying so hard but gets no credit for her hard work. He's not having any of it:

> Andy, be serious. You're not trying. You are whining. What is it that you want me to say? Do you want me to say "Poor you, Miranda's picking on you, poor you, poor Andy." Hm? Wake up, Six. She's just doing her job. Don't you know that you're working at the place that published some of the greatest artists of the century? Holston. Lagerfeld. De la Renta. And what they did, what they created, is greater than art. Because you live your life in it. ...Well, maybe not you, but some people. You think this is just a magazine?

Actually, it's just a magazine but some people care quite a lot about fashion. It's big business, predicated on convincing people four times a year

---

[25] https://pluralistic.net/2024/11/26/hawtch-hawtch/#you-treasure-what-you-measure

that whatever they've been wearing (because it's so fashionable) is now highly unfashionable. The new ugliest color was recently the hot new color.

In the movie, Andy decides to dress in high-fashion and cut down on carbs and work really hard for a boss who is really mean to everybody, presumably because she's been hangry her whole adult life and understands that her life's work actually is kind of empty inside. It's a great movie with a surprisingly happy ending. My wife, who used to work in fashion and still sets the standard for fashion at work, didn't care for it all that much.

It can be fun to get the Olds you work with to talk about their first jobs. Mine was delivering the morning paper in a part of the country where it snowed a lot. I also shoveled snow and cut grass and raked leaves and so on. My wife's first regular job was working at the B&G Milky Way ice cream stand at age 13. We recently were at her 40th high school reunion, and so we went there for some ice cream. She told the young girl behind the counter that this was her first job too and it was where she learned to count out change and be polite to strange ladies who worked here when they were your age. My wife also did a lot of babysitting for a nickel a year or whatever they paid back in the Seventies. When we were dating in high school she worked the gift wrap counter at a department store at the mall, which is how I know to crease the edges when I wrap a gift.

The fresh-out college graduates you hire may have never had jobs as teenagers. They may have been too busy during the summers with enrichment camps their parents paid for in order to pad their college application portfolios. College costs so much these days that there's no point in working a summer job to help pay for it. There isn't even any need to save up spending money if Dad is going to send you off to college with a credit card he pays, for emergencies, of course. It's princess 101 to continually redefine "emergency" to include pizza and shoes and Starbs. I've told my daughter that I'm taking that Visa card back when I retire, currently slated for age 79.

"Someone cooked here" is an expression that means someone else was in your partner's life before you, leaving their unique mark. It's obvious to most women when they visit a cishet young man's apartment whether he's had a live-in girlfriend before. It can be a good thing if someone else has already trained him to put the toilet seat down and take out the trash and so on. You can think of that prior relationship as an internship, which might even save you quite a lot of actual work. I had no sisters growing up, but I had a fair number of female roommates after college, so I learned my gendered role in a multi-gender living arrangement.

Unless roommate drama spills over into the workplace, you presumably don't care one whit about your young employees' living arrangements. You do care, though, whether they had summer jobs as teenagers. Always be sure to ask about such things during the interview process. If they have no stories to relate, you're going to have to probe a bit more about what they did all summer instead. You need to know before you start the on-boarding process whether you're going to be the first actual boss they've ever had. If you are, you're going to be the worst boss they've ever had.

There's a new office development in London designed to attract Gen Z workers.[26] As well as more traditional workout facilities such as a pool and gym, perks will include therapies such as music and art classes, breathwork, movement and meditation classes and access to clinically based nutrition. Of course, the building(s) will have air and water filtration to reduce toxins and will be fossil fuel-free and net zero on carbon emissions when in operation. There will also be 20,000 sq ft of creative and cultural space. Other features will include Pilates studios, hot and cold therapy rooms and napping pods, plus digital detox areas where workers can escape from screens. It's almost as if they want workers to never go home....

In most cases where young people have never actually worked, they probably had an internship during college. These are becoming more and more necessary, especially for academic high achievers who have excelled in the highly structured atmosphere of college but may flounder badly in the workplace. Internships, done right, teach young people to show up whether they feel like it or not. They learn to sit still all day long and accomplish the tasks that are being assigned to them, especially when those tasks aren't using their talents to the fullest. You'll want to see if you can tell whether they stuck it out for the whole summer or if they had to take a couple of weeks off to go on a family vacation. When I've had summer interns who ask for time off on their first day of work, I explain to them calmly but tersely that they "just quit their job" and have them give me back their key to the lab.

Unpaid internships are both unethical and violate the Federal minimum wage laws, so if you've got internships at your organization you need to pay the interns. Most of them won't deliver much value for that wage, but you're doing their next boss a service by teaching them some life skills. Ideally, the interns who work for you have already had some sort of job and/or internship before so you won't be starting from a blank slate. In some cases, you'll identify promising young people who you might want to hire when they graduate. You're probably going to want to limit your internship to rising college seniors.

I usually buddy up my summer interns with a graduate student who can use some help with their research project. Things that have become tedious will be new and exciting for the intern, freeing up time for the graduate student to do data analysis and write up results for publication. The graduate students also get some first-hand experience with managing the day-to-day

---

26

https://www.telegraph.co.uk/business/2025/02/08/napping-pods-and-breathwork-classes-the-round/

work of someone more junior. They learn to respond thoughtfully to naïve questions about what they're doing and why. They get some experience with a small project going sour because they didn't give proper instructions or properly monitor their young apprentice.

You probably can set up similar sorts of arrangements where your youngest employees learn to mentor interns for several weeks. There's a lot of babysitting involved, of course. It will be fun for you to watch them tell their charges to put away their phones because they're at work. During naptime you can ask your actual employees how it's all going. They will hear words coming out of their own mouths which straight-up plagiarize things you may have said about them a minute ago when they were new here.

The most important thing to do with interns is to give them tasks they have to figure out more or less on their own. You need to be able to determine whether the inherently unstructured nature of the workplace energizes them or causes them to collapse into a ball of anxiety. Failure is how all mammals learn. They need to get some experience at things that don't work the first time. Have them give things a try and see both what works and what doesn't. Then have them do a little PowerPoint presentation about all the many ways it didn't work. If they complain about having to work "overtime" to get their slide deck finished and their presentation practiced, tell them about the Congressional staffers who briefly demanded a four-day work week at full pay.

The association representing progressive Hill staff withdrew its letter calling for a rotating 32-hour work week for congressional staff, after significant bipartisan backlash.[27] You might think that the answer would be to put those staffers on a performance improvement plan. The key paragraph in "The Most Hated Way of Firing Someone Is More Popular Than Ever. It's the Age of the PIP." seems to be: "A common tactic for people placed on PIPs is to file for a leave of absence, often under the federally protected Family and Medical Leave Act. A leave stops the clock on the PIP. Even if they're not getting paid, workers can use the time to job hunt while still employed so there's no resume gap to explain to a prospective new employer. The leave could also give workers some leverage to allege retaliation if they're fired after they return." It's probably safe to assume that any and all malingerers know this.[28]

27

https://www.politico.com/live-updates/2025/01/17/congress/progressives-claw-back-letter-00199092

28

https://www.wsj.com/business/firing-someone-performance-improvement-plans-more-popular-the-pip-7cac7062

24 Yes, Mister Sir.

You'll be unsurprised to know that the Army has a well-developed system for determining who out-ranks whom. Two captains, for example, would be of the same grade (captain) but of different ranks depending on when they each pinned on the two silver bars. It's kind of like identical twins whose moments of birth determine which one is older, which presumably mattered at times and in places where inheritance went to the eldest son. There also used to be some cultures where naming conventions were rigidly proscribed, which now makes genealogy difficult because there are so many Peder Pedersons and Iver Iversons and Carl Carlsons and so on. Don't even get me started on Annie Thorisdottir, whose name turns out to be Þórisdóttir. She's the first woman to win the CrossFit Games twice. She trains four hours per day, six days per week, and also has experience as a gymnast, ballet dancer, pole vaulter and mother. Let's just all agree that she's the #girlboss and stipulate that it would be idiotic for anyone to try to invade Iceland. Annie could easily beat up any Air Force captain I knew back when I was one, and I was fit enough that I probably would have done CrossFit if it had been a thing in the late nineteen hundreds. I also had hair, as you can see here, but was required to keep it cut short.

The Air Force also has a well-developed system for how service members are expected to address each other. Two captains can address each other by their first names only if there's nobody else present of a different grade, what everybody calls rank. Otherwise they are to address each other as Captain Lastname or just Captain. This scheme is very convenient for those who don't remember names well, because the insignia of rank and name are right there in plain view. The rules for saluting are also quite specific. The more junior person raises their salute first and the more senior officer responds. The junior person is expected to hold their salute until the senior officer starts to lower theirs, but then react quickly enough to get their hand smartly down to their own side before the senior officer does. The junior person would address the senior officer as Sir or Ma'am or via rank with or without last name. The senior officer would always address the more junior person with rank or rank and last name.

Enlisted folks don't salute each other, and except for shouting in unison, "Sir, Yes Sir!" during basic training, privates never address sergeants as sir. At least that's my assumption based on movies. As an officer they would stick to the formal rules of address whenever I happened to be present. I don't think two captains salute each other, but can just give a little nod and say 'sup. My wife always liked driving onto base because she had a sticker on her car that indicated my rank and so the guards saluted her. She's a #girlboss these days, but there's no corresponding sticker on her car.

Your organization almost certainly has no such formal rules about how people of different "ranks" should address each other. This can be quite confusing for young employees, particularly now that the long-standing rules regarding gender roles and gender expression have finally been tossed out the window. It gets worse when an organization tries to pretend that they're all egalitarian and everybody is the same, a noble ideal that is kind of enshrined in various founding documents albeit with some caveats. I happen to favor as flat of a bureaucracy as is workable, but I fully understand that there must be some amount of hierarchy with a clear chain of command. I have a yellowed cartoon on my bulletin board where a boss at the end of a long conference table says, "All in favor of my motion, signify by saying 'Aye.' All opposed, say 'I quit.'" I also like the Nathan Arizona catchphrase, "Do it my way or watch your butt!"

Unless your new hires have military experience, they may have never been given a direct order. They almost certainly never have had to literally salute and say, "Yes Sir." They may have said, "Yes, Mom." when directed to clear the table or clean their room, but didn't accidentally say "Yes, Mom" when they were a cadet and meant to say "Yes, Ma'am" which is why it's better to say "Yes, Captain." At various points in your organization's chain of command, higher ups can issue directives, what the military would call direct orders, which must be followed. Failure to follow a direct order is grounds for court martial. Failure to follow a directive is grounds for firing. This can be a tough lesson for young hires. A meme that explains this has the caption, "How to be an adult at work. Replace 'fuck you' with 'OK great!'" I'm not sure you could get away with putting that on your office bulletin board, though. You'd be surprised what people will get butthurt about these days. In our chronically-messy kitchenette area I put up a cute sign that said, "Your mother doesn't work here. Clean up your own mess." Someone complained and we had to take it down. Whoever emailed that complaint probably got a small rush of power at being able to make the sign come down. It's been a couple of years now and the four screw holes are still in the drywall. I may try putting it back up again sometime and see what happens. It could provide an opportunity for some powerless n00b with mommy issues to feel like they have a bit of agency for a hot second.

One common mistake that bosses make is to encourage junior employees to address them by their first name. Don't fall into that trap. You wouldn't presume to call the CEO by their first name. If they call you by your first name you might be surprised that they even know that, but assume that there's an aide who whispers such things into their ear. Your doctor looks at your chart for such information just before they come into the examination room. The nurse may or may not have included a pronunciation guide for them. Eventually you'll get to the point where you're about the age of the moms of your new hires, so them calling you by your first name is exactly as awkward as when children address their parents by their names. I called my parents Mom and Dad until they became grandparents and got promoted to Granny and Gramps. I coined nicknames for each of my children within moments of their births, which I still use most of the time.

The fundamental problem with pretending there's no hierarchy and everybody is same-same so we all call each other by our preferred first names, is that sooner or later you're going to have to put on your boss hat and correct or discipline or terminate your employees. The faux familiarity of being on a first-name basis at work will diminish your authority. As a more senior member of the organization's hierarchy, you are clothed in immense power. At times you need to be able to embrace that mantle and your underlings should rightly fear and respect you. Pretending that you're all just a happy "work family" sets you up for the petulant rejoinder, "You're not my real mom/dad. Don't tell me what to do!"

I train PhD students for a living. When they finish their dissertations my students graduate to become my peers. I treat them as such, but they never call me by my first name even decades after graduation when they are at the tippy-top of their own organizational hierarchies. While they are students I call them by their first names. When they graduate, I call them Dr. Lastname. Both before and after graduation they address me as either Professor or Dr. MyLastname. The former is the more honorific of the two because we're all sooner or later Doctor but only I am Professor. My wife calls me Honey, which sometimes can be interpreted as Butthead.

My colleagues in the biomedical sciences all seem to have their students, undergraduate and graduate, call them by their first names. I find that quite jarring. It's also disingenuous because biomedical science couldn't possibly be more hierarchical. I'm pretty sure not addressing a physician as Doctor is grounds for termination in most clinical settings.

I don't know what the right forms of address are in your organization. Probably the right answer is to lean in on everybody's preferred pronouns.

People might need to wear lapel pins in lieu of insignias of rank, though. In case you're wondering, my preferred pronouns are "your highness" but I don't expect anyone to call me that. The dog seems to be saying, "Hurry up, old man." when I'm taking too long to feed her. I'll respond to just about anything, as long as only those at my rank and above use my given name. You'll have to constrain the choice of preferred pronouns somewhat or it will all be far too confusing for most of the Olds in your organization who can't read that small print on the lapel pins anyway. Get the Olds all confused and they'll just start calling everybody "Skippy" and then they can respond with, "Yes, Chief." which might end up being a workable system.

25 Unlimited vacation is an accounting gimmick.

The goal in life is not to avoid work, it's to get paid well to do work you want to do. Have fun. Make money. Those are not incompatible. To quote Dirty Heads, "A-a-aye, I'm on vacation. Every single day 'cause I love my occupation." Also, "Hard work, it pays off. I'm happy now, it's paying me." Finally, "Do this shit, I love it on the daily." I happen to have a job that both pays me well and gives me joy. I've worked really hard to get to this position and I get to keep doing this job as long as I want. I might think about retiring just before I turn 80.

I'm a tenured professor, so I come and go as I please. I tend to arrive in the office about 7 each morning, including Saturdays. I typically go home to walk the dog about 4 on weekdays and then do some things in my office at home, including late afternoon Zoom meetings, while she snoozes next to me in her dog bed. You might think that I have my summers off, but I run a research group so summer months are for working, as are spring break and semester break and various little holidays when the university is technically closed. If I feel like travelling, which I rarely do, there is always some scientific conference somewhere that I could easily justify going to with travel costs covered by a research grant. My wife is often cross that I never seem to spend all of the travel money in my grants. She likes to travel, so every couple of years I relent. Her idea of fun is to sit around and do nothing and then go out to eat. While I can do a thousand hours of small talk on a ten-day vacation trip, that's not relaxing for me.

As an Air Force officer, back in the day, I was allowed thirty days of leave per year. That sounds like a lot, but if you left the local area over the weekend or a holiday, those all counted against your leave balance. Hence, I never developed the habit of going on long-weekend excursions. I had an office job where I wrote radar equations, so taking a day off didn't require any sort of special permission or coordination, even for the short period during the liberation of Kuwait when I was on active duty during wartime. I have no skills that are useful in wartime.

Most organizations have a combination of holidays, personal time off, and paid sick leave. In some places, if you don't use up your vacation days by a certain time each year they do not roll over. This sort of use-or-lose blanket policy can make it really hard to find anybody at all in a government office near the end of the calendar year. Some organizations let some amount of leave roll over, or even better yet will give employees with a leave balance the option to get paid out for their unused leave in a lump sum at the end of the year. If your organization is a use-or-lose place, you may find that you have to encourage your hardest-working employees to take leave throughout the year. Unless it works to just shut the place down for a scheduled outage, you can't have everybody decide at the last minute to go on vacation at the same time or forget to plan ahead and all have to take the last week(s) of the fiscal year off.

Some organizations pretend they offer "unlimited vacation" but that's just an accounting gimmick to avoid having to pay out unused vacation time when someone leaves voluntarily (or not) and because accrued leave has to be accounted for on the books appropriately. Taking too much time off will affect any employee's productivity. The goal is to have your employees each take as much time off as they need to be optimally productive. That will be different for each of them, and will even differ for each of them at different stages in their life. I didn't work on Saturday mornings when I had little kids. If there was no soccer game or whatever, we would simply go mess around. We called it "boy's day" but tomboys were included in that, of course. The point was to give Mom a break. We imagined that we were out doing things Mom probably didn't approve of, but that may have only been getting Big Gulps or Slurpees at 7/11. Of course, I insisted that they choose colors of drinks that more or less matched my car's interior.

The last time I went on vacation I made a point of not checking my email, and I didn't even put an out-of-office message. There were no looming deadlines and I had alerted key people that I was going to be gone, but none of my co-workers have my personal cell number so I didn't get any calls or text messages either. I simply don't do social media, so people couldn't even check there for some sort of travelogue. Over ten days, I think I did check my email once, but didn't respond to any messages. People who know me know that I fully understand the asynchronous nature of email and that I'll respond when I think it's necessary. Or not.

This trip was mostly to visit my wife's extended family and go to her high school reunion, so I was primarily arm candy expected to make small talk (for 1,000 hours) and such. Had I wanted to do so, I could have spent quite a lot of time on a smartphone/laptop keeping up with work back in Virginia. I didn't want to, so I didn't. My wife had a great time, since it was ten days of sitting around and chatting and then going out to eat, which is her idea of fun.

She did a pretty good job of staying out of whatever crises were boiling over back in her office, but was only really out of contact when we were at her mother's house because there is literally no cell service there. I hadn't even brought along my phone charger, so after several days I simply turned my phone off.

In addition to encouraging your young employees to take enough time off so they will remain highly productive, you probably also have to give them firm guidance on disconnecting from the office when they're supposed to be taking time off. You're going to have to start by systematically modeling healthy behaviors. Step number zero is to not give any of your employees your personal cell phone number. Sorry if that just made you snort with derision or swallow your coffee wrong. Your organization probably has arranged things, perhaps unwittingly, so that the default answer is for everybody to use their personal devices at work. This situation may have just happened during COVID when most people were working from home (or wherever) and some were in the office and now who knows who is where and in what time zone on any given work day, night or weekend. It used to be unusual for your boss to call you at home. I suppose it would still be unusual for the boss to actually call, because who does that anyway, but text messages which should have been emails are far too common. Since your employees read emails on their phones anyway, the answer is probably to email them instead of texting or calling. You could get yourself a boss burner phone for when you need to call. When you do send an email after hours, be sure to use schedule send so you're not interrupting happy hour or their personal couch-rotting time over the weekend.

With that groundwork laid, step one is to set the expectations among your staff to email (with schedule send) whenever that can substitute for a text message. Selective cc's on an email chain are better than a group text. They should reserve that group text for complaining about the boss (you) or coordinating among themselves who's going to take vacation when. Your goal is to help them to learn to differentiate work-related communications from those that are more social in nature. Of course the boundaries will blur somewhat, perhaps more than they should, but this is just the first step. I understand that there are various professional and social messaging platforms, so maybe Slack instead of email or text. You can have a conversation with them about which tools to use to de-blur work and social boundaries. They'll need to know that if they message you over the weekend, you aren't likely to respond until Monday. You may or may not be rotting on your own sofa. That's not any of their business.

The next several steps in this conversation have to do with how to leave people enough alone when they're on vacation that they are able to come back ready to get back to it. Always-connected digital natives will often get anxious when they don't know what's going on. The answer might be a designated co-worker who keeps them in the loop. Whatever you do, though, don't start a group-text chain about this.

26 Don't wear your leopard print Spanx with those white pants.

Your female co-workers can be quite catty. Most people understand that if an office is all men it can easily end up with a frat house vibe, despite everybody wearing expensively tailored suits, and HR probably needs to step in to avoid a sequence of expensive lawsuits. Less widely known, is that if an office is all women the department culture can also go quite wrong in stereotypical ways. Not all that many grown-ass women remember "middle school girl world" fondly. Very few men even realize there is such a thing, except for those of us #girldads who read the mean-girl literature in order to help our floater daughters navigate these fraught years.

There are innumerable axes of human diversity, but the most important is still gender. Men and women are different. You want those differing perspectives within every unit in your organization. It tends to keep things from going stereotypically wrong, by forcing everybody to recognize that there are people who think differently.

The *Economist* recently studied this issue.[29] They include a plot which shows that ten percent more women than men are college graduates. You might think that doesn't really matter to you because everybody you hire graduated from a good college. "Differences in education lead to differences in attitude: people who attend college are more likely to absorb a liberal, egalitarian outlook. The education gap also leads to differences in how men and women experience life, work and romance. To simplify: when a woman leaves university in a rich country, she is likely to find a white-collar job and be able

---

29

https://www.economist.com/international/2024/03/13/why-the-growing-gulf-between-young-men-and-women to support herself. But when she enters the dating market (assuming she is heterosexual), she finds that, because there are many more female graduates than male ones, the supply of liberal, educated men does not match demand." My daughter is a professional in her late 20s in Washington, DC and I'm pretty sure she would agree with the quote from that article that men her age have a "little-boy" mindset. Many of the young, professional women who work for you are all experiencing this right now.

My wife just clued me in to an *Economist* podcast on the relationship between weight and success.[30] The teaser is, "Across the rich world there is a negative relationship between incomes and weight, as measured by body mass index. The richer people are, the thinner they tend to be. But separate the data by gender and a startling gap appears. Rich women are much thinner than poorer ones; but rich men and poor men are just as likely to be overweight or obese." She mentioned this to me on Pi Day, by the way. She's quite famous locally for her pies, especially the pie crust which my great aunt taught her to make. I was a big fat guy for a few years in my early forties, and then stopped eating pie and such. I quickly dropped back to a healthy weight which I've maintained for more than 15 years. My wife is still cross that I don't eat her pie anymore. She's been able to fit back into her wedding dress for a couple of years now.

My mother says she was overweight for a few years after college, but she started eating better and has been at a healthy weight for more than 60 years. She systematically destroyed all evidence, which I can attest to because I have recently scanned and archived the complete corpus of family photos and there are none of her from when she was ten or more pounds heavier than she wanted to be. My father was always active enough that he could have a piece of cake with his morning coffee and then go exercise before having actual breakfast. The dog used to clean up any cake crumbs, so she lost most of her teeth and had to switch over to soft food, which was a win-win for her.

The *Economist* ran the numbers, of course, and found that for an obese woman, losing weight could boost her salary by as much as obtaining a master's degree. Properly tailored men's suits do a good job of hiding their love handles, but nobody except their cardiologists really care about whether men are at a healthy weight or not. It certainly doesn't affect their salary. I found that when I went from fat to fit in about half a year people assumed that I was dying from cancer or something. They were concerned that I looked less healthy. Only two people asked me directly, though. Everybody else asked my wife to which she responded testily, "He's fine. He just doesn't eat pie anymore."

30

https://www.economist.com/podcasts/2023/01/05/the-relationship-between-weight-and-success

Part of my self-designed seven-year program to get in shape by the time I was 50 was to walk to and from work. I live just close enough to campus that that was possible, and because I prepare lectures and such mostly inside my head, walking turns out to be a productive time for me. If I'm thinking through some client's problems, it can be highly lucrative given my hourly consulting rate. I usually listen to music while I'm walking, but I could instead listen to podcasts, such as the WSJ one[31] with the tagline: *You just started taking Ozempic. Will you still crave that bag of potato chips?* with the teaser, "Big food companies and investors are watching as Ozempic and other similar weight-loss drugs flow to millions of people, upending America's diet industry and raising new questions about how consumers will eat."

A March 2024 WSJ piece[32] included the opinions of college students about whether *Wegovy* and *Ozempic* can help America's obesity problem. They are fairly helpful in understanding your young employees' thoughts on the matter.

- According to a study from the New England Journal of Medicine, obesity spreads through social ties. Having obese coworkers, for example, can normalize weight gain and promote unhealthy behaviors such as overeating and poor food choice.

- In the U.S., according to the Department of Agriculture, more than 23 million people live in food deserts, areas without access to nutritious food.

- The body-positivity movement, which challenges unrealistic beauty standards, has taken off on social media. This movement contributes to the obesity crisis.

- As the proportion of processed foods increases in diets worldwide, incidences of obesity, diabetes and cardiovascular disease will continue to grow, putting an ever-increasing strain on our medical system. Processed foods are simply too cheap.

- It is not only the lack of physical effort at work that causes people to gain weight but the changing American corporate culture. Large levels of stress lead to higher levels of after-work indulgence combined with increasing social pressure and longer work hours. These factors limit

---

[31] https://www.wsj.com/business/ozempic-impact-snack-food-companies-9eec87e5

[32] https://www.wsj.com/articles/can-wegovy-and-ozempic-help-americas-obesity-problem-e1fb1f6b

people's time, and test their motivation to exercise and eat healthy foods.

- Most people don't know enough about what's good for them to eat, what makes up a healthy meal and how to make sure they're not missing out on essential nutrients. Social media makes it worse by pushing fad foods and diets.

I hope you can begin to see that your young employees are going to blame this on you. You can even get into trouble by talking about it wrong. People aren't fat, they "have obesity" and also probably "have diabetes" and so on. It's not yet a protected class, but more and more obesity is considered to be a disease, which predominantly affects women.

I saw on the news that the *Super Size Me* (2004) guy just died at age 53. He only ate fast food for every meal that year for his documentary, so it wasn't like he had obesity or diabetes. I think it was cancer or something. We now know that up to half of cancers are obesity related, so there's that. It used to be that fast food was cheap, and healthy food was expensive, which explains some of why so many people have both obesity and poverty. Thanks to all that stimulus spending and the resultant run-away inflation, rich and poor alike have noticed that the price of a fast-food meal has about doubled since the Hamburgler-in-Chief left office the first time in 2021.

27 From the sky will come a great King of Terror in July 1999.

When you've been around the block enough times, it starts to seem to your co-workers like you can see around corners. You're actually just paying attention to patterns that repeat themselves with minor variations. There's no reason to be surprised by things that happen at the same time each year. Or quarter. Or week. But then Monday mornings seem to sneak up on some of your co-workers three or four times a moonth.

Deadlines don't sneak up on me because I can see them coming. What I mean is that I'm blessed with calendar synesthesia. The year has a particular shape in my mind, and I can see from a bird's eye view any part of the year. I've never quite been able to draw how I see the year. It's kind of potato shaped. Time moves counter-clockwise. Parts of the year that mattered most to me as a child take up more of the potato. I have to be careful about March because that was forgettable where and when I grew up. It's easy for me to skip over that whole month in my mind's eye. Both my daughter and my mother also have calendar synesthesia, although their shapes and directions are different. My mother says that when she retired, her year lost its shape.

Simply by premembering things that are coming up, you may earn yourself the nickname Nostradamus. It's not actually a compliment. He was a terrible seer. It was what he did for his second act, after he became famous as a physician whose patients didn't die from the Black Death. You might look up the meaning of the lyrics to *Ring Around the Rosies* sometime. I've instructed my heirs to sing that at the internment of my ashes. Assuming I've lived a long life full of joy and died with no regrets surrounded by family, there's no reason to be sad.

Bubonic plague is a bacterial infection, so it's easily treated with common antibiotics. Nostradamus may have made 500 years' worth of predictions, he left that one out. So when a plague ship came to town and the rats with fleas carrying plague came ashore because they were tired of hard tack and grog, the fleas who were tired of rats found delicious humans to nom-nom on and about a third of the good people of the city died. No doctor could do anything. Rich people who fled to their relatively rat-free country homes escaped. Nostradamus' wealthy patients brought him along, and presumably he had them drink some medicinal teas or whatever. They naturally ascribed their survival and good health to whatever their good doctor prescribed, and bragged about not being dead to all their friends. Doctor do-nothing may or may not have believed that his tinctures had curative powers. He had no concept of the germ theory of disease and that antibiotics don't do squat for viral diseases so stop insisting on those scrips, geez.

Both Drs. Oz and Phil owe their fame to Oprah. Their second careers as TV hucksters turned out well for them, even if they quickly had to punt on giving sound medical advice because you can't put on a daily show saying the same simple things over and over. Nobody would watch. Everybody is looking for a magic answer to what's worrying them. Seers and soothsayers fill this deep human need. Oprah has finally found the answer that she was searching for in all those episodes: *Ozempic*.

The hallmark of a terrible seer is that you can only interpret their predictions after the fact, which kind of defeats the whole purpose. Nostradamus claimed to be writing in some sort of code. It was also in the French of the day, which is now archaic. He very rarely pinned down the time frame. He made enough predictions that you can go back and fit them to many and various historical events. About the only one that was specific enough to provide actionable intelligence was that the earth was going to end in July, 1999. I was there. It didn't.

In some religious traditions you can raise as much hell as you want, as long as you repent just in the nick of time. Hence, if you are going to predict the end of the earth, I'm going to insist on a specific four-hour window so I can plan my day. Also, in order to convince me that you believe your own prediction, you need to give me all your stuff. That includes your credit cards because I'm going to max those fuckers out. That shouldn't bother you at all. If you believe your own predictions. Of course, if you're wrong I'm never going to believe you again. None of this Millerite "Great Disappointment" shit where the world didn't end and Miller pretended to go back to his bible and re-compute the end of days. I'm still amazed that "Seventh Day Adventists" are still around. They're a little weird, but relatively benign compared to Jehovah's Witnesses who will just keep coming to your house and knocking on your door until you say the magic words, "You shouldn't talk to me or you'll get disfellowshipped."

You might find it quite annoying if your co-workers start coming to you asking you to read the tea leaves for them. It's not about the tea leaves, BTW.

That's just the cold-reading gimmick. There are innumerable such gimmicks, including crystal balls and tarot cards and palm reading and so on. The best gimmicks divert the attention of the mark while you're making guesses and watching for subtle non-verbal cues. Funny hats and accents enhance the experience. It's also good if you can loop in semi-cooperative spirits or something, so as to deflect blame when you guess wrong. My favorite gimmick is iridology because I have to get right up close and peer into their eyes to assess the patterns on their iris which allow me to see their future. I can tell what they had for lunch and track their breathing, of course, but I can also look for very subtle tells in and around their eyes which are the windows into the soul or whatever. Palm reading is almost as good because while they're looking at their own palms, you're looking at them. If you hold their hands just right you can track their pulse, in addition to breathing and such like iridology.

I'm kind of a germophobe, so I think fortune telling via Zoom is better all around. The sessions will have to be scheduled in advance, of course, so you'll have plenty of time to google-stalk them, scrape their social media, etc. They will be amazed when you parrot back to them things they had posted themselves. You can simply have a second screen open while you're doing the readings, so you don't even have to memorize inane details about their so-called life. The key thing to know about fortune telling is that people pay money for advice about three things: money, health, love. Even if someone walks into a reading cold (hence the name cold reading) you can usually tell what's on their mind just by looking at them. If it's not obvious, engage them in idle chit chat while you're waiting for the spirits to come on line or whatever and they will typically yammer on about themselves. During the actual reading when you repeat what they just said a minute ago they will be amazed.

There's a bit of a skill to making predictions in that you always want to give yourself enough wiggle room. It's pretty rare for someone who has come to you to tell your fortune to call bullshit on you. In order to do that, they'd have to admit that they were wrong to come to you. A bit of wiggle room allows them to avoid that cognitive dissonance by fitting your predictions to what subsequently occurs. You also want the out of the spirits, or whatever, being a little vague sometimes. The spirit world is just funny like that. You're doing the best you can at interpreting their signs.

What I find most bizarre is that people think gifted seers would be giving readings via Zoom for a hundred bucks an hour or whatever. If I could predict the future, I'd be a day trader. I could make eleventy-bazillion dollars every day if I knew what stocks were going up and which ones were going down. It wouldn't even be interesting for me. I assume you would do the same thing. You certainly wouldn't be working in your current job. You'd be richer than Oprah. I predict that you'd tell people to get the hell out of your office because you have actual deadlines to meet.

28 Everybody should learn to use scheduled send.

When my oldest was a newborn, I got into the habit of sending my mother a quick email in the morning while I was drinking my convenience store coffee. It was 1992 and we were both professors, which meant that we had email at our jobs back in the days when almost nobody had email at home. She would print out the emails to take home so Gramps could read them, and then she would put them into a file. She saved almost three years of these "Maxwell Update" emails and I have recently transcribed them so that they are now preserved for future generations. My mother and I were having thoughtful discussions about child development, obviously without any pretense at full objectivity, but mostly it's interesting to know with some certainty what Maxwell was doing month-by-month as he developed. He was objectively far advanced beyond his contemporaries. Also quite cute.

Eventually everybody got access to email. That was fine for a while, but now busy professionals get far too much email. I was amused in 2016 when that orange guy tried to make a big deal about Hillary Clinton's 30,000 emails. I did the simple math and it was like three emails an hour or something. For the Secretary of State. I'm pretty sure my wife just got three emails while I was typing that sentence. Sec. Clinton had staffers who managed her email traffic for her, and only presented to her messages that needed her attention. They probably printed those out and gave them to her in a special folder.

I'm going to have to take another turn pretty soon as department chair. The part I'm looking forward to least is 5am email vomit. I typically triage overnight email while I'm waiting for the coffee to brew, deciding which urgent messages are going to get my attention before I head to the office and which can wait a couple of hours. There's no point in responding to a 2am email question from a student at 5am because they're not awake. Similarly, faculty colleagues who don't show up until mid-morning aren't going to get a reply to some late-night rant. I'll typically stop by their office and talk to them in person because that's a much more efficient way to assess how butthurt they are (on a scale of one to ten) and what they think I might be willing and able to do about it. I've been systematically cajoling my colleagues for two decades to simply stand up from their keyboards and take a few steps to talk to their office neighbor, rather than ricocheting angry emails around the aether, with everybody and their mother cc'ed. Don't you dare passive-aggressively bcc people in an email to me.

I've been using email since 1986 and I know how to weaponize such things. I know to never, ever send an email that felt good to write. I re-read my own emails before I press send, imagining that they'll get forwarded to the last person on the planet I'd want to read them. In some of the Maxwell Updates I was a little too honest about how slow his playmates were compared to him. They're all in their early thirties now, but their moms would still be offended.

I just saw an article in the Wall Street Journal[33] about how doctors are now charging for the time it takes to respond to their patients' emails. Insurance covers most of the cost, but there's sometimes an email co-pay. I can't describe how happy this makes me. Actually, I can describe it but I know enough not to do that in writing. Here's the Journal:

> More healthcare groups are charging fees to answer patients' electronic messages, often the ones you exchange via their portal. Doctors say it's only fair if they're spending time on the messages and note that an email discussion can often save you the time of having to come in.

I don't know what the current fee is, but the typical cost of an email message claim was $39 in 2021, including both the portion paid by insurance and by the patient. Let's allow for inflation and call it fifty bucks per email. That sounds fair to me, except that there probably needs to be some sort of surge pricing for urgent emails demanding an immediate response before I've even finished my morning coffee. People could easily avoid surge pricing by learning to use scheduled send. That would even allow them to change their mind about sending me a missive that will cost them fifty bucks or more. Again, from the Journal:

> The practice of charging for emails has steadily increased in the past few years, as the volume of emails that patients send has grown. A 2020 ruling from the federal Centers for Medicare and Medicaid Services added billing codes that let medical providers get

---

[33] https://www.wsj.com/health/wellness/doctor-medical-bills-email-37005e32

reimbursed for email correspondence that takes more than five minutes over the course of seven days and requires medical decision-making. That paved the way for private insurers that typically follow what CMS does.

I don't carry email around in my pocket, by which I mean that I don't have a smartphone. Hence, I read my email in one of my two offices. Emails that come in while I'm not sitting at one of those two computers will wait for me until I come and sit back down again. I recently was on vacation and went more than a week without checking my email. The sky did not fall. Also, I didn't even put an out-of-office notification. None of my co-workers know my personal phone number, so they couldn't txt me in lieu of or in addition to an email. People who wanted my attention all waited until I got back. But then I've been systematically training people I work with to not expect instant replies from me.

If I was able to charge money for responding to emails, the price would have to go up quite a bit for doing that while I was on vacation. I'm thinking a hundred bucks or more for that thing you think can't wait until I get back to town. Call it a roaming fee or something. If you so very desperately need my approval, me typing out O-K is going to cost you fifty bucks a letter. If you reflexively reply "Thanks" my "You're welcome!" would then buy my foursome a round of beers at the turn. There's excellent WiFi in the clubhouse, so I might respond to a bunch of emails while waiting for lunch to come out. You know that's what all the doctors are going to be doing.

Ivanka Trump just got herself into trouble in the recent trial where they all pretended their properties were a lot more valuable than Zillow's zestimates. She and her husband didn't realize that spouses emailing each other from their personal accounts constitute privileged communications, but if either one uses the company account, nope.

In Congressional testimony, it came out that Anthony Fauci's crew of Boomers discussed via their FOIA-able government email accounts the logistics of hiding information about COVID origins from FOIA requests.[34] Nellie Bowles says,

> On one level I'm charmed. This reads like my dad trying to commit secret crimes. It's like when the cops catch someone for murder because their browser history is all "how much fentanyl to kill my wife" and "how to carry 152-lb woman into car very heavy bad

---

[34] https://nypost.com/2024/05/22/us-news/explosive-emails-show-top-nih-adviser-deleted-records-used-secret-back-channels-to-help-fauci-ecohealth-evade-covid-transparency/

back." It's funny. But read these emails and remember: *The Washington Post* and *The New York Times* told us that all of this is a "conspiracy theory." They stand by that! There's been no retraction! There never will be. Fauci must be remembered as the nation's beautiful doctor, and our mainstream media will never back down on that. So we're all stuck with one true paper of record: the *New York Post*.

The only thing better than allowing me to charge an email fee would be to turn off the university email system at nights and on weekends and during breaks. Some European companies do that sort of thing. Imagine how restful it must be to know that none of your co-workers can send you an email when the office is closed. Checking your phone after a round of golf and finding that some stupid issue blew up while you were busy slicing balls into the woods takes away from the enjoyment of never keeping score when you play. People with nothing better to do on a beautiful weekend morning than hectoring the whole department need a hobby. Or a side hustle. Something other than emailing the rest of us who have actual lives and some remaining shred of work-life balance.

I feel like I'm doing the world a service by teaching frosh how to use email like a grownup. I email them an agenda about a day before each class, and they're expected to print it out, fill it out, and bring it with them so they're prepared for the discussion. They email me their papers as pdf attachments, and I patiently remind them to put their names both on their papers and in the filename. I mark up the pdfs and return them via email. They think this is odd.

29 The sky is falling, the sky is falling. We must run and tell the king.

When my kids were still quite young I began prepping them for life after college. I made it clear in many and various ways that they should not expect to move back home after graduation, because that's the time to strap on the old tin beak and get out there pecking with the rest of the chickens. I said repeatedly that "after high school you don't live here anymore" but we always like having houseguests and you'll be welcome to visit as often as you like. I also explained that it was going to take some years of effort and toil to work yourself back up to the standard of living you were accustomed to growing up, and that your first apartment after college was going to be gross. I said not to invite me over for dinner, I probably won't want to even sit down, but I'll be happy to take you and all your roommates out to eat. I wasn't comfortable sitting down in my son's first after-college apartment, but my daughter's first place was quite nice and she could afford it without having roommates. After we got her settled in and made "the last Target run with Dad" she snapped a picture of me sitting at her kitchen counter sucking a Gogurt and posted it to her Instagram to prove my prior statement wrong. I was happy to have been proven wrong, of course.

You probably have some fresh-out college grads working for you (or with you) that still live at home with their parents. Some of them may not have even thought to update the posters on the wall of their childhood bedroom that you can all see when they Zoom into staff meetings instead of putting on hard pants and showing up at the office. Some think they're being all grown up by taking over the family dining room as their work-from-home office, as if someone their age would have a 12-place dining room with a glass-front cabinet full of bone china and Hummel figurines.

Like many industries, college is being disrupted right now. Everybody figured out how to do on-line and hybrid classes during the pandemic, so that isn't an issue anymore. The pervasive angst right now is the looming demographic cliff. Starting in 2026 the overall number of college-age Americans will start to fall. Not level off. Fall. There's also a steady drumbeat in the media about whether a college degree even makes financial sense anymore, typically arguing from outlier anecdotes where somebody majored in something useless and then doubled down by going yet more deeply into debt via loans for some (even more) useless, predatory graduate program. Left out of the reporting are all those people who studied hard and got a good job and paid off their own damn loans. That the Biden administration was ignoring the courts and forgiving all sorts of student loan debt is also not mentioned in this context. Lots of the Olds were pretty pissed off that Gaza-encampment protesters[35] are getting their student debt cancelled.

But in the near future, there won't be as many college students, so there won't need to be as many colleges. Yikes, says every English professor. Law professors can at least go practice law instead; English professors don't have the option of practicing English. They would have already written the great American novel if they had such a book in them. I've recently read "To the Lighthouse" and it struck me as a little odd that there was no plot. I don't really need a Virginia Woolf scholar to tell me at great length how innovative it was for Woolf to write novels with no plot. I checked Wikipedia just now: "She is considered one of the most important modernist 20th-century authors. She pioneered the use of stream of consciousness as a narrative device." They do eventually go to the lighthouse, BTW.

College professors would like to give an assignment that goes like this: Pick a topic, write an essay, and say something interesting. But these days they can't — not even with graduate students. It gets worse; students seem to think their professors have fine-grain directions in mind but just won't share them. They'll ask how they're going to be graded. Their professor's actual answer is, "I'm going to read it, and I'm going to give you a grade." They don't like that at all. What they are really after is detailed, step-by-step rubric. They want that because their teaching-to-the-test K12 education has conditioned them to write in ways that fit with semi-automated grading via a detailed rubric. They can't understand that college professors want them to engage in reading and writing in a different way, as means of developing ideas and sharpening their thinking.[36]

---

[35] I think we can all agree that the wrong answer is to make protesting students write apology letters: https://gothamist.com/news/nyus-mandatory-ethics-homework-for-student-protesters-includes-the-simpsons-wikipedia

[36] https://www.chronicle.com/article/some-assembly-still-required

"Students are given little independence in school and, when they gain it in college, are overwhelmed rather than relieved, unmoored rather than motivated. After years of having their education treated as a performance, it's asking a lot of students to trust that it might be more fulfilling to approach it as a process."

I suppose if your kids are getting ready to apply to colleges in the next few years the competition for warm bodies to fill seats in core-curriculum English classes could be lucrative. The average discount rate right now is 52%, which means that most people pay about half of the listed tuition price. The competition is causing marginal schools to circle the drain. Just because they're non-profit, that doesn't mean that they can lose money (for very long) by offering too much financial aid and too many scholarships.

Even schools with high profile sports that generate television revenue aren't really immune to this, because athletics dollars stay in the athletic department. They never subsidize the English department, perhaps because in order to be truly competitive in the big-dollar sports you pretty much have to relax the literacy requirement. At least student-athletes can get fairly compensated via NIL deals, and so if they wanted to they could hire out-of-work English professors to tutor them and/or ghost write their 20th-Century English papers.

One strategy that many colleges are adopting to survive the demographic cliff is to treat students as customers, who are always right. As someone who employs college graduates this should freak you out. Student-customers who are always right are going to get excellent grades, whether they mastered the material or not. English professors, whose continued employment depends on glowing student evaluations of their teaching, are not going to properly criticize their customers' writing. Chemistry professors will hold out a bit longer because atoms share electrons according to well established rules and you can't really BS your way through that. There are right and wrong answers to chemical reactions. But some chemistry professors are tenured while more and more are non-tenure eligible. NTE faculty all know that their continued employment depends on glowing teaching evaluations, so they will tend to leave the hard stuff off the final and pass out A's like candy. They may even pass out literal candy (or cookies) on the day when students are asked to fill out course evaluations, because that has been shown to improve the scores rather a lot.

You may have heard about grade inflation where gentleman C's were given out by anti-war professors because young men who flunked out of college got drafted and sent to 'Nam. At elite universities right now it's pretty standard for 80% of the grades to be A's, and for the first time in two decades were not at war.

Here's why this matters to you. The desperate need to fill the frosh class to stay in business means pretty much anybody will be able to get into college.

Considering students to be customers and the ineluctable grade inflation that follows, means that you can't tell from their transcripts which students have worked hard and which have simply skated through. Also, most of the college graduates that you hire are going to be entitled little shits. You might be the first one ever who gives them honest feedback on their performance. They are going to react badly to that. There will be tears.

In 2008 Kelly Williams Brown (then 24) neologized the tongue-in-cheek verb adulting to describe everyday tasks such as laundry or grocery shopping that were the hallmarks of maturity. Gen-Zers never use the term, not even ironically. It's not in their vocabulary or their hopes and dreams. If anyone dares bandy around the term adulting, their digital tribe will close ranks and reassure them that there's no such word.[37]

Professors have gotten used to students crying in their offices, and usually have a box of tissues on hand for that. We understand that adulting is hard and getting your first-ever B+ can be traumatic. We've learned to feign sympathy and recite soothing words. You're going to need to learn to do this for the college graduates you hire. Perhaps a newly-unemployed Virginia Woolf scholar would be willing to offer you some advice. It could be a welcome break from weeks of writer's block for them.

Most organizations are currently relying on young Millennials to deal with these developmentally-delayed Gen-Zers when they show up without their tin beaks very much unprepared for corporate life. That's not going to cut it when the post-demographic-cliff wave hits. You need an old-school, in-house training program. A bootcamp of some sort. "Military Basic Training — often called boot camp — is designed to prepare recruits for all elements of service: physical, mental and emotional. It gives service members the basic tools necessary to perform the roles that will be assigned to them for the duration of their tour. Each of the military services has its own training program, tailoring the curriculum to the specialized nature of its role in the military." Adulting bootcamp needs to give your new hires experience with failure. You may recall the Kobayashi Maru, a training exercise designed to test the character of Starfleet Academy cadets by placing them in a no-win scenario. You'll have to figure out what that looks like for your organization. Not getting new-hires ready for daily life as a member of your organization is a no-win situation.

---

[37] https://www.yahoo.com/lifestyle/gen-z-lost-ability-manage-180000164.html

30 Extra college is optional.

The college graduates you hire were quite successful in college, or else you wouldn't have hired them. For many of them, the unstructured nature of life after college is disorienting. There's no syllabus where midterms and papers and other assignments are scheduled months in advance. There's no Spring Break or Winter Break or Fall Break or Summer Break when you can go home and catch up on sleep or go someplace sunny and go a bit wild and then come back all tanned and buckle down for the next several weeks. Instead of a report card with all A's you get a performance review with "areas for improvement" noted in your permanent record and if you don't show significant progress by your next evaluation you'll have to repeat a grade or some such thing. Oh, and it's fifty years until retirement.

One common reaction is to imagine going back to school. There's a drumbeat right now questioning whether a college education is worth it, given the ever-escalating cost of college and the dearth of young people entering the skilled trades. Mike Rowe makes many excellent points, but I think it's important to acknowledge that he doesn't actually do any of those dirty jobs on a daily basis. He's what you might call a weekend warrior, except that he's more of a war correspondent who shows up briefly to get some footage and then goes back to the studio to do some voiceovers. Full disclosure. Rather than taking over my grandfather's HVAC business I went to engineering school to get a whole pocketful of degrees and now I teach the subject. Also, my grandfather taught me to do plumbing, which I regret because if I didn't know plumbing I could call a plumber but since I do know plumbing I might as well just fix it myself. Frankly, I can't imagine doing plumbing every day for the next fifty years. I should also note that my grandfather once confided in me that he never enjoyed the work that he did for his whole life, despite being successful enough that his investments paid for my children's college, but he graduated high school during the Depression and he didn't have other options.

I talk a lot with college students about their graduate school plans, partly because my main line of work is mentoring PhD students and partly because students need letters of recommendations from people like me in order to get into graduate school. Here's what I tell them. First try to figure out what it is that you might like to do with your life, and then go get the education necessary to do that. You need a college degree to get most non-dirty jobs these days, but extra college doesn't widen your career prospects, it narrows them. The point is to narrow things down to the jobs you actually want. I point out that it's dumb to go to medical school if you don't want to be a doctor. It's dumb to go to law school, full stop. Graduate school is not a place to hang out while you figure out what you might like to do next. Get a job that pays you while you figure that out.

I went to college on a full-ride Air Force scholarship, but my wife paid for four years of private college all on her own and that was right when college started to get really expensive. I owed the Air Force four years of active duty service. My wife had student loans, which we were able to get paid back in about five years, although the last big chunk we were able to pay back when my grandfather died and my mother sold his yacht. I did my PhD while I was on active duty with the Air Force, since my job was to sit at a gray steel desk and write the equations that let us figure out how to make things hard to detect on radar. The Air Force had a program where they would pay 80% of my tuition, although I would incur two years of active duty service commitment each time I used that benefit. I got all my coursework for the PhD done within two years, and that service commitment fell within the four years I already owed for the undergraduate scholarship. The way PhD programs work, when you're done with coursework and just doing dissertation research, the tuition cost is negligible so I paid that myself. I didn't make a career of the Air Force, but it was a good way to pay for school.

Many years later when my wife went back to graduate school part time, she was able to use employee benefits for most of that. I don't recall ever noticing the tuition costs affecting our family budget. Presumably I was more focused on the looming cost of college for our then high-school-age children. My parents had set up 529 college savings plans for each of their grandchildren, which turns out to be a really smart way to do things because any money the children or parents save up for college works against you when your "expected family contribution" is calculated. I insisted that my children take out some student loans so that they would have some skin in the game. The arrangement was that if they graduate college on time and get a job, apartment, etc. (i.e. strap on the old tin beak and get out there pecking with the rest of the chickens) my mother and I would pay off their loans. If they didn't graduate and tried to move back home, they'd be on the hook for that debt themselves. To quote Brittany S. Pierce from Glee, "Tough love feels a lot like mean." but it worked for both of them and they finished college on time and got out there pecking with no debt.

We did feel like suckers whenever the Biden administration announced that they were forgiving another chunk of student loan debt. What about plumbers with credit card debt? What about gambling debt? What about car loans? I don't think people who inspired Mike Rowe's various cosplays should have to pay law school loans for history majors who couldn't find jobs that didn't involve making soy lattes for regulars who majored in something sensible. Over-extend yourself betting on sports and you pay that back. Take out loans for a car you can't afford and you get to have more roommates than you want to save on rent. Not everybody's grandfather will leave behind a sailboat that can be sold to pay off loans.

The answer for your twenty-somethings who are thinking about doing some extra college is to start by taking a class or two. Ideally, your organization will have a program which will cover some of the costs for that. You might even be able to make allowances for remote-work days or flex time that facilitate going to a class during the daytime, although there are many graduate programs which make themselves accessible to working adults by holding classes in the evenings. Some organizations will have restrictions about which sorts of classes are eligible for tuition reimbursement, although sometimes you can help by attesting to the relevance of what your employee wants to study in the context of your department. HR may be under instructions to reflexively deny most requests as a money-saving strategy, so you can demonstrate your commitment to the people who work for you by effectively pushing back on that.

If and when your employees do decide to go back to graduate school full time, they're going to want a letter of recommendation from you. You'll be in a much better position to write them a strong letter if they've taken a few classes part time already. Here's another thing you can do. Put aside a little money in your discretionary budget to pay for GREs, LSATs, MCATs and such. Not just the tests themselves, but test-prep materials and the like. You don't want your employees to feel like they have to sneak around in preparing for these. You want them to know that you support them in their career development, even if that means they'll be leaving the organization to go back to school. They probably won't realize that your primary motive is getting a heads up well in advance so you can plan for the day when they ghost. Have a little congratulations party when they get their scores back and again when their acceptance letters arrive. You'll then have plenty of time to be sure to backfill that job before they leave.

My son is a professional actor in Chicago. The entire theatre ecosystem collapsed there during the pandemic, and it's probably never coming back. Fortunately, he had a day job in a startup game-hosting company that was able to pivot to an on-line model when the lockdowns hit. Many times during the last few years he might have considered going back to graduate school to get an MFA or some such thing, but knew neither Granny nor I would ever pay for that.

31 Out of an over-abundance of caution.

The mid-afternoon sky outside my office window is blue but the streetlights are on. There's an eclipse underway right now, but it's only 80% here so meh. I remember making a pin-hole viewer out of a shoebox in 1979. I remember Donald Trump looking up at the sun without eye protection in 2017. The main thing this year seems to be that scientists have arranged to crowd-source video from amateur astronomers all along the path of totality from Texas to Maine. They'll be able to stitch all of that video together to get an unprecedented video of the sun's corona. I might watch that video next week some time.

Everybody talks about the importance of STEM education, but far too many schools are punting on this rare opportunity to have their students go out into the school yard and actually learn something. They're sending kids home early or having Zoom school, out of an (over) abundance of caution.

> Abundance of caution. You hear this phrase a lot in our era of absurd safetyism, which is reshaping modern childhood. An abundance of caution is the reason kids no longer spend time alone or play outside, depriving them of some of life's most fulfilling experiences. To be clear: when you look at an eclipse, your instinct to squint may not kick in—which can damage your eyes—but cases of blindness are vanishingly rare, and there are simple precautions that can be taken.[38]

The pending eclipse has been all over the news for the last several days. It was a nice break from wall-to-wall coverage about how badly a couple of wars and political campaigns are going right about now. One reporter even did a

---

[38] https://www.thefp.com/p/school-safetyism-classes-closed-solar-eclipse

package about how it is bad for the camera on your iPhone to point it at the sun. The local meteorologists all bugged out for the path of totality, and then did brief reports from there so their trips could be expensed.

I'm certain that many elementary schools had their kids do color-cut-paste worksheets about eclipses, not appreciating the danger of paper cuts. And paste eating. You'll poke your eye out running with those dull little round-tipped scissors if you're not careful. No matter how carefully you cut construction paper, though, you'll be utterly blind[39] to the wonders of the worlds above unless you go outside and safely take a look for yourself. Not to put too fine of a point on it, you need to go out and experience the feeling of shared wonder and togetherness of doing such things in a group. Think back to how it felt the first time you attended an event IRL after the pandemic lockdowns. Depriving young people of shared experiences blunts their emotional development. It also dulls their ability to recognize the full range of emotions in others, and that becomes your problem a few years down the road when they come to work for you.

You probably have pointy-tip scissors in your office, trusting that the purported grownups who work there know not to run with them. There's probably no paste or whiteout in the supply cabinet anymore, though. You might be the only one left who has mastered the key photocopying skill of knowing just how long to let whiteout dry so it wouldn't smear on the glass. I used to have whiteout in a selection of colors that matched different kinds of stitched-binding laboratory notebooks and various other specialty papers. What young people find most strange about the workplace is that the rules aren't written down anywhere. There's literally no instruction manual for how to use whiteout, although I just googled that and found "Whiteout Survival codes for April 2024" which refers to "a mobile strategy game where your goal is to survive a glacial apocalypse."

I know a lot of chemists, but I don't know much chemistry. My research laboratory has no chemicals in it, other than some Formula 409 under the sink. Nevertheless, the chemical safety inspector insists that I have a sign on the door indicating which dangerous chemicals are stored in the lab. Spoiler alert, it's all zeros. Without such a sign, out of an over-abundance of caution, the fire department will assume the worst and stand outside watching the place burn down waiting for the hazmat team to arrive from the next town over.

It used to be that if your house was struck by lightning, the fire department would come right over and do their best to make sure your neighbor's house didn't also burn down. You were being punished by the Almighty, so yours

---

39

https://www.ign.com/articles/google-searches-for-eyes-hurt-spike-amid-solar-eclipse

would be left alone. Ben Franklin's lightning rods were rather controversial for that reason.

It's not really fear of something bad happening that has led to an over-abundance of caution. It's fear of getting blamed for not doing everything you could to prevent something bad from happening that paralyzes bureaucrats. In a secular society it's no longer fashionable to blame God when there's a cancer diagnosis. People naturally grasp at an explanation for things, the simpler and more deep-pocketed the better. Also, there are way too many lawyers these days. Young people have never known a time before the security theatre at the airports. They wouldn't think to question whether that makes air travel any safer.

I was just discussing faith healers with my frosh. These charlatans claim some special connection to the Almighty which allows them to cure all manner of invisible maladies in front of audiences, large and small, assuming everybody makes a generous donation to demonstrate their faith. Peter Popoff was pwnd back in the day when James Randi brought a radio scanner to the auditorium and recorded his wife reading off the prayer cards that people had filled out before the service. He had a radio earpiece, but pretended that he was getting the deets from Jesus' dad. Randi played the clips on the Tonight Show and Popoff went bankrupt. In preparation for the class I had recorded Popoff's current show on some obscure cable channel. He's playing smaller rooms these days, but it's the same old act albeit without the radio prompting. It's not sophisticated. It's old-fashioned mentalism tricks.

The question that I posed to my frosh, now four plus years post-COVID, was why didn't the world's faith healers combine forces and pray away the pandemic? That seems like an all-hands-on-deck situation to me. I also pointed out that during the COVID lockdowns, faith healers were prevented from holding in-person healing services. That's like having a fire department who stands by and watches your house burn down.

I would like to have seen a healing service where you had to present a positive COVID test in order to be admitted to the auditorium. First some singing and praying and whatnot in order to be sure that anybody with a false-positive test actually had COVID. Then, after the offering and then healing parts of the service, give everybody another COVID test and they should all be negative. After that, send the preacher and his crew around to all the city hospitals, nursing homes, etc. Out of an abundance of caution, the preachers could wave their wands or whatever during homeroom so kids could go to actual school. We could even have them show up during an eclipse to un-blind any kids who looked at the sun without special glasses.

There's a problem with all of this, though. Faith healers never take responsibility for failing to heal. They blame the victim whose faith wasn't strong enough and even though the preachers did everything they could they take no responsibility. Typical bureaucratic response. Take away people's agency out of an abundance of caution, but then when something bad happens don't own that failure. I'm sure you know lots of people like this in your organization.

32 THE RENT IS TOO DAMN HIGH.

I have a small mortgage on a giant house. We bought the house thirty years ago, but refinanced during the Great Recession when interest rates bottomed so I still have some years left to write a laughably small check each month. It's a fixed-rate mortgage, so my payments will never go up even as the dollar continues to be devalued and the apparent cost of everything else keeps going up.

I assume that your young employees complain about the cost of their rent and, of course, their roommates who they only cohabitate with to split the rent. They may lament that they'll never be able to buy a house. They may try to argue with a straight face that it's somehow better to rent than to buy. Because reasons.

I live in an affluent college town where the custodians, food-service workers and administrative assistants typically commute from the next town or two over where the cost of living is more manageable. It's also a tourist town, and the seasonal industries often import temporary workers from other countries. I was looking for a locksmith a couple of years ago and happened upon the residential hotel where they are housed while here on their "cultural exchange" or whatever they were told it was. I know well the motels where local housing-insecure families live. The area churches cooperate to provide meals via "motel ministries" and in the summer deliver meals to food-insecure kids who are out of school. During the school year there is a robust backpack program to provide supplementary food to school children. There's a food pantry across the street from the College that anybody can make use of year round. During the winter months the area churches take turns providing meals, overnight lodging, laundry, etc. to the surprisingly large un-housed population. When I'm on my way to the office I can usually tell which church is hosting folks that week because the nearest bus stop is busy. Most of them are headed off to work, BTW.

I'm not all that price sensitive, but even I have noticed how much more expensive healthy food has gotten lately. Even unhealthy food is a shock to the wallet these days. A few years ago my mother and I finally convinced the other grownups in the family to stop exchanging gifts. We all already have too much stuff, and more money than we know what to do with. It's a chore to try to think up something we might want so someone can buy us a gift. My mother and I think of shopping as a chore, BTW. My wife considers shopping to be recreation, so she isn't fully on board with the new scheme. What my mother and I actually do, though, is donate money to food banks in the other's name. I have one in South Dakota that I like, and have been in the habit of sending them a check each year which amounts to 1,000 meals a month. They're very efficient, so that's not as much money as you might think. With inflation, though, I think I'm going to have to increase the amount I send. The need just seems to keep increasing.

I hope your organization encourages your young employees to give back to their community in meaningful ways. It used to be that charitable contributions were tax deductible, but when the standard deduction was cranked up a few years ago it no longer made sense to itemize. Since my wife and I don't coordinate on who's donating what to whom, this simplifies things for us quite a bit. The left hand doesn't know what the right hand is doing, as they say. I also don't like to keep track of such things because I'm donating for entirely selfish reasons. It makes me feel good to do good.

This is on my mind this morning because yesterday when I arrived at 7 am the custodian flagged me down to tell me that there had been a student camped out in the lecture hall she was trying to service for the day's classes. He had gone off somewhere, but his things were all still there. The custodians come in a few hours earlier than I do, so she knew that this student had been living in the science complex for some time. He wasn't just pulling an all-nighter.

We have a campus police force. They carry actual firearms. I would never, ever call them for something like this. Poverty is not a crime, dammit! We're a residential campus, so something serious must be going on for a student to be un-housed. The good news is that there's a formal mechanism to submit a "care report" when a student needs help:

> Care Support Services provides outreach, advocacy, and support services that assist and empower students in identifying and managing interpersonal, academic, and wellness concerns. When students face significant challenges to their mental, physical, and social health, we help in identifying and accessing resources both on and off campus to meet students' needs.

There's a Director, Associate Director, Assistant Director and Administrative Coordinator. "*Please note our e-mail is only monitored during business hours and is not intended for use in the case of an emergency."* I happen to know that a care report was submitted some time ago and the Care Support Services office knows who the student is. So far, so good.

Yesterday I noticed that the student had decamped from the lecture hall and set up camp in a small conference/study room just down the hall from my office. I recognized his balloon animal and backpack. This morning when I arrived a little after 7am, his things were all still there. It's not unusual for students to study very late and then leave their belongings behind while they go back to their dorm to get some sleep. But I recognized the balloon animal and backpack. A couple hours later he came back and has been alternatively dozing and studying and perhaps even going to class. I would have noticed if anybody from the Care Support Services office stopped by to perform their primary function.

When my wife was in college, and paying for it all herself, she went through the process the summer before her junior year to get emancipated and thus be eligible for more financial aid. That meant she rented an apartment herself, even though both her father and her mother and their blended families lived in town. It wasn't a very nice apartment, but it was only for a few months. Recently, it came up in conversation that she got quite sick that summer and so my parents had her come and stay at our house for a week. I had no memory of this, which struck me as odd. I eventually figured out that it must have been during the month that I was in California doing ROTC training. It made me even more cross about her father refusing to contribute to her college expenses. During the school year she worked two jobs and then was a live-in nanny for three kids in exchange for room and board. I went to college on a full-ride ROTC scholarship.

When I periodically complain about having too much money, my daughter always says that I can pay her rent if I want to. I then respond that I wouldn't want to deprive her of the satisfaction of paying that herself. She's earning quite a lot of money and living well beneath her means in a rent-controlled studio apartment which costs more than twice as much as my tiny mortgage on my giant house. If she ever needed help making rent, we would quietly and without comment help with that.

As more and more states and localities institute higher minimum wages, but yet rent continues to go up, there may be a better solution to how little we pay our custodians. Expect them to do more things. I don't mean do more with less, I mean expect them to perform routine maintenance tasks in addition to emptying the trash, mopping the floors, etc. When light bulbs burn out, they are not empowered to change them. They aren't even empowered to send in a work order to have a licensed electrician come and swap them out. The same goes for routine plumbing issues, which I know because I arrived one morning and went to lift up the toilet seat in the "executive washroom" near my lab to give back some coffee and only half the seat came up. It had broken right about where one's butt crack would go. The custodian had cleaned the toilet that morning, but wasn't empowered to put in a work order, so I did that. When the plumber came and replaced the seat I had him give me the old one, which I now bring to my mechanics of materials class so the students can speculate on what combinations of forces and moments led to an internal stress distribution that caused that particular fracture.

I think a scheme like this could be implemented without increasing the custodians' workload. If they change lightbulbs and maybe even toilet seats, we'd need to have fewer electricians and plumbers on staff. The savings could be used to pay the custodians more. As they acquired more skills, their pay would presumably reflect that. Eventually, some would be able to put down their mops for good and take on skilled trade jobs instead. We're a university, after all, so providing opportunities for people to learn new things and graduate to better jobs should be a no-brainer.

Good news! I just walked past the little room where the student hobo has been for the last day or so. He and his things are gone. He left behind the purple balloon animal, though.

33 Does anybody really know what time it is?

Once upon a time somebody made the first clock face, and then had to decide which way around was ever after going to be known as clockwise. If it was a wind-up clock it may have been simply that that first clockmaker was right handed and obviously wanted to wind the clock with their dominant hand. Maybe some early clock makers did it one way and others did it the other way. Some cultures read right-to-left, after all. Some countries even drive on the wrong side of the road and use the metric system to price petrol in Euros per litre when everybody knows that 55 mph makes no sense in the Dakotas.

Most people seem to agree that clockwise settled on our current direction because of sundials. Setting that first clock would have used a sundial to get noon just right, and it probably took many days to get the gears and whatnot the right size to have the hand(s) end back up at noon several (sunny) days in a row. I assume there were lots of people who were distrustful of mechanical time because they had been telling time from their trusty stick for generations. Why would anybody want to pay good money for a newfangled gadget when time is free. Wasting free time winding a clock and oiling its gears seems kind of dumb. Why would I want to know what time it was when it's dark outside anyway?

Mechanical timepieces are the fault of the railroads, who Mussolini did not make run on time. Those who actually lived in Italy during the Mussolini era have borne testimony that the Italian railway's legendary adherence to timetables was far more myth than reality.[40] Obviously, one can't run a railroad without schedules, and that means standardized time. If every station keeps track of time using some sort of traditional stick-and-shadows system, everybody will be in a different time zone. I suppose that was fine until the telegraph meant that people with different noons could argue back and forth

---

[40] https://www.snopes.com/fact-check/loco-motive/

about what time it was. It's not so different from setting up a Zoom call when you're not really sure where your work-from-home slacker colleagues are.

Daylight savings time was instituted to save energy during World War I. Federal income tax was instituted to pay off that war debt. Both were one-time deals that would be temporary, just until the war to end all wars ended all wars. Everybody seems to hate the transitions to and from daylight savings time. All dogs everywhere call bullshit on having to wait an extra hour to eat when the clocks are set back.

I think the problem is that we're changing the clocks in the middle of the night. Here's what I think would work much better. In the Spring when we gain an extra hour, do that at 8am Monday morning. In the Fall when we lose an hour, do that at 4pm on Friday afternoon. Who doesn't want an extra hour Monday morning? Who doesn't want to get off work an hour early on Friday? You over there, put your hands down. The answer is nobody.

I was a Captain in the Air Force during the first Gulf War, which only lasted about a minute. They gave me a medal for writing radar equations on the chalkboard. To be fair, it was like the participation trophy in kids' soccer. They gave that medal to everybody who was on active duty. I should point out that I have no skills that are useful in wartime, although I can tell you how to make your crossover SUV more difficult for police radar to detect. I'm also kind of a smartass, so I used to wear a Mickey Mouse wristwatch with my uniform. I may have carried a plastic GI Joe lunchbox to the office, and dressed in camouflage battle-dress-uniform in order to sit at a gray steel desk and do my equations.

Most of the young people that work for you have never worn a wristwatch, except as a fashion accessory. They use their phones to tell time, and their phones automatically update the time twice a year in the middle of the night so they have no excuse for being late to work when Daylight Savings Time ends. Their phones are also their alarm clocks.

Time blindness is the newly-invented disability being claimed by young people who can't ever seem to show up on time. According to the NY Post, a young woman who went viral for asking about "time blindness" accommodations during an interview has since doubled down on her request after she was branded "entitled" and ruthlessly mocked online. Sarah Trefren posted a TikTok whining that she was "yelled at" for asking what accommodations there were for people with time blindness and who "struggle being on time" during a phone interview to apply for a trade school. The school she was applying to had a perfectly sensible rule that if a student was late more than four times they were kicked out of the program. Now a meme, the video has inspired numerous parodies where other TikTokers discuss their fictional struggles with time blindness.

You probably have some hourly employees who can't seem to show up to work on time most of the time. You probably have had to kick back their timesheets for correction when they expect to be paid for a full shift yet they didn't clock in as scheduled. You may have had to bite your tongue to avoid making some crack about needing a Mickey Mouse watch or a Hello Kitty alarm clock. Yes, I had a Hello Kitty alarm clock on my nightstand for several years. It had been my daughter's, but she felt she was too grown up for it at one point and re-gifted it to me. Eventually I had to get a more grown up alarm clock, by which I mean one with much bigger numbers that I could read at night without my glasses.

Sooner or later somebody is going to file a grievance against their boss for creating a hostile work environment which has old-fashioned analog clocks that workers are expected to know how to tell time from. How can anybody be expected to fill out a timesheet with actual numbers on it when the office clock just has those two sticks that move around and around and sometimes aren't even the right time so I shouldn't have to show up for work when it's still dark outside. Grievance procedures move at a time scale that can best be described as glacial, BTW. Much like Las Vegas casinos, there are no clocks in the HR department. Your time-blind malingerer will be long gone by the time their grievance is resolved.

I was quite happy when my kids gave up playing soccer. I have no affinity for the beautiful game, and I find the idea of extra stoppage time quite annoying. I've always been quite punctual and do not like to be kept waiting. My kids each learned the hard way that when Dad said we're leaving in five minutes, I meant five minutes. When Mom said we're leaving in five minutes that could include up to a half an hour of stoppage time, so there's no danger of getting left behind.

My wife had this crazy idea that if she set all her clocks ten minutes ahead then she would never be late. I would get in trouble if I helpfully changed the clock in her car when Daylight Savings Time turned on or off, because then it was my fault if she was late. Her friend Laura always told her sister that birthday parties and whatnot started a half an hour earlier than they actually did, because Laura's sister was chronically half an hour late to everything. What Laura didn't realize was that her sister did the same exact thing to her. In my family, when a Holiday Dinner started at 5:30 that meant that we sat down to eat at 5:30. Show up a few minutes late and we'll already have started. Show up too late and we will have already finished, but there's probably some pie left so help yourself.

34 Talent, preparation, hard work and luck.

There is this rule of thumb called the ten-thousand-hour rule which Malcom Gladwell describes in his book[41] *Outliers: The Story of Success* where he asserts that the key to achieving true expertise in any human endeavor is simply a matter of practicing, albeit in the correct way, for at least 10,000 hours. A fair number of purported experts in various fields have taken to keyboards quibbling with the math. It's a helpful rule of thumb, which highlights that among the four things necessary to reach the top of your field, hard work is the one you have the most control over early in your career. You can hedge your bets on the lucky one by checking the on-coming traffic before you pick up a penny in the gutter. You only know for sure if it's an unlucky one when you get run over by a bus.

Since it's a nice round number that makes the math work out, let's assume that the magic answer is putting in an extra 10,000 hours of hard work, having been born with the requisite talent and afforded the preparation necessary to get you to this point and with a fair amount of luck along the way, a streak which you hope will continue. Most people who reach the tops of their fields put in that extra 10,000 hours of effort over the course of about a decade. If math isn't your strong suit, that's an extra 1,000 hours a year for ten years. Since the standard work year is 2,000 hours at 40 hours per week for 50 weeks with two weeks of well-earned vacation, what we're talking about here is 3,000 hours per year which is 60 hours per week on average for a decade. Go ahead and check my math.

I often joke with incoming graduate students that it's flex time and they

---

[41] Gladwell M. Outliers: The Story of Success. Little, Brown and Company; San Francisco, CA: 2008.

should feel free to work any 80 hours per week they want. I then tell them that we don't actually mean 80, but we sure don't mean 40. They're all very talented and we wouldn't have admitted them to the PhD program without the proper preparation, but they're training to compete in one of the most competitive games known to mankind. It's a global competition, and even if they're a one-in-a-million outlier, there are several thousand humans just like them. When I was coming up in this game (and before I had children) I found that I could work 70 hours per week sustained. Now that my children are grown I probably do about that most weeks. I have a highly functional home office in addition to my campus office, and since I get paid to solve people's problems or to come up with better ways to explain difficult problems, I may be fully engaged in my work when it looks (to my wife) like I'm just sitting there doing nothing. Or raking leaves. I don't punch a time clock, but I do bill a few hundred dollars per hour for my expertise.

It's scary for a young person to be told that they have to work 60 hours per week until they're thirty-something in order to be a success. It depends on what you mean by success. My colleagues in teaching intensive undergraduate departments have a lot more free time than I do. They aren't competing for grant funding to run research laboratories where the primary workforce is graduate students who are paid from grants. They aren't obsessed with being at the bleeding edge of their fields so that research proposals will be funded. They can't charge a few hundred dollars per hour to a grateful client for solving their problem while raking the backyard. It's a different way of life.

The message you want to get across to your young employees is that they need to set career goals for themselves, and then set about doing the hard work necessary to meet those goals. Only 100 Americans get to be Senators at any one time. Only rarely do Senators fail upwards into that job and then get to keep it for more than one term. Only 60 outliers were NFL starting quarterbacks for at least one game last season. Saturday Night Live has only ever had 164 cast members, and the enormous machine of Second City in Chicago affords rare opportunities to make the big leap.

I'm just spitballing here, but there are probably about 500 Fortune 500 CEOs. Some of them might have inherited the job or whatever, but the vast majority of them worked their butts off to get the top job. They also had to have been lucky. Your message to new college grads who want to be CEOs should be to work their butts off, but more importantly they need to know that it's statistically unlikely that they'll be the one to grab that brass ring so they really should be working hard building a career where the work along the way gives them fulfillment.

My son made a go of it as a professional actor in Chicago, whose luck ran out when the COVID-19 pandemic shut down the whole theatre ecosystem there for a couple-three years. His high-school golf-team buddy made a go of it for several years but never quite earned his PGA tour card, and now golfs with clients when he's selling them investment advice. Since I played a lot of golf with them when they were teenagers, I know by now they had expected to be winning the Pebble Beach Pro-Am, one as the champion golfer and the other as the famous actor who was also a scratch golfer.

In April 1744 John Rattray was victorious in the first ever golf tournament and so earned the title 'captain of the goff' for winning the £15 silver club. Rattray, as captain, had the authority to settle disputes between fellow golfers and was responsible for superintending the course in the year of his captaincy. These regulations, which were signed by Rattray and which—on matters of order of play, outside interference, water hazards, holeing out, making a stroke, and the stroke and distance penalty for the loss of a ball—remain an integral part of the modern game. Rattray's sole signature does not guarantee that he was wholly responsible for them, though his prominence within the company and Edinburgh society at large makes him the most likely candidate. Under these rules he went on to win the silver club for a second time in April 1745. His older sister, Grizel Ratray, is my ancestor but she came to Virginia before 1720. Today, only one person at a time gets to be champion golfer of the year and imbibe from the claret cup. Lots of golfers put in uncounted hours over many years to try to achieve that goal.

The way I start conversations with young people about their career aspirations is to simply ask them, "What do you want to be when you grow up?" That seems to work better than to ask them what they want carved on their tombstones. I hate questions like, "Where do you see yourself in five or ten years?" In my case I don't want a tombstone since I expect to be cremated. Five or ten years from now I hope to be still doing what I've been doing for decades already. Deep down I hope I never actually have to grow up. I like taking joy in the work that I do most days.

Remember the career jungle gym? You'll have to tell your youngest employees that there's no set path up a career ladder. There will be stretches when you're working your butt off and you don't seem to be making much progress. You'll often have to maneuver sideways in order to be able to move upwards again. There will even be setbacks where you get knocked back down a rung or three and might even start to feel like it's not worth the climb anymore. That sucks. Bad luck happens to everybody at some point(s) during their climb. Giving up isn't the answer, though. Not being a champion golfer or SNL star or Senator or CEO doesn't mean you've failed. Those are merely particular rungs on the jungle gym, and something else you didn't think of back when you were imagining those goals might be better in all the ways that matter to you.

I'm self-aware enough to know that the thing I like best about my job is spending time with students. Last week was Spring Break and I didn't get to have any talking turns, which kind of bummed me out. I was busy doing the usual things that professors with research programs to run do, but I like it lots better around here when there are lots of students. Fortunately my graduate students are here working during Spring Break, so I had them to talk to about their research projects, because they are all in the middle of their 10,000-ish hours of extra effort that it takes to be outliers.

35 You Expect Me to Pay to Park at My Place of Employment!?!

I was in the office pretty much as usual throughout the pandemic. I was about the only one there, so there were no distractions and I was able to get quite a lot of work done. Lockdowns turn out to be helpful when doing the final edit on a book or two. The only other person who was on campus as much as me was the guy from parking services who walks around giving parking tickets. I assume he was in a bit of a panic because parking services is required to be self-supporting, and with most faculty and staff taking the work-from-home option they were likely facing a rather serious budget hole. The only way to make that up is to aggressively write tickets. They even changed the signs on the road outside my office window to "Reserved at All Times" so they could ticket at nights and on weekends. The fines for those places are a plus-up from the usual "Faculty and Staff Parking" zones. I didn't bother having a parking pass because I come in early enough to snag a spot on one of the few remaining un-metered streets near campus.

For many years I mostly walked to campus, even though that's three miles each way. It's quite good exercise and I write inside my head so it was a productive time for me. I would then sit down at the keyboard when I got to the office or my home and type out the words that were in my head. I stopped walking after my father died because I need to be available if my mother needs something urgent. I bought an electric bicycle, which turns out to be as fast as driving once you account for the time it often takes to hunt for a parking spot.

Some years ago they built a new parking garage, which included both the parking services offices and a campus police station. When they rolled the cost of the bonds for that into the fees that faculty and staff pay to park—at their place of employment—they found that the cost was going to be too high for those at the lower end of the pay scale. So they decided to introduce a tiered fee structure, structured such that the more someone earned the more they paid. My wife and I each pay $500/year to park. At. Our. Place. Of. Employment. That's the opposite of a perquisite.

My response to this new socialist parking regime was to nope out of the system. I believe my exact words were, "Fuck it. I'm just going to walk." Everybody said, either out loud or inside their heads, "You're too fat and/or old to do that." I'm kind of stubborn, so that may have hardened my resolve. Also, this was a deliberate part of my self-designed seven-year program to get in shape by the time I was 50. Since the magic answer to weight loss is diet and exercise, I also systematically deleted from my diet sources of empty calories. I started with pie and ended with red wine. My wife is still mad at me for not eating pie. Her friends are low-key pissed off that I dropped 30% of my body weight over the course of a semester and have kept it off for more than a dozen years. I know from off-hand comments that they were tracking my weight loss as I walked to and from campus, which makes me a bit uncomfortable because I don't think they should have been checking me out like that.

I'm sure you're wondering what this all has to do with global warming, which Al Gore warned us about. He had a PowerPoint and everything. Even South Park now admits that ManBearPig is real, so it's natural to ask what any of us can do about it. Your primary contribution to adverse climate change is your daily commute, so the best thing is to live close to your work. Ideally you would live close enough that walking and/or biking is a viable option, but unless you live in a little college town that's pretty unusual. For most people, their second-highest source of greenhouse gases is due to air travel. One redeye flight can be as bad as your annual commute. Minimizing air travel is much easier now that many meetings can be done via Zoom, so all you have to do is not ruin it by vacationing far away. You probably don't use all your vacation time anyway, so go ahead and mark that down as saving the globe.

The third thing you can do to save the planet is to eat lower on the food chain. You've been meaning to eat better anyway, so save mankind, cut down on your grocery bill, and look better in those hard pants you wear to the office. Also, try to eat more locally. Start with obvious things like don't drink Fiji Water in Vermont and don't eat Ben & Jerry's in Fiji. Container ships are the most-polluting vessels on the planet. Along the same lines, eschew fast fashion. Invest in a quality professional wardrobe that you can wear for multiple seasons. But start building that wardrobe after you're a little closer to your goal weight, unless you have the kind of disposable income that would allow you to take several carloads of high-end outfits to Goodwill over the next few seasons because they're all just too big on you now. Such a strategy can both make you happy and spread joy to others, so you do you. It's your money, so spend it how you like.

As annoyed as I am about the cost of parking at my place of employment, it's not any sort of hardship. Even with the tiered scheme, though, the cost of parking for those at the bottom end of the pay scale is a real problem. I can work from home pretty much whenever I want. I can arrange my comings and goings so I never need a parking pass. Spending as much as two hours per day commutercizing enhances my productivity. I can watch the weather and bug out early if the morning weather guessers misled me about the afternoon chances of precipitation. I could even call a taxi or an Uber to get a ride home if my wife is in late meetings and I needed a ride. I understand that none of this applies to hourly staff. I further understand that this freedom to come and go as I please is an earned privilege that my youngest employees will assume they can adopt without yet having put in the decades of work required to earn it.

My wife noticed one of her new staff members was quite upset because parking services was requiring that the annual parking fee be paid up front rather than taken out as a monthly payroll deduction. Despite being at the lowest tier, it was a real hardship for her. She was probably out-of-pocket with some new outfits so she would look professional in the office where, frankly, my wife sets a very high bar for professional dress. My wife didn't hesitate to take out her own credit card and pay for her staffer's parking pass, and then made it clear that this was simply a gift with no strings attached or expectation of repayment. The only condition was that she was expected to keep coming to work as usual. It's absurd to expect employees to pay to park at their place of employment.

I learned to drive at age 13, in an orange VW Bug with a pumpkin stem on it. I got a license to drive when I was 14, which means that I was able to drive myself to high school. My high school was downtown and there was no student parking, so we all battled for on-street parking wherever we could find it. My daily driver for part of that time was a 1973 Plymouth Satellite station wagon, a car so massive that I've seen one win a demolition derby. Give me a foot on either end of that beast and I could get it into any available space on a side street, because the alternative was circling the block(s) to find another and you don't want to know what kind of gas mileage that tank got. I still scoff at cars with self-parking technology.

It strikes me as quite odd when young people these days don't seem to be in any hurry to get their drivers' licenses. I insisted that my own children get trained up and licensed the minute the law allowed. I found driving them to and fro quite strange. The idea that I was supposed to be idling at the curb when they came out of whatever activity they had previously been driven to is backwards. I'm the grownup. You sit on the curb and wait for me to arrive. I wonder how many moms thought about alerting child protective services that I was making a 16-year-old wait outside the school for several minutes?

You may have been hiring college graduates who never bothered to learn to drive. Good luck getting them to show up at the office when the weather is bad. Maybe they still live at home and Dad can drop them off on his way to work.

36 OLD BRIDESMAID DRESSES CAN MAKE EXCELLENT HALLOWEEN COSTUMES.

My wife has a tight friend group that gelled at a two-year-olds playgroup thirty years ago. I'm happy to report that they've recently agreed to not invite each other to their kids' weddings. Weddings aren't fun for me. I don't eat cake. I don't drink alcohol. I don't dance. Even in a quiet room I find small talk with strangers tedious. At those big round tables in a reception hall with music and dancing and drinking and cake, I can't effectively converse with anyone but whoever happens to have been seated next to me at the table for random people the parents of the bride/groom know. Because I won't have fun, I will be declared to be no fun. My wife isn't wrong. We eloped on Leap Year Day.

I loathe all hotels, so you can imagine how I feel about destination weddings. Unless the destination is the tourist town where I happen to live. In that case, invite as many out-of-town guests as you like. My wife can even get you a reservation at the campus chapel, which is small so it keeps the guest list down. It was originally an Anglican worship space, so the pews face the aisle, which makes it easy to see the bride come up the aisle and the newly married couple go back down the aisle. More importantly, everybody can get a good look at their new in-laws across the way. Perhaps the last time I travelled for an out-of-town wedding was in the late 1980s. I didn't actually attend the wedding ceremony because whoever packed my suitcase forgot my dress shoes. Scratch that. I went to a beach wedding on the Outer Banks, NC in the late 1990s where some of the bridesmaids wore shoes and some didn't. Rather than going somewhere for a honeymoon, the bridal party had rented a fancy beach house and stayed there after the ceremony out front.

I understand the concept of spending enormous amounts of money on a child's wedding in order to show off to your friends and business associates how much money you can blow on such things. It's the culmination of years of birthday party competitions where the kids' enjoyment is secondary to the show, in person and on social media. We used to win the birthday party competition handily twice a year, mainly through thoughtful creativity and themes that nobody had thought of yet but then lamely tried to copy. Putting a birthday cake on the kitchen floor and letting one-year-olds have at it doesn't translate to a giant pink mansion. Giving everybody hard hats and shovels and having them dig for treasure in my dirt pile does an excellent job of working in that peat moss. Beating all the boys by not barfing at the *Fear Factor* birthday party still gets talked about. The seven-year-olds who each got to paint a section of the upstairs playroom however they wanted are now 29, and sometimes come over so I have them go check on their artwork.

I assume you've been to your share of weddings and have many birthday party (horror) stories. If you pay attention, you'll notice that many of the young people who work for you are right in the middle of their going-to-weddings years. Some are helping friends plan weddings. Some might be planning their own weddings. Some might be trying to figure out how to stay out of trouble and/or avoid drama during the wedding planning process. I would tell them to just elope, but the moms might not think that's a great idea. Dads will be on board, and might be quite happy to chip in on the down payment for a condo or something *in lieu* of a big wedding. The best advice that I can give to grooms-to-be, however, is that their role is to demonstrate their commitment to their betrothed by paying such close attention to her ever fluctuating opinions on all manner of seemingly insignificant details that when you are asked your opinion you can correctly parrot back whatever she thinks she wants at that particular moment in time. "Whatever you want is fine with me." is exactly the wrong thing to say. The secret to a long and happy marriage is listening so very carefully that your seemingly independent opinions mirror those of your better half. It's not a democracy. You can decide how to decorate your man cave, as long as it looks OK from the street when the garage door is open.

What you'll find most amusing about watching your young employees plan weddings is knowing that they've never even hosted a sit-down dinner party. When a grown-up asks, "What can I bring?" the answer is always, "Nothing." You bring a bottle of wine or other hostess gift of course, but you don't expect to drink that at the party. You also don't chip in for the cost of the meal. Offering to do that would be an insult.

I understand the whole wedding registry concept but having a cash option strikes me as gauche, a word which here means awkward or lacking in social graces. It would be like passing the collection plate down the pews during the ceremony. Nevertheless, it seems to be more and more common for young couples to announce that they're paying for the wedding themselves (even though one or both sets of parents kick in sizable chunks of change) and then put out some sort of plea for crowdfunding. They might as well go ahead and sell tickets. I didn't want to go anyway. My wife will send a nice gift from the registry.

I should clarify that I'm fine going to the actual wedding ceremony itself, particularly if it's in an actual church. I kind of like the religious-tourism aspect of church weddings. For co-workers who I don't know socially, it can give me rather a lot of helpful insight into their psyches by watching their extended family interact in that kind of formal setting. If the reception is punch and those little sandwiches down in the fellowship hall, followed by cake, I might even stick around and chat with the various grandparents.

Funerals are rarely big expensive productions these days. I watched Queen Elizabeth's funeral all the way through. I'm curious what Interim King Charles' funeral will be like. The standard church funeral still seems to be an appropriately somber ceremony followed by a stand-around-and-chat reception in the fellowship hall run by one of the church circles. I've been pretty clear (in writing) about my final wishes. What's in my file in the fireproof safe with the wills and trusts, is a one-pager where I say in no uncertain terms that, "I don't want a funeral. I'm not coming to my funeral. I understand that I don't technically get a say in the matter." I make some suggestions for hymns, but not readings. I am somewhat more emphatic about being cremated and think it would be fun for any kids to sing *Ring Around the Rosies*, with or without all falling down in their fancy clothes, when my ashes are dumped in the hole.

Weddings and funerals. That will be what your young employees need big chunks of their PTO for. The funerals will likely be hard for them and may take some time to process. Unless you've been to their church wedding, you probably have no idea what faith tradition, if any, they were brought up in. Sometimes you get a sense because of which religious holidays they've taken off over the last couple of years, or if they've given up coffee for the whole month of Ramadan, something I have mad respect for.

Everyone everywhere has wondered, "How long 'till I die? Then what?" Every religion everywhere provides answers. To the second part. Actuarials know the first part, but not for any particular individual. You can expect weddings and funerals to trigger rumination about these issues. I have a suggestion that you can suggest: genealogy. The question that's really being asked in this context is, "Who am I?" Genealogy can help to answer a closely-related question: "Who do I come from?" It turns out that during the COVID-19 lockdowns, people all around the world spent much of that time crowdsourcing their family's details up into one of the several genealogy platforms. I recommend the Mormon one, FamilySearch.org, because it's free and also easy to click up, back and sideways in a family tree. I also use the version of Ancestry.com available via my campus library. WikiTree is pretty good and totally free. Geni.com is a front for MyHeritage.com, so don't make an account. You can jump start the process if you happen to have chatted with their grandparents at their wedding and asked them questions. This hobby might keep them busy until they have kids.

37 FOREVER IN DEBT TO YOUR PRICELESS ADVICE.

Hey. Wait. I got a new complaint. Sometimes it sucks to be a good listener. The youngest people in the office may have convinced themselves that you have nothing better to do at work than to hear all about what's bothering them. This. Very. Minute. I'm not talking about things that you did or didn't do or could or couldn't do or might or might could do. There's always something that algorithms have just force-fed them through their phones to keep them engaged and outraged. Because that's what drives ad dollars for the socials. You mostly use social media to keep up with actual friends, so you're not outraged about today's particularly outrageous something somewhere.

Recently some students at Vanderbilt did an old-school sit-in during midterms in the building where the chancellor's office is located in "response to the college administration shutting down a student government vote over whether the school should divest funds from Israel." It's good to see them gathering IRL with other students and expressing outrage with solidarity. That's a big improvement over sitting alone in their dorm rooms ruminating over why everybody else's highly curated lives on social media look more fun than my so-called life instead of studying for midterms. I'm not quite sure that they all understand how universities work. Back in the day, students who opposed the Vietnam war might go so far as to burn down the ROTC building. Four of you might get shot by the Ohio National Guard, though. I assume at this point you're humming Crosby, Stills, Nash and Young. War is bad. We should stop having wars.

At elite universities the typical grade-point average these days is three-point-alot. That makes it hard for employers to differentiate so-so students from excellent students. The WSJ does an excellent job of explaining why grade inflation is your problem.[42] College students who get an A for no

---

[42] If You Give a College Student a Cookie... by Allysia Finley on 21 April, 2024

effort will graduate with honors and think they don't have to work hard to succeed.

"Then, when you give them a job, they'll ask to work only 30 hours a week. If you say yes, they'll use their extra time to organize a union. If you recognize their union, they'll ask for extra paid days off and eight weeks' vacation."

Meanwhile, at Vandy in 2024, there were two crisis points during the 21.5 hours of protest. The university administration had *Panera* sandwiches sent in for the officers who were guarding the office of the chancellor, but didn't order enough to share with the hangry protesting students even though they all have plenty of dining dollars left to spend this time of the semester. They also shouldn't allow white bread on campus, obvi. That wasn't why some of the students called 911, though. It was because their friend, who was part of the sit-in, had to change her tampon. She was "being denied the right to change her tampon that has been in for multiple hours, which leads to an increased risk of toxic shock syndrome." They tweeted out the video of their speakerphone call to 911, as well as when they angrily plead their case to an exceedingly patient Vandy administrator in a sweater vest.[43] "She does not feel safe," someone says off-screen, punctuating it with claps. There was nothing preventing the student from leaving the protest to go attend to whatever personal business. She just wouldn't be able to come back in. Here's the takeaway message from Bari:

> Just like middle-aged women who think dressing down the manager will somehow earn them a full refund, these students have convinced themselves that by linking arms and screaming "shame" at their college's chancellor, they are stopping a war in the Middle East.

When my daughter was quite young and was cross about something I didn't do that she wanted me to do right now, she would cross her arms and stomp her foot. I would calmly suggest that she try stomping her foot a little harder to see if that might work.

Nonviolent protests may or may not solve the particular issue that's causing the outrage. It can be very helpful in building communities of like-minded humans who can then organize to enact change. I assume that you often find it hard to get all worked up about some issues. I have no personal experience with feminine hygiene products, although I've been quite hangry in my share of meetings which seem to go on and on for no particular reason. It's almost as if people are using the meeting to protest having to go

---

https://www.wsj.com/articles/if-you-give-a-college-student-a-cookie-fb5f617d
[43] https://www.thefp.com/p/tale-of-a-tampon Lots of excellent reporting by Bari Weiss and her crew at The Free Press.

back to their offices and get down to work solving some problems. As a #girldad, though, I understand that the wrong response from someone like me is to tell young people that they shouldn't be upset about the things that have clearly upset them. I've never been ostracized for wearing the wrong color scrunchie on a Tuesday. I was in ROTC, though.

You're presumably offering your sage wisdom and advice for free, but I'd recommend taking some guidance from fortune tellers who get paid real money to proffer sage wisdom and advice. First you listen to what they are telling you. You only have to half listen, because there's a relatively narrow range of things people get upset about. Usually it's relationships, money or their health. Your young employees are healthy and they aren't going to be eligible for a pay raise until their next performance review, so that kind of narrows things down. They do so much of their socialization on their phones that they probably don't know how to do it in real life. They haven't yet developed the social skills to interact effectively in real life when there's a power imbalance. It hurts their feelings when the university doesn't instantly divest from (checks notes) Israel even though they've all inconvenienced themselves by sitting on the floor kindergarten style without anyone even bringing them a *Green Goddess Caprese Melt* on a toasted baguette.

There's an obvious, if curmudgeonly, way to deal with campus protests. Assign students more school work to do.[44] What must they be majoring in to be able to camp out in protest for the last couple weeks of the academic year? "STEM departments tend to have a lot of grant money and don't particularly want to deal with annoying undergraduates, so they put rigorous courses on the board to weed out weaker students. Humanities departments, by contrast, have to justify their relatively meager budgets in terms of student interest, which means they need to try to give the people what they want, which is easy classes."

In his 2022 follow-up book, "The Dumbest Generation Grows Up" retired English professor Mark Bauerlein complains for 310 pages about Kids These Days. Since they've had smartphones and whatnot most of their lives, Millennials don't read books. They didn't read much when they were kids. They didn't read for pleasure in high school. Even elite colleges didn't make them read the Great Books in college, and now that they're in their 30's they Still. Don't. Read. Wikipedia helpfully reminds me that LeVar Burton hosted "Reading Rainbow" for more than 20 years, teaching reading skills, habits, and attitudes. The magazine-style format took kids on real-life journeys with celebrity guest readers and "Kid on the Street" book recommendations. Again from Wikipedia, which Prof. Bauerlein presumably thinks isn't a proper source, "Reading Is Fundamental, Inc. is the oldest and largest non-profit children's literacy organization in the United States. RIF provides books and

---

[44] https://www.slowboring.com/p/college-students-should-study-more

reading resources to children nationwide with supporting literacy resources for educators, families, and community volunteers."

Since you probably don't have as much time to sit and read as us professors do, here's the TL;DR: It's been true for a while now that most young people have never been and are not now in the habit of reading for pleasure, and because of that they're missing out on important things. Reading literature that has stood the test of time gives you first-hand experience with people who think and act differently than you and the people you usually hang out with. It gets you inside the heads of all sorts, good and bad, and that allows you to understand that most people are not the flat 2D caricatures they are presented as in social media. Heroes aren't all good; villains aren't all bad. Every saint has a past; every sinner has a future. Humans are much more complex than children understand. Reading lots and lots of good history and literature is how young adults come to understand this, and that is important for navigating the complex world of adults.

Prof. Bauerlein mostly blames his Humanities colleagues who didn't fight the good fight to prevent the watering down of Humanities curricula and that's why nobody wants to take their classes anymore. He goes on about that for perhaps longer than he should, but then nobody was forcing me to read his book. He does come to a point, though. Lack of long-term exposure to art and literature and history and music and religion, and also avoidance of those works of those old white guys, is what has left young adults feeling so anxious and unmoored. They can't be expected to figure out for themselves which things of whatever medium are most worth immersing themselves in. They accept an absurd framing of the world as oppressors vs. oppressed and they don't really even think to question the underlying assumption that if only all the bad guys could be cancelled, or whatever, everybody would henceforth always be happy. My wife blames Barney, but the larger issue is that this sort of uneducated (Millennial) potato can't be reasoned with because they aren't reasoning about the world. If you say to them, "That's simply not the way the world works." their feelings will get hurt because they want to imagine that that's exactly the way the world works. It's a very child-like worldview that can be quite out of place in an adult place of business.

My daughter and I watched Pretty Little Liars together. I wasn't emotionally invested in the on-screen drama, but I could see immense value for her in having the characters dealing with extreme versions of the issues that any young girl has to navigate. Middle school girl world is fraught. I was having some trouble following the plot, so my daughter had me read the seven books that the TV show was based on. That gave me the back-story, but the seasons we were watching together had long since left those plots behind. I also had some trouble distinguishing the various characters, so she wrote their names with a sharpie on the cast photo on the cover of one of the books so that I could have that at hand when needed. I'm still not entirely sure who A was, but I have a favorite quote, "Are you sure she's gay, she hardly even looked at me." More recently, I've watched a fair amount of Real Housewives with my daughter, as well as a scripted drama that focused on the behind-the-scenes issues on so-called unscripted reality TV. Now about 30, my daughter often uses her intuitive understanding of real people gleaned from such sources to better navigate the adult world. My daughter wasn't an avid reader growing up, but she is now. Prof. Bauerlein argues that kids who don't grow up reading for pleasure will never develop that habit as adults. I think that's totes skibidi.

According to their CEO, Google "is a business, and not a place to act in a way that disrupts coworkers or makes them feel unsafe, to attempt to use the company as a personal platform, or to fight over disruptive issues or debate politics." The fever may or may not have broken and so hopefully we can all get back to doing our jobs, counting on our company leadership to "keep the psychotic workplace Stasi shit at bay." Fear of inadvertently uttering wrong-think and getting disappeared for it takes all the fun out of being in the office.[45]

Ivy League snowflakes blowing off the last few weeks of the semester to protest, demanding that their university endowments divest of certain stocks and whatnot, should probably check with their own parents about the family stock portfolios that make it possible for them to attend Ivy League schools and not even bother to buckle down the last few weeks of the semester and earn their degrees.

At the Columbia protests, Johannah King-Slutzky told reporters on camera, who then both tweeted and fact-checked her statement, that "I guess it's ultimately a question of what kind of community and obligation Columbia feels it has to its students? Do you want students to die of dehydration and starvation or get severely ill even if they disagree with you? If the answer is no, then you should allow basic—I mean, it's crazy to say because we're on an Ivy League campus, but this is like basic humanitarian aid. We're asking for, like, could people please have a glass of water?" The NY Post headline is "Keffiyeh Karen whines for glass of water, proving pro-terror students are total weaklings" and notes that this sounds like a parody of leftist whining.[46]

I still find it a little strange that students in college these days don't seem to learn how to speak truth to power. When my daughter figured out that crossing her arms and stomping her feet wasn't going to work, she learned to use her words instead. I made some effort to not discourage her as she was learning to boss me around effectively. When she was a teenager I told her

---

[45] https://www.piratewires.com/p/mission-accomplished

[46] https://nypost.com/2024/05/01/opinion/keffiyeh-karen-johannah-king-slutzky-proves-pro-hamas-students-are-total-pushovers/

that, "Boys don't think, you have to think for them." and when she went off to college I explained that one of the things she needed to learn there was how to manipulate frat boys. As a senior, she talked her way into a closed section of a class on negotiation. She is very effective at protecting her team of young women when some man in the company tries to get her team to do his work so he can then take credit for it. She deliberately and strategically overshares with her "emotional support old men" at work in order to build a robust network for herself and her team and so they are properly informed of all things Taylor Swift.

I hope tween Swifties who watched football with their dads all season, watched the Masters with them as well. When their dads marveled at the unattainable ideal of the Augusta National landscape compared to their backyards, their daughters could explain that that's how they always feel on Instagram.

Your young employees will be non-deliberately and un-strategically oversharing with you, but by half-listening to what has them outraged on any given workday you can begin to understand what's keeping them from staying on task. You have to somehow resist the urge to tell them how insignificant their worries are in the grand scheme of things. They're in an echo chamber. That means they are largely immune to opposing views. But it also means that pretty much everybody they know is worried about the same thing(s). Hence, that one person who feels the need to over share with you is giving away the game plan for the whole team. You can feel free to generalize widely from your one data point. What you choose to do or not do with that intelligence is up to you.

Probably what will work best for your career progression is to use that understanding to advise the more senior members of your organization on what "kids these days" are up to. There's a sharp break in the flow of information from the jungle gym rungs below you to the ones above. I think it's safe to assume that the big bosses aren't following the TikToks of the new hires. One of your many superpowers might just be to explain to both sides what the others think and why. I'm certainly not suggesting that you connect up with your young employees on social media. That would be cringe. Half-listen and then generalize.

If you feel up to it, you might even want to organize some sort of team outing to help them build skills and make the world a better place. One of the times my daughter stomped her foot was when her older brother got to go along with Granny and her church circle to fold donated underwear at the battered women's shelter. "I want to help poor people!" she shouted. She got lots of turns going along to help poor people when she was just a bit older. The young people who work for you probably don't realize that it takes the typical abused woman seven tries to leave her abuser. If you ride together to the shelter, play *Salt-N-Pepa – Shoop* in the car. Feel free to sing along. If they ask what that's from, tell them they should binge the 2021 *Netflix* miniseries, *Maid*. A single mother turns to housecleaning to make ends meet as she escapes an abusive relationship and overcomes homelessness to create a better life for her daughter.[47]

---

[47] https://www.imdb.com/title/tt11337908/

38 I have nothing to hide. You're wearing pants, aren't you?

There are many things about digital natives that freak out the Olds, but top of that list seems to be the lack of concern about privacy by those who seem to live their lives entirely online. I tell my frosh that I oppose beer pong because recent studies have shown that binge drinking temporarily suppresses one's immune system and that ping pong ball may have bounced under that nasty second-hand frat house sofa. I also tell them that there are no drunk pictures of me in college, because people didn't have cameras on them all the time back then.

You might think that it's not your problem if your young employees want to Instagram pics of their brunch. But what if they're having bacon and eggs instead of avocado toast? Should that information be used to adjust their health insurance premiums? I'm going to say, "No." even though I eat very healthy these days.

Recently there was an article in the New York Times[48] detailing how car companies sell fine-grained information about drivers to their insurance companies, routing the data through third-party data brokers for plausible deniability. This is totally separate from discounts that insurance companies offer to customers who have agreed to have their driving habits monitored. "Modern cars are internet-enabled, allowing access to services like navigation, roadside assistance and car apps that drivers can connect to their vehicles to locate them or unlock them remotely." The Times continues, "Automakers and data brokers that have partnered to collect detailed driving data from

---

48

https://www.nytimes.com/2024/03/11/technology/carmakers-driver-tracking-insurance.html

millions of Americans say they have drivers' permission to do so. But the existence of these partnerships is nearly invisible to drivers, whose consent is obtained in fine print and murky privacy policies that few read." That's not even a little bit OK.

> READ CAREFULLY: By reading all or part of any of this or other essays in this collection, you agree, on behalf of your employer, to release me from all obligations and waivers arising from any and all NON-NEGOTIATED agreements, licenses, terms-of-service, shrinkwrap, clickwrap, browsewrap, confidentiality, non-disclosure, non-compete and acceptable use policies ("BOGUS AGREEMENTS") that I have entered into with your employer, its partners, licensors, agents and assigns, in perpetuity, without prejudice to my ongoing rights and privileges. You further represent that you have the authority to release me from any BOGUS AGREEMENTS on behalf of your employer. Also, I'm a sock puppet, geez.

At this point I'm going to have to start quoting Cory Doctorow[49] who is perhaps my favorite blogger/author/thinker on these sort of issues. "Learning, growth, and fulfillment all require a zone of privacy, a time and place where we are not observed. Far from making us accountable, continuous, fine-grained surveillance by authority figures just scares us into living a cramped, inauthentic version of ourselves, where growth is all but impossible." The young people who work for you need to learn and grow. They can't always be worried about how well their brunch photographs, although they probably should be worried about whether those drunk-eye college pics are going to haunt them when they're older.

It's one thing to freely post to social media, whether or not one understands the risk of tossing so very much information out into the aether. It's quite another thing to be monitored at work via various internet-connected technology that your boss issues you and expects you to carry or wear. Doctorow again: "Even where these tools are nominally designed to help you do your job better, they're also *explicitly* designed to help your boss keep track of you from moment to moment." and "It's bad enough that your boss has decided that you now must turn part of your home into an extension of your workplace at no cost to them. Then they add Bossware to your computer so they can spy on you (and your family), adding insult to injury." Creepy creepers who make this shit include "InterGuard, StaffCop, TimeDoctor, WorkSmart, Teramind, and many others." I didn't realize that Office365 uses "sentiment analysis" to predict whether I might cause trouble,

---

[49] https://pluralistic.net/2024/03/15/wellness-taylorism/#sick-of-spying

so I guess it's a good thing that I never clicked on those links to upgrade.

I've been teaching a frosh seminar on pseudoscience for thirty years. We talk about all sorts of crazy things and the students write two-page briefing documents for "The Senator" which they email me as pdf attachments so I can grade them and email back comments on them. I understand that gmail reads all my message traffic, but I am comfortable with that because they read all my message traffic and so the context of what the government should do about Bigfoot or Aliens or Psychic Detectives is clear. What's funny, though, is when I stop by my lab on the way to class and my graduate students ask what the topic *du jour* is. The apps on their smartphones often pick up on some of that and they start getting fed ads for crazy shit.

Meanwhile, here's a reddit post[50] that caught my eye, titled "You're being targeted by disinformation networks that are vastly more effective than you realize. And they're making you more hateful and depressed." (Ides of March, 2024)

> TL;DR: You know that Russia and other governments try to manipulate people online. But you almost certainly don't know just how effectively orchestrated influence networks are using social media platforms to make you—individually—angry, depressed, and hateful toward each other. Those networks' goal is simple: to cause Americans and other Westerners—especially young ones—to give up on social cohesion and to give up on learning the truth, so that Western countries lack the will to stand up to authoritarians and extremists.
>
> In 2014, the IRA and other Russian networks began establishing fake U.S. activist groups on social media. By 2015, hundreds of English-speaking young Russians worked at the IRA. Their assignment was to use those false social-media accounts, especially on Facebook and Twitter—but also on Reddit, Tumblr, 9gag, and other platforms—to aggressively spread conspiracy theories and mocking, *ad hominem* arguments that incite American users.

Your social-media savvy employees are being systematically targeted by a sophisticated PR campaign meant to make them more resentful, bitter, and depressed. It's not just disinformation; it's also real-life human writers and advanced bot networks working hard to shift the conversation to the most negative and divisive topics and opinions. China is now joining in to try to divide Americans by combining AI with real images to exacerbate political and social tensions in the U.S. "The reality is that you cannot distinguish

---

[50]https://www.reddit.com/r/GenZ/comments/1bfto4a/youre_being_targeted_by_disinformation_networks/

disinformation accounts from real social media users. Unless you know whom you're talking to, there is a genuine chance that the post, tweet, or comment you are reading is an attempt to manipulate you—politically or emotionally."

This becomes your problem when your employees get unwittingly manipulated and it affects their mental wellbeing at work. Although I don't do social media and I carry a camera-less flip phone, I'm not Luddite. I develop new technology for a living, and AI is in everything we do these days. But Cory Doctorow again: "Contrary to the ahistorical libel you've heard, the Luddites weren't angry or frightened of machines – they were angry at the machines' *owners*." Your problem is shitty Bossware that your boss wants you to inflict on your human charges.

39 You Go Girl!

Since everybody has times in their professional life when they feel a bit stymied, it can be helpful to have actual stories of people who have gone through tough times and kept on going. All of the women in the snippets below are from a single family tree which I have researched thoroughly enough that I can attest that these stories are pretty typical. I've compiled these stories for my eventual grand-daughters, but they are also useful as a reality check to the recent spate of stories glamorizing divorce as narcissism disguised as feminism, a product of the "woman empowered by everything woman does" paradigm wherein all choices made by women are the product of liberation, hence feminist, hence good. @katrosenfield sez, "There is no error or disappointment that can't be yass-kweened away. Heaven forfend a woman admit that she made mistakes or has regrets. Everyone makes mistakes; everyone has regrets." Of course, when you're on your deathbed you do want your primary emotion to be curiosity, rather than regret.

Cicely Reynolds arrived at Jamestowne Colony in August 1610 on a ship called The Swan. She was ten years old. She didn't come with her family, except perhaps a brother. When she was sixteen she married Thomas Bailey and they had a daughter, Temperance, in 1617. When Thomas died of malaria, three-year-old Temperance inherited his 300 acres. The widow Bailey married the widower, Samuel Jordan, whose 700-acre plantation was next door. The good news is that everybody at Jordan's Journey survived the 1622 massacre that wiped out a third of the English colonists. The bad news was that Cicely was widowed a second time the next year. She was pregnant with Samuel Jordan's second child, and suddenly in charge of more than 1,000 acres. The creeper minister who had just buried her husband proposed marriage. She declined. He sued. It was the first breach of promise suit in America. She eventually married William Farrar who was helping her manage her plantation, but he wasn't after her money because he had his own 2,000 acre headright for paying to bring over 40 indentured servants. As a child, Cicely was a servant. She was also besties with Pocahontas. As a woman, Cicely was the original Southern Belle who is said to have introduced the art of flirting to America. At a time when women didn't typically own property on their own, she was probably the wealthiest woman in the Colonies.

As their youngest was finishing high school, Emma Green and her husband were packing up the house to move yet again. Her husband was a miller, but that industry was being disrupted by electrification and consolidation and the Depression. The next job lasted not quite a year and the one after that her husband couldn't do because of advancing lung disease (from being a miller) so they bought a little country store in Schindler, SD and moved back home. Emma's oldest daughter was a school teacher, but when the school system couldn't meet payroll she took a job in the western part of South Dakota. There was a one-room teacherage attached to the one-room school. She married a local man who had a good job as a heavy equipment mechanic in the nearby mines, but then the mines closed and the bank would only partially cash her paychecks because the school system had no money. They moved back to South Sioux, SD and bought a grocery store. Emma's husband died, so she was left to run the store on her own. Her baby boy married his high school sweetheart and they had a baby girl, Denis Anne, in 1937. Denis Anne's mother was sick with Hodgkin's disease for a long time and died at age 30. Emma offered to sell her store and move in with her son to keep house. The other grandmother also wanted to take in everybody's favorite grand-daughter, but they were about to move to California. In the end, Denis Anne went to live with her father's big sister and her family above the store in South Sioux. At some point her name became Denise, but she mostly went by Denny.

Iona Hathaway was a bearcat on wheels, but you didn't hear that from me or my mother. I'm pretty sure she had no idea that she was descended from Samuel Jordan, who was probably on the Sea Venture in 1609 when it shipwrecked on Bermuda in a hurricane that was the basis for Shakespeare's last play, *The Tempest*. Iona grew up in Iowa where her father had done quite well homesteading and then bought four adjacent acreages in South Dakota. If you know how to look for such things, which I do, you can find bits and pieces of Hayes Chappell's courtship of Iona in the local newspapers. Hayes and Iona married and had two children, although she was only two months' pregnant with their daughter Hazel when Hayes caught pneumonia working on the prairie farm and died. Iona's father and youngest sister and two of her brothers were all on adjacent farms, so at least she had a support system. She remarried and ran a small-town store with her new husband and had two more children. Hazel married a local farmer at age 16 and they moved into town before the farm economy was decimated by the Dust Bowl. Her husband led the first successful sit-down strike in America, but the giant meat-packing plant refused to re-hire the union leaders for three years, so they were too poor to have their second child in a hospital and new-mom Hazel did the doctor's laundry to pay off his bill. Her husband would walk a mile or more for odd jobs that paid him two or three dollars.

There's a statue of Mary Dyer next to the state house in Boston overlooking the Common where she was hanged because the Puritans didn't take kindly to women preaching the Gospel where men could hear. They had previously banished her or else, so she apparently chose else. There's no statue of Anne Needham, who was admitted to the Boston church as member #100 in the winter of 1630/1. After being cast out and restored to the Boston church, she was dismissed on 6 April 1653 to the church in Malden, and on 22 January 1670/1 (as "Anne Hitt an ancient widow") she was admitted to the church in Charlestown. She died at Charlestown on 30 November 1688, "aged woman." She was obviously suffering from post-partum depression in 1637 when Gov. Winthrop wrote, "A woman of Boston congregation, having been in much trouble of mind about her spiritual estate, at length grew into utter desperation, and could not endure to hear of any comfort, etc., so as one day she took her little infant and threw it into a well, and then came into the house and said, now she was sure she would be damned, for she had drowned her child; but some, stepping presently forth, saved the child;" Winthrop gave an even longer account of an unsuccessful attempt to drown another child, this one being three years old in 1642, and this is one of the grounds for the excommunication a few months later.

Anne Bradstreet was overwhelmed by the sickness, lack of food, and primitive living conditions of 1630 New England. Her father was the steward for the Earl of Lincoln and had afforded his daughter an unusually complete education. She was frequently ill and apparently developed a vaguely morbid mindset. She was continually distressed by the culturally ingrained condescension toward women. She struggled to raise eight children and take care of her home, but she still found time to write. I recently bought a book of her poetry. The Puritans believed that suffering was God's way of preparing the heart for accepting His grace. Anne once said "If we had no winter, the spring would not be so pleasant: if we did not sometimes taste of adversity, prosperity would not be so welcome." I agree that when we are faced with trials we can learn and grow from what we have learned. She would say that trials are not to throw us off track, but to appreciate the miracles that are to come.

Ora Empress Newell died in 1909 after giving birth in Burma where her husband Ambrose Rice was an agricultural missionary. The baby didn't live very long either, despite Ora's widower and three little kids coming back home to Iowa where Ora's sister Ada moved in to take care of the kids. Ada and Ambrose eventually married and had four children, two of whom lived to be more than 100, which isn't all that surprising because Ora and Ada's father was the oldest man alive in 1954 at age 108. Also, one of Ada's sons went to Burma with his family as an agricultural missionary.

Carrie Paulson was born near Oslo, Norway in 1861. She came to America with friends when she was 18 years old and first settled in Chicago. She was able to bring her mother, sister, niece and nephew to America. She married Nels P. Nelson in Wisconsin in 1884 and bore six children in a pioneer log cabin. She lived to be 95 years old, sadly outliving two of her sons. Edwin Nelson had his arm ripped off by a threshing machine in 1913, a few weeks after he had taken out a $12,000 life insurance policy with his mother as beneficiary. Albert Nelson died in 1919 in Norge, VA from malaria or perhaps stomach cancer. After the Civil War an unscrupulous railroad developer had tricked a bunch of Norwegian immigrants into moving to Virginia because the farm economy had collapsed. Albert's widow, Tillie Nelson, moved back to South Dakota with her two young children. She kept house for, and then married, the widower Charlie Nelsen and had more children. The blended family with more or less the same surname(s) made things a little confusing but I guess you can use the same monogrammed bath towels. Tillie married a third time after Charlie died.

King Henri Membertou said he was more than a hundred years old. He was very tall and had a beard, which made him stand out among the surviving members of the Mi'kmaq tribes in Nova Scotia whose numbers had dwindled to perhaps 2,000 by the start of the 17th Century. They had been trading with the French throughout the 16th Century and so there were a series of epidemics. If you don't believe that King Henri lived to be 110 years old, then Grace Membertou would have to have been his grand-daughter rather than his daughter. Princess Grace went back to Europe with some traders about 1607 and married John Granger, Jr. Their son, Launcelot Granger, Sr. was born in 1609 in England. Launcelot Granger, Jr. came to New England and he married Joanna Elinor Adams in 1654 in Massachusetts. I wonder if they met when they were growing up back in England. I wonder if Joanna knew her husband's grandma was originally from Arcadia. Several generations down the Granger line, Anna Granger married Asael Chappell, and in 1815 their son Martin Henry Chappell, Sr. was born. Martin Henry Chappell, Jr. was a few months old when his father died, but lived to age 78. Of course, that means he was alive to see his son, Franklin Hayes Chappell die young and leave Iona a pregnant widow.

I've come across a surprising number of ancestors who fought in King Philip's war, but even more surprising is Miss Pokanoket Prentice, born in 1646. Several sources believe she is the daughter of King Philip (Pometecomet) who was the son of Massasoit—leader of the Wampanoag who kept the Pilgrims alive so they could pretend to have the first Thanksgiving. After King Philip's war, some of his descendants were shipped off to the West Indies as slaves, some ceased to exist, and two daughters were believed to have married into the families that won the war, one to a Starkweather and one to a Stanton. That means that when Joseph Stanton, Sr. married Miss Pokanoket Prentice, their son Thomas Stanton was the grandson of King Philip. The Stanton branch of the family joined up with the Hull branch and then Sarah Hull married David Hathaway and had a son Ebenezar Hathaway in 1843, who was the father of Judy Iona Hathaway. She was a bearcat on wheels, but you didn't hear that from me or my mother.

Mary Letitia Varner was the daughter of Isaac Varner and Phoebe Ann Clark. Her family lived in Belmont County, Ohio, in 1850 and had moved to Linn County, Iowa, by the time of the 1860 census. She seems to have been married five times so there may have been issues with her cooking. The middle husband, Jonathan O. Jones, may have instead lived to old age in the next county over. Close reading of census documents show a young farmhand in the household who becomes her husband by the next census. It's tricky, though, because she had a lot of different names, and sometimes went by Libby and sometimes Mary Letitia. Also, Jonathan Jones is a pretty common name.

On 26 Sep 1692 Rebecca Chamberlain, age 67, wife of William and mother of 13 children, died in Cambridge Prison. The Salem mass hysteria had spread to two dozen other nearby towns including Billerica, and second-wave accusations of witchcraft were often based on grudges, jealousy or revenge. Rebecca died before she could be exonerated. Another Rebecca, but this time in Connecticut thirty years before Salem, was hanged as a witch. She is assumed to be the child of George Steele, a founder of Hartford, because he included her sons Micah and Moses Mudge in his will and they are assumed to be his grandchildren. That she married at least 3 men is undisputed. Jarvis Mudge was the second husband and died as her first husband did after a few years of marriage. Her third husband was Nathaniel Greensmith. Rebecca was accused of being a "lewd, ignorant and considerably aged woman" by her minister. After Nathaniel sued his wife's accuser for slander, Nathaniel himself was named. She and Nathaniel Greensmith were indicted in 1662 as having familiarity with Satan, found guilty and hung on Gallows Hill in Hartford. The Connecticut General Assembly formally exonerated them in 2023.

Joanna Borridge was married to Thomas Cogan when she was about 16 and over the next twelve years would become the mother of at least four children. Her husband died in March 1654 and the following month her father-in-law, William Cogan wrote his will leaving his house and land to "Joane Cogan my daughter and to the heires male of her bodie" if his daughter Eleanor Deane had no male heirs. Joan had a small son whose name does not appear in the records. She was left with little means to provide for her small children and soon married Obadiah Miller, a man she came to hate. Not long after their marriage, while living in Taunton, she was brought before the grand jury for fighting with him and in 1655 he took her to court for calling him names: "Obadiah Miller complaynes against Joane his wife for abusing him with reproachfull tearmes or names as calling him fool, toad & vermine and threatninge him; as also for that yesterday shee fell uppon him indeavoringe to beat him at which tyme shee scratched his face and hands. The case being examined it was found that Joane the wife of Obadiah Miller was guilty of very evill behavior towards her said husband; it beinge proved by the testimony of John Lamb and Thomas Miller. John Lambe testifyed he heard her say shee would knock him on the head; and that shee did often call him foole and other reproachfull tearmes. Thomas Miller testifyed that when his brother Obadiah and his wife lived with him, she did comonly call him foole and vermine and he doth not remember he ever heard her call him husband and that she said shee did not love him but hated him; yea shee here said shee did never love him and shee should never love him. For which her vile misbehaviour towards her husband shee was adjudged to be taken forth to the whippinge post; there to receive soe many stripes on the naked body as the commissioners should see cause to inflict on her; whereuppon shee was brought forth; but by her humiliation and earnest protestations for better carriage towards her said husband the punishment was remitted and this sentence passed, that for the least miscarriage to her husband after this tyme shee should be brought forth agayne to receive a good whipping on the naked body well laid on."

On the sunny morning of September 19, 1677, shortly after the men had gone to work in the fields, a large band of Indians attacked the fort at Hatfield north of the palisade before their victims could get to its shelter. Twelve innocents, mainly women and children were killed and a number of others were wounded by the Indians, who also put the torch to the barns and houses. The raiders also carried off seventeen captives, including Martha Waite, wife of Benjamin Waite and their three little girls, and Hannah, wife of Stephen Jennings and her two children. Benjamin Waite and Stephen Jennings went all the way to French Canada in the dead of winter and found their captive wives and children at a poorly guarded wigwam. The party of captives numbered twenty as two children had been born during the four-month captivity and several had died or been killed in the long, northward journey. The survivors were ransomed and brought home. Waite was killed and skinned by a large contingent of French and Indians on February 29, 1704 during the famous Deerfield massacre. Stephen Jennings was killed on July 20, 1710 with his son, Benjamin Jennings, near Brookfield, Massachusetts. You may have read James Fenimore Cooper's "The Last of the Mohicans."

The Boscobel Dial in Wisconsin dated 28 Nov 1889: "There was considerable excitement among the people here all day Tuesday over the disappearance of Assistant Postmaster Adolph Meyer. He had last been seen at 10 o'clock Monday evening, and it was believed by many that he had committed suicide as he has been in poor health for some time and intimated that he would make away with himself. Telegrams to neighboring cities failed to bring tidings of him and a search was made in the river bottom. However late in the afternoon a lady in his house discovered 2 letters wrapped in a muffler and shoved up the leg of a pair of his drawers which hung on a line in the backyard. One of the letters was addressed to his wife, and one to Neldo Francisco, his brother-in-law. In his letter to Neldo he stated that he was going to 'Leave this cursed whisky town' and go to Kansas and try to make something of himself and he wanted Neldo & his father-in-law to take care of his wife and 4 little children until a year from next December, when he would let them know where he was." It looks like he never returned to his family and by 1905 Hattie lists herself as single and then by 1910 as widowed. Adolph George Meyer may have died on September 6, 1894, at the age of 26, perhaps in St. Louis or maybe Kansas City. He was likely suffering from late-stage Hodkin's disease, which is the same thing his grand-daughter, Marjorie, died from leaving Denis Anne to be raised by her father's big sister. The good news is that Hattie's brother and father did step up and take care of her and her children. Hattie moved to Parker, SD to take care of her grandchildren when her daughter-in-law died.

Tele and Margaret (Van Ruschen) Hinders were both born in Germany. They each came to America at age 9 and settled in Illinois where they met and married. They worked hard and built a life for their children and grandchildren in America. All nine of their children lived to adulthood, but two died as young adults. Minnie Hinders died in 1907 from typhoid fever. The newspaper says there were 50 carriages at her funeral. Harry Hinders died in late November 1916 in a car crash, reported in the newspaper as, "Four of the occupants of the machine escaped without any injuries, but Harry Hinders, who became slightly tangled in the blankets in the front seat, was unable to jump clear of the auto. As it turned slowly over, a lever pierced his skull, cutting a rectangular hole into the cerebrum, badly tearing the brain tissue. The young man was unconscious all of last night, but regained his senses this morning. Shortly after the accident had occurred, all hope of his recovery was given up, but he was so much better this morning that there are now hopes he may live. The car was not perceptibly harmed by the accident, except that the windshield was demolished. It was run on its own power back to the city and soon repaired." Harry's father, Tele, was driving the brand-new Ford and Harry's younger brother, Bill, was one of the passengers who was unhurt.

Brita Knutsdatter Rokne was born on July 11 1828 in Norway. She married Swen Edson (Svein Aadson Tesdahl) in Oct 1848 in Vos, Norway. The family immigrated to America in the spring of 1857 with their four children, Christine (8), Odd or Ed (6), Jorund or Julia & Ingeborg or Emily (2). They had another child Martha in Illinois on Oct 26, 1857 and then settled in Deerfield, Wisconsin where they had two more children, Betsy & Anna (who died in infancy). While in Wisconsin, Swen was drafted in the Union Army. Pvt. Edson served for 8 months and 13 days in Company C of the 16th Wisconsin Infantry before the war ended. In the spring of 1866, he brought their family to Minnesota where they had another child Anna, in July of 1866 at Fort Ridgely near New Ulm, MN. They built a homestead in Brighton Twp., Nicollet County, MN where they had two more children, Caroline & Lewis. On March 29 1879 at the age of 51 Brita died of consumption and is buried at Swan Lake Lutheran Church in Brighton Twp.

Iver and Marit (Petersdtr) Iverson left Norway on 11 April 1875. They sailed from Kristiansand harbor, destination Minnesota. They had their two boys, ages three and almost-two, as well as a baby girl, who was just a few months old. When they arrived in America the immigration official said, "There's too many Iversons. Pick a different name." Marit remembered fondly the beautiful green valley where she grew up and chose Green for the family name. She was also probably pretty tired after a very long boat ride with two rambunctious boys and a five-month old girl. You go girl!

40 THE ELUSIVE GOAL OF THE CIVIL RIGHTS MOVEMENT CONTINUES TO BE A COLORBLIND SOCIETY.

I recently watched the 2004 movie *Hotel Rwanda*, which takes place during the genocide of 1994. The Hutu military initiated a campaign of ethnic cleansing against the Tutsi minority, killing a million or so men women and children. Often with machetes. Paul Rusesabagina, a hotel manager saved the lives of more than 1,000 people who sought refuge at the hotel from Hutu death squads. He stayed in Rwanda for two more years after the genocide, but then Rusesabagina applied for asylum in Belgium and moved to Brussels with his wife, children, and two orphaned nieces in 1996, rightly fearing for his life. He was awarded the Presidential Medal of Freedom by George W. Bush in 2005, but was kidnapped in 2020 and taken to Rwanda where he was put on trial for terrorism because he was an outspoken critic of President Paul Kagame of Rwanda. Happily, he was released from prison in 2023 after 939 days in detention, and was able to return home to his family in San Antonio, Texas.

When Rwanda was a Belgian colony, the Belgians invented the concepts of Hutus and Tutsis. They had some bullshit about Tutsis were taller and had narrower noses and were a bit lighter skinned, but nobody could ever tell who was which unless they looked at the stamps on their identity papers. Tutsis were always the ones who had government jobs with the Belgians. After independence, the Hutus were looking for payback, or maybe it's just that dictators always need an enemy. Cycles of ethnic cleansing and retaliation and payback and so on are horrifyingly common in the world. The answer to the question, "Can't we all just get along?" seems to be Nope. Jesus weeps.

I have kind of a hard time getting my brain around the idea that the Belgians could invent arbitrary racial categories and then pit those two races against each other leading to genocide. As a Red Sox fan I have been known to say to Yankees fans, "Is that some sort of birth defect or do you just not know any better?" It's a good-natured gibe, not a serious question. I fully respect Yankees fans who grew up cheering for the evil empire. My son is a natural-born member of Red Sox nation; I'm a naturalized citizen. He was born a few blocks from Fenway Park; I lived and/or worked within sight of Fenway park for 11 years. The Sox were never very good when I lived there. The Sox have been World Series champions repeatedly since my son started caring deeply about such things. Recently the Baltimore Orioles were quite good, which we both found kind of amusing. My now-grown son currently lives just south of Wrigleyville.

I find that I'm not emotionally invested in the outcome of baseball games these days, although I do quite like several of the rules changes that have sped up play. I'm interested and will watch, but don't care enough to stay up past my bedtime. Maybe if the Sox were in the World Series, but probably not. I'm mostly just cheering for the laundry anyway, because players change teams so often these days, and several of the big-market teams are throwing money around exactly like the Yankees used to do back when they were winning all the time and we hated them for that.

The two-block street in front of Fenway Park was recently re-named. It had been called Yawkey Way after the long-time owners of the Red Sox, who were racists. The Red Sox were the very last team in the majors to integrate, only finally hiring a black player, Elijah Jerry "Pumpsie" Green, in 1959. That's 12 years after Jackie Robinson broke the color barrier with the Brooklyn Dodgers, BTW. Jackie Robinson was passed over by the Red Sox after a tryout widely believed to have been a sham. Robinson believed that Tom Yawkey was the biggest bigot in professional baseball.

Boston was apparently still a pretty racist town when I lived there in the 1980s. The riots over desegregation of the public schools were only a few years before that. It wasn't until 1987 that a federal appeals court ruled Boston had successfully implemented its desegregation plan and was in compliance with civil rights law.

I personally think it's quite important for schools to be well integrated, because so many social organizations are self-segregated. Kids need to grow up together with kids who look different from them, with the hope that they'll realize organically that superficial differences in appearance don't matter. I was delighted to watch my own children develop friendships with classmates from various backgrounds, ethnicities and such. Many of my son's close friends were Orioles fans. I fully support all parents' rights to make educational choices for their own children, but I find the ongoing existence of private academies kind of sad. These schools were created during Massive Resistance to school integration when the response in Virginia was to close the schools instead of integrating. Affluent white parents then created a private (white) school system so their kids wouldn't get behind on their schoolwork, miss out on prom, etc.

Rather than moving inexorably forward toward the shared goal of a colorblind society, there have recently been people pushing hard in the opposite direction.[51] The word that's used is "anti-racist" but it's really just a new form of racism, i.e. neoracism. It's often wrapped in the mantle of the civil rights movement, but its aims are the opposite of what MLK and his allies were (peacefully) demanding. "The only remedy to racist discrimination is antiracist discrimination. The only remedy to past discrimination is present discrimination. The only remedy to present discrimination is future discrimination." — Ibram X. Kendi, *How to Be an Antiracist*. Jesus weeps.

Loving your neighbor as yourself doesn't mean ignoring that your neighbor has a different lived experience than you. In Luther's small catechism he explains the ten commandments. "You shall not bear false witness against your neighbor. What does this mean? We should fear and love God, so that we do not lie about, betray or slander our neighbor, but excuse him, speak well of him, and put the best construction on everything. God commands us to speak truthfully and charitably about our neighbors so that others view them in the best possible light." Who is my neighbor you might ask? It's everybody. Being a good Lutheran can be hard, but at least there isn't all that institutional guilt that Catholics have to deal with.

Part of the anti-racist mantra is that whenever racial disparities are noted, the cause is automatically racism. If nobody racist can be pointed to, then the fallback is structural racism. Structural racism can be blamed even if, in fact, nobody involved is racist. It's a logical fallacy to have one go-to explanation for everything which can't be disproved. The five-dollar word for this is non-falsifiable hypothesis, and it automatically disqualifies something from logical argument, rational public policy, and scientific thought.

The answer to racism is, in fact, to stop being racist. Sox fans and Yankees fans can enjoy the game together. Hutus and Tutsis can govern a democratic Rwanda together. We can all just get along. But first we have to stop demonizing the other and insisting on an eye for an eye. We can celebrate diversity without pitting tribes against each other. The magic answer is to view others in the best possible light and expect them to do the same to us and the rest of the neighborhood. You knew Mr. Rogers was coming:

> I have always wanted to have a neighbor just like you, I've always wanted to live in a neighborhood with you. Would you be mine? Could you be mine? Won't you be my neighbor? Won't you please, Won't you please? Please won't you be my neighbor?

51

https://www.axios.com/local/boston/2025/0131/bu-closes-antiracist-research-center-ibram-x-kendi-leaves

41 We will, of course, adore whoever you bring home.

I would have liked to have known my grandmother, but she died at age 30 when my mother was only seven. She and my grandfather were high school sweethearts. They were pals before that. Marjorie died from Hodgkin's Disease, which is now easily treatable, but in the 1940s about all they could offer was periodic blood transfusions. My mother has no memories of her own mother because Marjorie was so sick for so long, so stories that she tells me are second-hand although sometimes backed up with photos and archival evidence which I have been systematically accumulating.

Here's a picture of Marjorie in her high school band uniform, which is labeled Tommy. She always kept her hair quite short, so most people would assume this was a picture of a boy. Once when my future grandparents and two of their pals were over at a parent's house for dinner, the mom actually thought Marjorie was a boy. Her hair was tucked up under a hat and her pals all called her Tommy because she was in a tomboy phase and the four of them palled around together. They used to do thinks like wax the trolley rails on a steep hill and then watch when the trolley couldn't make it up the grade. The moms were all a bit shocked when Tommy showed up at graduation wearing a beautiful green dress.

On the following page is another picture from those years where Marjorie and a friend are posing with big smiles and arms around each other's shoulders. Note that both young women are wearing overalls, but Marjorie's are so brightly patterned that I wish it was in color. She's wearing a hat with very short hair and it kind of looks like she has a big-ole ring on her ring finger. Marjorie was all set to go off to art school in Minneapolis after graduation, but she couldn't stand the idea of being apart from her sweetheart so they eloped. They were married in the church rectory and Marjorie's sister was a witness. Both mothers were pretty upset, but they got over it.

In my mother's baby album she is identified as Denis Ann, which we both thought strange because she has always gone by Denise. The mystery was solved recently when I was reading my great-grandmother's diary from those years and in the entry where her son came to tell her about the birth of my mother, she spells it phonetically as Dennes Ann. Somebody changed Denis to Denise after Marjorie died.

My conclusion from all this is that Marjorie was pushing back against rigid gender stereotypes of her day. She may or may not have even realized that her new daughter was from a long line of strong, independent women on both sides of her ancestry. I've been systematically collecting and curating these stories on behalf of my eventual granddaughters. My kids both tell me, "It's going to be a while, Dad." They both seem to be cishet, but I've been clear with them all along that we will, of course, adore whoever you bring home. There are some lash-ups that complicate the logistics of getting me tall, multi-talented grandbabies, but that's a minor matter.

In a recent Gallup poll, 30% of Gen Z women self-identified as LGBTQ+: "Increases in LGBTQ+ identification in recent years have occurred as members of Generation Z and the millennial generation have entered adulthood. Adults in these younger generations are far more likely than those in older generations to identify as LGBTQ+." Gallup breaks things down further, "More than one in five Gen Z adults, ranging in age from 18 to 26 in 2023, identify as LGBTQ+, as do nearly one in 10 millennials (aged 27 to 42). The percentage drops to less than 5% of Generation X, 2% of Baby Boomers and 1% of the Silent Generation." The Silent Generation simply didn't talk about such things. The youngest generation of employees you're now dealing with never seem to shut up about such things, as you may have noticed.

Gen Z's endemic aversion to risk has created a strange new relationship style that no one—not even them—really wants, called situationship, an increasingly popular term used to describe any unlabeled, undefined romantic relationship. For many young people, any form of communication that requires someone's immediate attention has become generally stigmatized. Texts are fine, but don't expect prompt responses. Out-of-the-blue phone calls are for emergencies and are frequently answered with a mix of confusion and concern. Gen Zers are setting themselves up to be one of the loneliest generations in recent memory. The blame seems to lie with some combination of too much time on social media exacerbated by pandemic isolation and a lack of childhood independence.[52]

I don't claim to know much of anything about on-line dating. I'm married to my high school sweetheart. Our first date was 24 October 1981. I assume that I phoned her to ask to go to a movie. We went to Taco Bell afterwards. We often have Mexican food in honor of our first date, because we only have wedding anniversaries every four years. My actual wedding proposal was, "Wouldn't it be amusing if we got married on Leap Year Day." Our tenth anniversary is in 2028.

I assume that the young people who work for me have personal lives. I don't have any interest in them, though. If they get married I don't want to be invited to the wedding, but my wife will be delighted to get the happy couple a gift. If they have babies I'm quite interested in seeing pictures and hearing anecdotes, mostly because I don't have any grandbabies yet. I wouldn't presume to offer relationship or parenting advice, though. There's one exception. My advice to expectant fathers is: "There's only two things you can't do. You can't gestate. You can't lactate. Otherwise man up." I am quite sympathetic to work-life balance issues, and I quietly praise my colleagues with young children who are successfully juggling the complicated logistics of two careers and three little kids. I often comment how much I enjoyed having children and how glad I am that I didn't miss out on it because in the blink of an eye they're grown up and gone. When my colleagues bring an infant with them to the office for whatever reason, I always make a point of telling them that goo-gooing at their baby was the highlight of my day.

I have typically had no idea who my late-twenties daughter may or may not be dating. I know the names of her gay friends simply because when she says, "Cole made me meatloaf." or "I went to brunch with Cody." She sees me (and my mother) getting too excited about the prospects of (great)grandbabies and quickly clarifies why that's not happening. She has offered to explain to me all about the DC dating scene, but I declined.

I imagine that you're far too young to be eagerly awaiting the arrival of grandbabies. You may or may not know anything more than me about on-line dating. I do hope that you have enough sense to stay out of all such drama which may be going on in your young employees' social lives. There is no upside for you to be anywhere near any of that. You don't have time for that kind of drama, and you could easily find yourself entangled in really messy HR messes. As a faculty member I am what's called a mandatory reporting official. That means that if a student or staff member confides in me about certain

---

52

https://slate.com/life/2024/11/gen-z-situationship-relationship-dating-risk-ghosting-chappell-roan.html highly personal things, I am required by law to report it to the proper officials in the proper way, even if the student or staff member begs me to not tell anyone. I even have to report Title IX issues that I hear about second or third hand. Doing that wrong is one of the few justifications for firing a tenured professor. I tell the students in no uncertain terms not to confide in me.

My office door is always wide open and my laboratory has a wall of glass that overlooks a busy atrium with a Starbucks. The words I actually say are, "I'm not your mother. If you set the house on fire the number is 911. Don't call me." I sometimes relate the story of the Oregon coed who sued the University when they let her football (or maybe basketball) player rapists off the hook because they were so good at running/jumping/etc. and so the University used her confidential counselling center records against her in court. In principle I could give lots of excellent advice to young people out in the world for the first time navigating the dating scene and whatnot, but in practice I find it best to just stay out of all that. It's easier for me because I'm a man. I'm not much of a hugger. I don't show outward emotion. I have resting bitch face, of course, but you can't infer emotional state from that. It's just my face.

On the inside I'm rooting for all of the young people who work for me to find personal fulfillment in their social lives, but I strive to be like Sergeant Schultz on Hogan's Heroes, "I see nothing." I'm happy to see that that's a TikTok meme.

I'm happy to report that my daughter now has a serious boyfriend. So far the only potential relationship issue seems to be that he doesn't like Jello. He does like Banana-Flavored Laffy Taffy, though. I can work with that.

42 Doctor, it hurts when I do that. So don't do that.

Young people think they're invincible. Physically, I mean. They all seem to be emotionally quite vincible these days. Middle-aged people typically have enough miles on their bodies that they understand their own physical limits, which is psychologically healthy. If a young person's knee hurts they expect it to either get better on its own right away or they're headed off to urgent care. When a middle-aged person wakes up and their knee hurts, their typical response is, "My knee hurts. I might as well get up and go to work." As long as it's not getting steadily worse, a middle-aged person can get used to their knee hurting. Ideally our knees wouldn't make those noises first thing in the morning, but we're not exactly young anymore.

One of the lasting legacies of price and wage controls during WWII is company-sponsored health insurance. It was a way for companies to compete for talent when they couldn't offer more money. It didn't take very long for people to get used to the idea that health insurance for employees and their dependents was a standard fringe benefit of a good job. The pre-existing conditions trap made changing jobs problematic, because once you get to a certain age that trick knee that's starting to get a lot worse would discourage job hopping.

Obamacare changed many things about health care. Doing away with the pre-existing condition trap was pretty significant, but decoupling health care from any job totally changed the way young people think about such things. Since almost everybody under the age of fifty has defined-contribution pensions rather than traditional defined-benefit pensions, retirement isn't tied to your job either. It's important to understand that these two traditional mechanisms to discourage job hopping are simply not in play anymore. Also, almost nobody expects to stay at the same job their whole career these days.

For the last thirty years I've been telling my graduate students that I might be one of the few people they ever know who stays at the same job for fifty years.

When you first hire new college graduates they are almost certainly still on their parent's health insurance and phone plans. Obamacare set the adulting milestone of getting your own health plans at 26. At what age young people get their own phone plans is up to their parents, but I can say from personal experience it's really amusing to watch a grown child sit down and figure out what that's going to cost them. If I knew how to take pics with a flip-phone I would have taken one.

Eventually your young employees will age out of their parents' health plans and will need to sign up for what your organization offers. Well, technically they don't have to do that because there are various Obamacare options that are distinct from what employers offer. They may assume that both the process and the ramifications of their choices of health plans are similar to getting their own phone. You're going to have to explain how much more serious the health insurance choices are. You're probably going to want to start the conversation with pet insurance.

Veterinary medicine is changing rapidly right now. I'm old enough to have once said to my vet, "I paid $100 for this dog, so don't even think about sending me a bill for more than that." She was a good dog. I have friends who spent quite a lot of money on chemotherapy for their fur babies and now have the dogs' ashes in urns on their mantle. When my last dog died after a long happy life, going from tubby to frail in a few weeks so it was probably cancer, I buried her in my backyard. She may have helped me dig part of the hole. She was a good dog, too. My current dog is a little Yorkie who got rehomed with me when my mother downsized because I have a big yard. The last straw for my mother may have been the $1,300 vet bill for extracting most of the dog's teeth. I'm having none of that. I scoop her gloop from a can three times a day and if teeth want to fall out on their own that suits me just fine. I don't carry pet insurance, so I'd be out of pocket on dental surgery or whatever. I also may be a bit behind on required rabies shots, but that seems a reasonably low risk given her lack of teeth. Also, she's already beyond her breed's life expectancy, which my wife googled first thing when the dog moved in here.

The main thing that's happening in veterinary medicine right now is that private equity is buying up practices from any vet who will sell. You may not realize that it's harder to get into vet school than med school. You could argue that it's harder to be a vet because there's more than two anatomies and your patients can't tell you (in words) how they're feeling today. Both types of medical school are quite expensive, of course, and those loans aren't going to be just forgiven. When private equity buys out a practice, they then begin putting the screws to the vets to make them profits. The only way to do this effectively is to cram services the pets may or may not need, like convincing rich old ladies to pay for dental surgery. This scheme is facilitated because more and more companies offer pet insurance as a perk.

When you take your car in for service you expect an estimate of what it's going to cost to make it all better. When you show up at the hospital there is no corresponding estimate, even though they have an actual price list for everything. A chargemaster is a comprehensive list of charges for each inpatient and outpatient service provided by a hospital. Each poke, prod, lab test, exam, surgery, procedure, room charge or supply is an item within a hospital's chargemaster[53] which contains thousands of items and services with their associated charges. An individual hospital's charges vary based on its unique range of services, adoption of new medical technologies, capital investments and other local factors, and there's no way to shop around to find a hospital that fits within your budget. Only the uninsured are subject to the prices in the chargemaster because insurance companies have all negotiated rates which are the basis for determining an insured patient's actual out of pocket cost after the deductible which you also pay. In the automotive world, the analog to the chargemaster is the MSRP sticker price, which is a starting point for negotiation rather than a price that you expect to pay. The chargemaster isn't on any window sticker, though. If there's a price for holding your own newborn grandchild, I think that should be posted publicly. My wife would happily eat that up charge. I could probably wait a day or two to begin doting.

So talk with your young employees about pet insurance, especially out-of-pocket costs and deductibles. There probably are some monthly employee costs, which show up as payroll deductions. They should include in their pet-parent budget costs of boarding their hairy dependent when they travel. Depending on their work schedule and commute, they may need to include costs of pet-walking services and/or doggie daycare. Food, grooming, loss of security deposit, etc. The costs can add up. Some future jobs might not include this as a perk.

Then you'll be ready to guide them through evaluating health insurance coverage options for themselves. They probably have a variety of options for different plans at your work, but have them also price out some Obamacare options. Someday they might get laid off or deliberately take unpaid leave for personal reasons, and they'd need to jump back on their parent's health care or get Obamacare for themselves right away. It's important for them to know that getting sick or injured without health insurance can be financially ruinous. Nearly one-third of GoFundMe campaigns are dedicated to raising money to help pay medical debt. If medical debt is discharged in bankruptcy, it'll be like a zombie apocalypse on their credit report and then good luck ever buying a

---

53

https://www.mainlinehealth.org/patient-services/patient-billing/price-transparency/chargemaster house with a fenced yard for that furbaby.

43 THE PRINCE OF CRANKS.

Minnesota Congressman Ignatius L. Donnelly was bummed when he lost his re-election bid. He didn't want to go back to the land of 10,000 frozen lakes, so he spent his time hanging out in the Library of Congress reading all the books in the Jules Verne section. You'd think that would cause him to embark on a new career as a lobbyist for the nascent submarine-building industry, but instead he took Plato's account of Atlantis literally and wrote a book "Atlantis: The Antedeluvian World" arguing that all known ancient civilizations were descended from that continent that sank into the sea. You may have seen the Disney version(s).

Here's the key quote from Plato, "But afterwards there occurred violent earthquakes and floods; and in a single day and night of misfortune all your warlike men in a body sank into the earth, and the island of Atlantis in like manner disappeared in the depths of the sea." That seems to fit pretty well the volcanic eruption which obliterated the Greek island of Santorini and destroyed most of the Minoan civilization via tidal waves bad enough to have been memorialized in Egyptian hieroglyphs. But where did Plato hear the story from? It turns out that he described Critias reporting what his grandfather was told by Solon who heard it from Egyptians when he visited there back in the day....

It can be hard to keep track of how you have come to know the things you know. It can be even harder to admit, even to yourself, that many of the things you believe are wrong. By contrast, it's relatively easy to tell when somebody else is wrong. The hard part is not immediately telling them how very wrong they are. This is especially hard with n00bs who don't yet know enough to know how little they know. You'll often find yourself exasperated with those that want you to explain why things are as they are and why we do things the way we do. That's just the way it is. That's just how we do things. I don't have time to explain it all to you right now. Nobody leaves an interaction like that satisfied.

As you get to the stage in your career where more and more of your time is spent mentoring others, you're going to have to get into the habit of questioning yourself. Not in some sort of "impostor syndrome" way because you know your shit and have earned your current rung on the jungle gym. What I mean is that you want to be helping others to learn how to do things and not just to do what you tell them to do, and the key to that is articulating why various things are done as they are. That requires you to both question the underlying logic of standard operating procedures and to invite your mentees to question that logic as well. Inviting people to question you takes a full dose of self-confidence. It's also freeing because you are freely admitting that you don't know all the answers. Nobody knows all the answers. We're figuring this all out as we go along. That might have been part of Plato's message. Don't get too full of yourself.

When you've been with an organization long enough, you end up being one of the few people around who remember the old timers. Hopefully you listened to enough of their stories back in the day that you can pass along some of that accumulated wisdom to the younger generation. So much of that lore is simply not written down anywhere. Much of it may very well be embedded into the current structure and operations of the place, but without the underlying reasoning, the way things are will often make no obvious sense. Dialogs are the answer.

I teach by telling stories about people who made choices and enjoyed/suffered the consequences. This strategy has worked for millennia, of course. Much of received wisdom has been passed down through generations this way before being written down. The advantage of the oral tradition, though, is that you can adapt and adjust your stories to best reach any given audience. A literal interpretation of Plato's dialogs by an ex-congressman in the 1880s is absurd.

One of the reasons I get excited at the start of each semester is that there's a whole new group of students who haven't heard my stories. My wife has heard my stories, of course, and she often rolls her eyes at me when I'm working through the updated versions that I'll be regaling my classes with in the coming days. I'm not just pulling things out of a can, and until a few years ago I had never even written them down, so as these things are rattling around inside my head I talk through them out loud. Apparently it's not all that interesting to some people to hear these variations on themes for the bazillionth time. Plato wasn't married and he never thought that love was necessary for a marriage. Hard disagree. Patiently listening to stories over and over is a sign of true love.

My students' parents and/or their future selves are paying real money to listen to my stories. Also, they might show up on the final exam, so they're at least somewhat motivated to pay attention. Your mentees have no such external motivation to pay attention to your stories. The trick is going to be how to make your stories engaging enough that they will listen and memorable enough that they will remember. You're probably going to have to exaggerate somewhat. Not to the extreme that Donnelly did, of course, but you have to resonate with your audience.

Aesop's Fables were cautionary tales which often have anthropomorphic animals at their moral heart. Aesop may or may not have even existed, per se, but these stories continue to provide valuable life lessons for both children and adults. Sometimes you can twist them just a bit to make an important point. For example, when I'm describing to graduate students the level of effort necessary for them to succeed at their chosen career, I say that, "It's not slow and steady that wins the race. It's fast and steady."

It can also work to make reference to pop culture touchstones, although those are always a moving target. I recently explained to my frosh that, "Madonna was the Taylor Swift of her day." I'm continually probing to see which cultural references they get. I have to remind myself that they wouldn't have seen any R-rated movie that's more than a few years old and they don't watch TV in the way people my age do. The good news is that you can feign ignorance and ask them to suggest shows for you to binge. You might even be able to have some sort of public tote board where people vote on what "everybody" is watching right now. It's not like it was even a few years ago when every so often a large portion of the population all watched the same thing at the same time and then talked about it around the water cooler at work the next morning. Even Super Bowl commercials aren't a big deal anymore. You can go pee whenever you want and watch the best commercials online however you wish. When you tell your Gen-Z employees that it was the Janet Jackson half-time wardrobe malfunction that spurred the development of Youtube, they'll have no idea what you're talking about.

I assume you know that in Zoom meetings everybody is also on their phones. If you put one of your young employees on the spot, they'll be getting real-time assistance with their answer from most of the other young people on the call. More senior members of the team almost certainly have their email open on their second monitor, and if their microphone isn't muted you can hear them clicking away. You may or may not be aware that this is also happening during in-person meetings. Even in moderate-sized lecture classes, it's obvious to me who is paying attention and who is doing something else on their phones or laptops. I often break up the class into chunks, with little stories in between. I can tell when some of the class need a few minutes to finish transcribing what I've been writing on the whiteboard or finish formulating a question and screw up the nerve to ask it out loud. I've been doing this for decades.

If you're going to get people to pay attention to your dialogs, you need their full attention during meetings. If they've got their laptops open and their phones at hand, the best you're going to get is continuous partial attention. Everybody thinks they're better at multitasking than they are. Nobody can pay attention to both what you're saying and those damn devices. Part of the reason you tell your stories without slides or other visual aids is to prevent people from flicking their eyes back and forth between your screen and theirs.

It's bad manners to not look at someone when they're talking to you. The Fully Present Rule isn't just about politeness, though, it's about maximizing the potential of each interaction you have with each team member. When everybody dedicates their complete attention to the interaction at hand, it creates an atmosphere of respect. It communicates the importance you each place on the other persons and the subject being discussed. The advice from experts is to establish the rule that complete attention to the present task is required whenever in a designated "Fully Present Zone." Such a zone could be a specific meeting room, office, or virtual space. When my students are taking an exam, I write on the whiteboard, "Phone all the way off. Brain all the way on. Third eye blind." It's not about cheating, it's about being fully present for the task at hand.

With nothing else to distract them, you have a fair chance that people will listen to more of your stories. You'll have to be explicit about how it relates to the issues that they're facing, though. You might even have to tell them the moral of the story up front, e.g. be sure to keep all your receipts or you're not going to get your travel reimbursed. You may or may not have mechanisms to incentivize them to keep track of what you tell them. It's not like you expect them to take notes while you're going on about some old guy who worked here all those years ago and then regurgitate factoids on a midterm. That one guy who paid for an Airbnb up front and then his travel voucher got kicked back might get their attention, though. You'll want to make it a better story somehow to make it truly memorable. Maybe include a tidal wave or a volcano. If there's a subplot of some Disney movie that they've all seen, work that it somehow, of course.

44 I wish I had a million dollars.

The Dow Jones Industrial Average just hit $44,000. I have a clear memory of when it first hit $2,000. For some reason I also remember the first time the price of a new car on *The Price is Right* was above two grand. The average price of a new car is well above forty grand these days, so I think I'll just keep driving my hoopty. It was my father's car and when he died six years ago, nobody in the family wanted it so I paid my mother the blue book value of $5k for it. It's the perfect old-man's car to drive my mother and her friends to church on Sundays. Sometimes they ditch me during the last hymn to go to brunch, though.

One of my father's hobbies during retirement was fiddling with his investment portfolio. Not day trading, because he got his insights from various investment newsletters that came in the actual mail, and he plotted his strategy in pencil on yellow legal pads. He was moving money between different mutual funds, not buying and selling individual stocks. For many years I was worried that he would fritter it all away and I would have to support my parents, but his investments did well enough to pay for my kids' college and now my mother complains that she has more money than she knows what to do with. I have no particular interest in the stock market, per se, but I do pay close attention to what's going on and what might be moving the market. I also am a careful student of a wide variety of scams designed to separate fools from their money, and routinely talk about them with oldsters to help inoculate them from being conned. Eventually my father got into the habit of running any changes to his portfolio by me to get my opinion. Just before he died he asked me to help my mother manage their investments.

In retrospect it's quite odd that my father was into the stock market. He was born at home because his parents were too poor to go to the hospital. His mother did the doctor's laundry for quite a while in order to pay off his bill. My grandfather was one of the union leaders who led the first successful sit-down strike for better wages and conditions, at a large meatpacking plant. The rank and file went back to work in short order, but the union leaders were out of work for three years during the depths of the Depression. One source of my parents' affluence was my mother's father, who took up what work was available when he graduated high school during the Depression, built a successful HVAC business, and bought some commercial and residential rental properties. My parents also benefited from a once-in-a-lifetime demographic quirk where they had generous combinations of defined-benefit and defined-contribution pensions. They also lived modestly. Since I'm executor of the trust, I happen to know that I'll be getting a low-seven-figure inheritance sometime in the next fifteen years, even though I already make far more money than I spend and have no interest in retiring before I'm 80.

I sincerely hope that your 401k and other investments are doing well. You may have gotten out of the habit of looking at your statements when the stock market did that V-shaped thing during the pandemic, but they should have recovered by now so go ahead and take a peek. Assuming you didn't buy a bunch of properties you shouldn't have during the housing bubble, you may also have quite a lot of equity in your home. Most families don't talk openly about money and inheritances and such, so you probably don't have any idea what your parent(s) have specified in their will(s). Do have them annotate the family photo albums though. Sooner or later somebody is going to want to know who those people in them are. Genealogy is the most common hobby these days. Pickleball is a distant second.

Since you're an actual grownup who might know about such things, your new hires are going to look to you for advice. During the on-boarding process they're going to have to make some decisions that could have profound financial ramifications when they're pushing 80. Repeat after me: low-load ETFs, low-load ETFs, low-load ETFs....

None of the people who offer investment advice on TV or on-line or via books, newsletters or weekend seminars can predict the future. If they have inside information that will move the markets, they will go to jail if they act on that information or tell someone else to act on that information. Successful investors like Warren Buffett sit atop large efforts to determine which companies to acquire, which stocks to sell, etc. His company then acquires and/or sells in order to build wealth for the company, which regular folks can invest in to share in that effort and expertise. But if you were to ask the Oracle of Omaha what to do with your money, he would say: low-load ETFs.

In 2008, Warren Buffett issued a challenge to the hedge fund industry, which in his view charged exorbitant fees that the funds' performances couldn't justify. Buffett won that million-dollar bet. His logic was that once you include fees, costs and expenses, an S&P 500 index fund would outperform a hand-picked portfolio of hedge funds over 10 years.[54]

Since my wife and I each earn quite a lot of money and we live well beneath our means, our checking account balance periodically balloons. In principle I could go out and buy a new car, but I don't want one, so I simply say to my wife, "Why don't you dump another $50k into your Vanguard fund?" She clicks a few buttons and our checking account is back down to a comfortable range for another six months or so. She actually wants to retire some day, and carries the super-longevity gene, so I expect that this is money she'll be spending after I'm dead. Our finances have been fully co-mingled for decades and everything is in order via our wills and trust, but it's simplest if that money is all under her control.

When you're giving advice to your young charges, you should point them towards Vanguard. The average Vanguard mutual fund and ETF (exchange-traded fund) expense ratio is 83% less than the industry average. "Vanguard was built differently to make sure we stay focused on keeping your costs low." That's not just a tagline. You can think of it as a non-profit, which was so innovative back in the day that the other investment giants sued them for being unfair and hurting everybody's profits. Vanguard has lots and lots of mutual funds to choose from, and they are all helpfully categorized with a risk metric from 1 to 5. Young people should go with funds that are 4 or 5. You probably want something in the 3 or 4 range. Those nearing retirement should go for lower-risk options.

There are so many options that it can be a little daunting, so go with a simple ETF that tracks the S&P 500 for your bread and butter investment. Disclaimer: "All investing is subject to risk, including the possible loss of the money you invest. There is no guarantee that any particular asset allocation or mix of funds will meet your investment objectives or provide you with a given level of income. Diversification does not ensure a profit or protect against a loss."

Another mantra: buy and hold because you're investing for the long term. The stock market will have its ups and downs over the short term, but the sort of diversified portfolio you get in an ETF insulates you from the collapse of any individual company. Those Enron employees who had their retirement nest eggs in Enron shares went through some tough times, even if they avoided jail time for that systematic fraud. It was horrifying to watch the broader markets drop precipitously during the housing market collapse and the COVID-19 pandemic, but the markets recovered fairly quickly. The part that surprised me is that there was so little inflation after sequential rounds of quantitative easing. I'm not price sensitive, but even I'm shocked when I go to

---

54

https://www.investopedia.com/articles/investing/030916/buffetts-bet-hedge-funds-year-eight-brka-brkb.asp the grocery store these days. Although, I had been waiting fifteen years for inflation to finally show up, so I have that small comfort I guess. One more time: low-load ETFs. Buy and hold.

45 Highly Magnified and Thoroughly Educated.

Many years ago, a Wogglebug came into my classroom to get warm. He liked it so much that he stayed three years, becoming thoroughly educated. I once placed him onto the document camera and projected his likeness onto the screen. As much to his surprise as mine, when the Wogglebug stepped down from the screen he remained highly magnified. You may have heard of my prized student because he's the Head Professor of the Royal Athletic College of Oz, and is quite famous for the invention of school pills. Students merely take one pill per class period in order to master both required and elective subjects, which frees up the rest of the daylight hours for achieving athletic perfection which is what leads to lucrative NIL deals. These things can't be left to serendipity because even royal colleges depend on wealthy alums to fund their ever-expanding real estate empires.

University administrators are often thoroughly educated because they started out as professors, but teaching well turns out to be quite hard work so they've failed-upwards to a much more lucrative gig. They all think of themselves as highly magnified. Indeed, they all rate each other quite highly, so it's not surprising that they get all butthurt when the faculty assigns them the grades they have earned. Sometimes it's via the charade of a five-year performance evaluation, but usually it's when they do something so obviously inept that a large fraction of the faculty feels the need to tell them so via email. For example, for hundreds of years administrators neglected to have faculty they've hired provide proof that they earned the degrees they hold so everybody needs to drop what they're doing in the middle of the semester and provide their official transcripts because someone might someday do a random check of the personnel files and if that proof is not there we might lose accreditation. For those of us with our diplomas on the wall and our dissertation on the shelf, such a demand is rather insulting.

It turns out to be quite shocking to look at college transcripts from the era before grade inflation and school pills. Sometimes you can get your more senior co-workers started talking about their non-athletic college experiences. "What was the hardest course you took?" usually works as a prompt. They won't be at all shy talking about how many C's they got and how happy they were about those grades. Try to get this conversation rolling when your youngest colleagues are present and you can watch them react in horror. You'll see them all thinking, "How did the Olds ever get jobs here?"

There's no such thing as the Gentleman's C in the Ivy League anymore, because 80% of the grades are A's. I don't know why they even bother assigning grades anymore. It's like youth soccer where everybody gets a trophy, and orange slices. You might want to get into the habit of looking over the transcripts of any potential new hires fresh out of college, and then asking them during the interview process, "What was the hardest course you took?" They won't be at all shy talking about how few B's they got and how angry they were about those grades.

The root of grade inflation was the wartime draft in the 1960's. Ivy League professors who were opposed to the war knew that any students who flunked out would get drafted and sent off to war. Ivy Leaguers all seem to agree that only the poor and uneducated should have to fight wars, so a consensus developed to never flunk anybody out. These days the issue is that an ever-increasing proportion of faculty members are not on the tenure track. We call them non-tenure eligible (NTE) faculty, and they have none of the protections typically associated with being a professor. Their contracts are renewed (or not) each term, according to the need for classes they teach and the whims of various administrators.

In many areas of specialization there has been an on-going egregious overproduction of PhDs by the Ivy League schools, so there's a never-ending supply of thoroughly educated historians, biologists, etc. Almost none of them are ever going to get to be tenured professors, even though that's what they were all led to believe when they went off to graduate school. Their only hope of maintaining a shred of professional dignity is to take whatever contingent teaching job(s) they can cobble together and hope against hope that if they work hard enough and are obsequious enough someday some dean will bestow upon them the opportunity to jump to the start of the tenure track treadmill. That sort of pathway to citizenship happens just often enough to allow NTEs everywhere to suspend disbelief.

I find that I'm offended by the whole idea of pretending there's "separate but equal" tenure-eligible and non-tenure eligible categories of faculty. NTE's tend to be mostly women and of color. Senior tenured professors tend to skew male and white. I've been one of those for more than twenty years and expect to keep on keeping on for another 20. The protections of tenure mean that I can provide proper pushback to administrators who have done, or are proposing to do, something really dumb. I wouldn't do it via email, though. I typically tell them directly to their face. In a collegial manner, of course, except in rare cases when I will say, calmly but firmly, "I'm not going to do that and you can't make me." Tenure allows me to insist on doing what's best for the students and the institution as a whole.

NTE faculty all know that their continued employment depends on getting favorable teaching evaluations from their students. These are done anonymously towards the end of each semester and these meaningless numbers are highly magnified in importance even when the response rate is around 20%. Students are also encouraged to include written comments where they can get back at mean professors who didn't give them all A's or who made them work for their A's. They will, however, say nice things about professors who brought goodies to class on evaluation day. Ideally fortune cookies with the answers to the final exam on the little slips of paper inside.

Senior tenured professors who grade as they've always done are running into problems when another section of the course is taught by a desperate-to-be-renewed NTE who inflates grades to gain favor with students. It's even worse when an NTE waters down content in a prerequisite course in order to gain that favor. I suppose in an English class it's not so terrible to skip a difficult book, but in something hierarchical like math or chemistry we've long since settled on a curriculum where each course builds deliberately on the ones taken beforehand. Eventual employers expect our graduates to have mastered certain sets of material, as has been the case for hundreds of years. They also expect to be able to look at a transcript and differentiate excellent students from those who skated through with minimal effort.

Even professors like me don't grade as firmly as we know we should. It is true that C's have become B's and B's have become A's. Since we don't give A+ or A++ or A+++ there's no way for employers to tell which of our students are truly exceptional. It used to be that such information was explicitly coded into letters of recommendation, but we're all concerned about the liability of putting down in writing any subjective assessment of a student's shortcomings. Once upon a time prospective employers would simply pick up the phone and ask professors for their candid assessments, but the unhelpful dumbasses in IT just yanked all the desk phones on the erroneous assumption that we'd all use Teams instead. It's exactly the kind of boneheaded move that causes administrators to get all butthurt when professors tell them in no uncertain terms how stupid that was.

Don't ever hire someone who's never gotten a B. They will freak out the first time you correct them in the mildest possible manner over the most trivial sort of issue. There will be tears. There will be outrage expressed for all the world to see on social media. It will all be your fault, even though the actual fault is with pervasive grade inflation.

46 It takes quite a long time to build a lasting legacy.

The pyramids in Egypt are so old that when they were built the Sahara wasn't a desert. It was grassland, with lakes and rivers and hippopotami and crocodiles. At the time of the Old Kingdom things were starting to get drier and that caused the area population to coalesce along the Nile and then when the rains stopped coming altogether the extravagance of great pyramids couldn't be afforded anymore. Also, pyramids are a terrible way to preserve your wealth and your mummy for use in the afterlife. All the pyramids were robbed almost immediately.

There's no mystery about who built the pyramids, or why they did and when they did. The literal Rosetta Stone means we can read the hieroglyphs carved and/or painted on the tombs themselves, including the polished granite tippy-top where they were pretty careful to claim ownership. We can also read the graffiti of the workmen. Amazingly, there is even surviving papyri discussing the logistics of the far-flung public works projects that these national construction projects represented. Some people still like to quibble about the details of how the pyramids, obelisks, etc. were made, but there's lots of solid archaeological evidence right there to look at. It seems strange that they were able to carve so much stone with only soft copper chisels and transport so very many large stones without wheels, but Pharaoh was both god and king so it was pretty much an all hands on deck kind of thing. Yes, the copper chisels got dull pretty fast, but that just means that you need about as many sharpeners as you do chiselers. Yes, it's hard to drag stone blocks which weigh as much as an SUV without wheels, but if you put it on a sled and wet the ground a bit you'll find that six or eight guys can do it easily enough. You have to make sure that the ramp wraps around the pyramid, though, or building the ramp will be as big an effort as the pyramid itself. The amazing part about pyramids is that they were under some pressure to get them done before Pharaoh died. When teenage Tutankhamen died in a drunk-driving chariot accident, he had to be buried in a borrowed tomb that was probably being prepared for his mother. King Tut was so insignificant that before his tomb was discovered, there was active scholarly debate about whether he even existed. His father had tried to change the State religion, so there was some effort to erase all memory of that dynasty afterwards.

I'm the sort of person who plants acorns on the prairie. Also maple and blue spruce seedlings. My parents sold our lake cabin in South Dakota when they retired, but I still check Google Earth now and then to see how "my trees" are coming along. I'm a little peeved that the new owners cut down some of my maple trees when they added on to the cabin that my father and I built in the late 1970s. They also removed part of the stone wall that I built to enclose the perennial garden that my mother and I planted. I built that over the course of three summers, since we only went there on weekends between Memorial and Labor Days. It was about three feet high and a total length of about 100 feet, made with stones I had carried up from the lakefront. I mixed the mortar in an old Radio Flyer wagon with a garden hoe. Each time I finished a section my mother would say, "That's nice, honey. Please stop now." I finished what I had started out to do, before I went off to college in Boston, and planted Boston ivy at the base of the wall which did quite well despite the harsh climate. I keep hoping Google Streetview will go down that little gravel road so I can get some close up views of the former alfalfa field I terraformed all those years ago.

I've been in my current job for more than thirty years. I came here to build something special. I hope you have similarly been able to devote large chunks of your professional life to building things that will endure. I've had lots of colleagues who were here for a handful of years and then went off to do something else. Some of them I miss having around. Others I'm glad I don't have to deal with anymore. One colleague just ghosted last week, but we simply added a second position to the search we were running anyway and will backfill without missing a beat. Bye Felicia.

When we hire someone new, a common source of annoyance is a stereotypical reluctance to learn the history of the organization. There have been various massacres and a Revolution (win) and Civil War (loss) here, so there's been some fits and starts, but my organization goes back to 1619 when my ancestor was in charge of building and organizing both a college and a town. My department goes back more than 50 years, and I knew most of the people listed on our 1972 recruiting poster, which I have framed in my lab. Our current configuration and set of policies/procedures has resulted from the thoughtful decisions made over more than four centuries. N00bs who think they know better and want to wipe the slate clean to start over get on my nerves.

The other thing that can be quite tiresome about new hires is when they insist on being told what to do rather than having me explain to them why we do what we do. Can I get an Amen? I'm always playing the long game, so it's worth it to me to have them understand the logic of our policies and procedures. Especially when they seem to make no sense. We all know many of the things we do seem illogical, but that doesn't mean there isn't logic behind what we do. It takes longer for me to explain the steps to follow than it does to just do it myself, so I need the people I hire to be able to start taking some baby steps right away. And then to begin to see how things fit together so they can figure out the next steps on their own.

But how do I get new hires to think on their own? I'm glad you asked. One tried-and-true strategy is to deliberately leave gaps in your own knowledge. I run a moderately-large research laboratory, where graduate students are the primary labor force. Although I'm the principal investigator responsible for deciding what everybody does and that it gets done according to our sponsors' expectations, I don't know how to operate any of the equipment in my own laboratory. I know what to do and why, but exactly how to make an apparatus perform its specific function, dunno. New students can ask more senior students or they can just figure things out. Once they start to get some data I can help them make sense of it and give them guidance on what to try next, of course. If they can't operate in that sort of paradigm they can't work for me and will have to switch to a different research group or else get sent down with a master's degree.

Initially, students will come to me having completed a set of tasks and I'll suggest the things to do next. At some point the conversation will switch and rather than suggesting next steps I'll ask them what they think they should do next. Once they get comfortable interacting like that, I start giving them pushback on what they suggest as next steps. They will have to defend what they want to do next. This comes more or less naturally to some students, but students from China, for example, have a built-in, irrational respect for authority and so challenging their Professor is really scary for them. They have to get past it, though, or they won't succeed as scientists. For some students all I have to do is tell them once that it's perfectly fine to call bullshit on me and they're off to the races. It's fun for me to get ordered around by my graduate students, because my goal is to have them be successful enough in their careers that they can fund the next generation of students here in my lab. In that sort of situation, my former students become my boss, which is really fun.

Back to your snowflakes who have no appreciation for how much collective work it has taken over (many) decades to build the organization they joined a hot minute ago. Whatever you do, don't give them checklists to follow. They can bang out a detailed recipe all day long, but are often hopelessly lost when things don't go according to plan. "I did what you said and it didn't work." is a common complaint, but what they really mean is that it's your fault it didn't work. There's an art to baking a high soufflé. Even when you do everything right it might fall. That's just the way it is.

47 Agent Cookie Baker reporting for duty.

Most people find that business travel isn't very fun. I find it amusing to watch a n00b go through the mentally deflating process for the first time. Initially they are all excited that they've been approved to go somewhere and not have to pay for it themselves. They quickly look up flight options and quirky Airbnbs and exotic dining options and even side trips they hope to squeeze in if their meetings don't take all day. At some point before they get too excited, I let them know that they can't just book things on their own and they need to go through the travel agent that we have contracted with. I sometimes helpfully hand them a business card with our agent's phone number on it. Sometimes I'll email them a link to our travel regulations.

I'm old enough to have sat at a travel agent's sad little desk while she click-clacked away at her terminal to find me a flight. The only modern analogy for that is going to the DMV or standing in the auto parts store while the counterman looks to see if they have the part you need on the shelf or if you should just go back home and order it yourself. It's quite funny to watch a young person use the "phone" function on their smartphone to call a travel agent who looks up flight information and relates options by voice for flights that are all right there on the smartphone already. I don't travel very often, but generally my wife books my flights. She even keeps my boarding pass on her iPhone so I can often tag along in the short line because she has gone through TSA PreCheck.

My wife also makes my hotel reservations, because she has Marriott superpowers and gets the points on her Marriott Visa card. I usually forget to tell n00bs that the travel agent was supposed to book their hotel as well, and they'll have to call back. Only sad corporate hotels, though. Buried deep within our travel regulations is a prohibition against Airbnbs and the like. Of course there's a justification process if staying in one of those saves the organization money, but I don't recall anyone ever doing that successfully. It could happen.

Your youngest employees probably aren't old enough to rent a car. That's fine with them because they prefer to Uber in unfamiliar cities anyway. Good luck getting reimbursed for that. The system won't reimburse for tolls without a proper receipt, so you're going to be better off taking an old school taxi in from the airport. You'll have to wait in line for that. Don't worry, though. When you check out of your hotel to go back to the airport, you might find a taxi waiting at an upscale hotel down the block. Or not.

And then there's per diem, a Latin phrase which means you're going to want to fill up on that sad continental breakfast before you head to your meetings because your daily meal allowance will only just cover your Starbucks fix. You forgot to get a receipt, didn't you? You won't be getting reimbursed then.

In 1998 I travelled all the way across the country to the 90210 (Orange County, CA) for a weeklong conference. The weather was miserable. Some quirks of the Federal budget meant there was a huge number of no-shows. My middle-seat redeye flight back across the continent was diverted and so on. I vowed to make every effort to minimize business travel, and found that people were happy to visit me here in a popular tourist destination. After 9/11 travel became even more cumbersome and unpleasant, so I doubled down on staying around. I nearly succeeded in going a full ten years without getting on an airplane, but then Airbus had some sort of travel freeze and so instead of them coming to Virginia for our final presentations on a Smart Intelligent Aircraft research project, I had to go to Germany for the weekend. I spent more time in airplanes than I did in the country, and while I was there I saw the inside of two airports, two aircraft factories, and two hotels overlooking aircraft factories. I let my passport expire during COVID.

I've only ever bought one house. It was 30 years ago. We got an excellent price on it because the original owners had done such a tragic job of decorating it. Now that the kids are grown it's way more house than we need, but our modest mortgage payments mean downsizing would likely cost us more. Rather than paying off the mortgage early, we refinanced at the depths of the Great Recession when interest rates hit a global minimum. In those days you had to lock in the rate via phone, which my wife did from the dentist's chair. We'd certainly get an excellent price if we spruced things up and sold, because inventory is really low and demand is still pretty high. My mother sold her house and downsized three years ago, and her house sold in two days with seven offers above asking. Things moved so fast that the stagers were bringing furniture in before Junkluggers finished taking leftover furniture out. We didn't repaint, or even clean. No repairs. I felt a little bad so I ran a quick vacuum, though. The real estate agent was the mother of my daughter's friend Abbey Layne, who had been over to play at the house over the years. My mother didn't begrudge the agent her 6% commission, even though it was pretty easy money for Abbey Layne's mom.

When my wife and I bought our one-and-only home thirty years ago, we hired a buyer's broker. He bent the rules by giving us a copy of the current MLS book for the area. We had moved to this town several months before and were renting a house while we figured the place out and waited for the right house to come on the market. My wife had made friends with someone who had bought the previous year, and from them we knew that the house we were considering making an offer on had been on the market then. Understanding the particular circumstances involved allowed us to make a below-market offer that was accepted. In retrospect, our broker didn't really earn his half of the 6% commission, but that's paid by the seller anyway.

My daughter tracks real estate for sale in town, even though she doesn't live here. My dream is for her (and her brother) to move back home and one of them can have our house to raise their family in. I'm sick of painting that white picket fence and the grand piano, dining room furniture, etc. can all convey as far as I'm concerned. My wife also tracks real estate for sale in town. She doesn't play the piano or paint, and she'd love the opportunity to buy all new furniture. I have no idea whether she'd bring along that $7,000 Pilates reformer that's upstairs in the former nursery.

You may have heard that mortgage rates are up but real estate commissions are coming down. Forbes says that: "A powerful real estate trade group has agreed to do away with policies that for decades helped set agent commissions, moving to resolve lawsuits that claim the rules have forced people to pay artificially inflated costs to sell their homes." This seems to be the end of the 6% commission almost always paid by the seller. It may be the beginning of the end of Real Estate Agent as a viable career option. In the same way that anybody can track air travel options with their phones, real estate listings are readily available online, as is advice about local schools, tax rates, commuting times, weather, etc. Buying or selling a house is a big enough transaction that there needs to be some professional looking out for your interests, but that could simply be a real estate lawyer who has their paralegal prepare the contracts and walks both parties through the sign here and here and here closing process.

Some professional athletes go into contract (re)negotiations without being represented by an agent. While it may save them a ten percent fee, it seems foolish to forgo that professional advocacy and oversight. But that's about the only time you might need an agent anymore these days, so you can join your young employees in snorting derision about having to book travel through an agent, and bake them some cookies as a housewarming present when they accomplish the American Dream, with or without a buyer's broker. They do need an actual lawyer though, not AI-generated forms, because this is the single biggest purchase they are ever likely to make.

48 WHY YA WALKING SO FUNNY, CARTMAN?

You probably have some co-workers who end up down social-media rabbit holes and want to talk your ears off about their unbelievable insights into life, the universe and everything. You might think that such people should have their internet privileges revoked. I'm here to tell you that crazy predates the interwebs. The universal phenomenon that's in play is that people want to feel special, and one way for demonstrably unexceptional people to feel special is by being among the special few who are in on some big secret.

Here's a secret for you: flying saucers are not saucer shaped. When private pilot Kenneth Arnold reported seeing a string of nine, shiny unidentified flying objects (UFOs) near Mount Rainier in 1947 he said they moved like saucers skipping on water. The newspaper headline shortened things to "Flying Saucers" and so UFOs are saucer-shaped.

The government looked into UFOs and collected reports from the general public. You can look up the *Project Blue Book* files easily enough at the National Archives and the Internet Archive and elsewhere. Some say that it was never really a serious effort because any good intelligence would still be super-de-dooper secret. After all, Vice President Truman didn't know about the Manhattan Project because President Roosevelt and the generals didn't think he needed to know about it. President Truman did need to know, so he was read into the program and then had to decide whether to use two or three of the gadgets *in lieu* of an invasion that the generals said would cost a million lives. Classified information is highly compartmentalized.

There simply isn't any physical evidence of crashed flying saucers, of whatever shape. But then any such evidence would be highly classified because any alien races who could come here are obviously way more advanced than we are now, let alone at the start of the jet age in the 1940s. I tease my friends at NASA that it follows logically that if we're getting our advanced aerospace technology by reverse-engineering crashed UFOs, then NASA is merely a front organization designed to hide that fact. They don't think it's very funny. It's a little funny. Also, don't you think there's something just a bit off about

Elon Musk?

The Air Force says that the Roswell Crash, a few weeks after Kenneth Arnold's sighting, was not a "flying disc" like they first said, but it was a super-de-dooper secret balloon. We apparently had high-altitude balloons which were listening for the sound of Soviet nuclear tests, and we didn't want the Ruskies to know about that. Somebody thought it was better to say it was aliens, but then the cover story got changed to "weather balloon" and all the bits and pieces of Mylar, balsa wood, and whatnot were collected and sent off to someplace where secret junk gets disposed of. People who had seen the detritus were sworn to secrecy, which means if they ever blabbed they'd have to pay a six-figure fine and go to jail for a decade.

There was a lot of ridicule surrounding UFOs back in the day, but there were a handful of influencers who made a fair living at it. My fav was Dr. George King, who was having trouble making a living as a spiritualist medium, but hit it big when he found UFOs. "He was contacted by an extraterrestrial intelligence known as 'Aetherius' in 1954, and founded The Aetherius Society in 1955—to promote and act upon the wisdom of highly evolved intelligences from other planets who communicated with, and through, him for over 40 years." That's a humble brag from his official bio. From among all humans, he was chosen by the leaders of the interplanetary confederation, headquartered on Venus, as the "Primary Terrestrial Mental Channel" through whom literally hundreds of Transmissions have been given by higher beings from beyond this world.

I also have a fondness for Howard Menger. He wrote books and went on speaking tours and eventually married one of his groupies. He describes his 1956 trip to the moon thusly,

> Finally we came to another large dome-shaped building, where we halted and our guide told us we could get out on the moon's surface where we could breathe the air with little or no difficulty. That pleased the group, for we were eager to stretch our legs.
>
> My first impression was that I was in the desert. The air was warm and dry. I could see little wind funnels forming on the ground, drawing up dust particles like tiny whirlwinds. I looked up at the sky. It was a yellowish color. When looking I had the queer impression that if I walked some distance I would fall off, since the horizon seem foreshortened.

We now know that it's quite dusty on the moon and that dust is a problem for astronauts and their equipment, it's not windy there at all. Menger also goes on at some length about a hottie from Venus who naturally had the hots for him. All in all, it's very sweet.⁵⁵

We don't say UFOs anymore, we now say UAPs. It's exactly the same. Congress recently held hearings about UAPs, with whistleblowers and everything. As if dealing with the COVID-19 pandemic wasn't enough for our government to do, Congress had inserted language into the Inflation Reduction Act or the Infrastructure Bill or the Chips and Science Act or some such thing, which required the Pentagon to spill all that super-de-dooper secret alien tea. Here's the October, 2023 headline: "Most UFO reports likely to have 'ordinary' explanations, government says, as investigation continues." Nothing to see here, sheeple, everybody go about your business. It's more or less a repeat of the Edward Snowden leak from a decade prior when there was a suspicious lack of information about UFOs.⁵⁶

I have to assume that Stanton Friedman, RIP, was even more disappointed in the Snowden leaks than I was. Friedman had spent fifty years working full time to uncover evidence of flying saucers. He died in 2019 of a heart attack at the Toronto Pearson Airport while traveling home from a speaking engagement in Columbus, Ohio. Presumably he was about to make some big reveal and had to be silenced.

When I was a child there were nine known planets in the universe. Pluto has since been demoted, but the Hubble and now Webb space telescopes have made it abundantly clear that stars with planetary systems are the norm rather than the exception. There's more than enough habitable planets for every dead Mormon to get their own. Unless you ascribe to some sort of young-earth creation story, picking either of the two in the Book of Genesis, you probably agree that there are other planets with technologically advanced races on them. Why haven't they come here? Perhaps they have, and all evidence of it has been covered up by a super-efficient, world-wide, multi-government conspiracy. Perhaps it's just that our galaxy is nothing special and our planet is nothing special and hence we're nothing special. That could be a good thing, because we might make great pets or be fun to hunt for sport or we might be delicious. In the latter two cases, galactic anonymity is for the better. Also, space is vast. The center of our galaxy, where all the cool kids live, is 50,000 light years away. That's why we can see the Milky Way in the night sky from our un-special cul-de-sac in the exurbs.

---

⁵⁵ King and Menger and various other Contactees are interviewed in the 1992 film "Farewell, Good Brothers" which I recommend.
https://www.imdb.com/title/tt0145641/

⁵⁶
https://www.theguardian.com/world/interactive/2013/nov/01/snowden-nsa-files-surveillance-revelations-decoded

49 Aren't you, like, worried?

Apparently the GenZs are all anxious all the time because they had smartphones when they went through puberty. There are all manner of hockey-stick graphs used to prove this. The brainiacs at the social media companies used their big brains to hijack the brains of all their users in order to maximize advertising revenue. All the other tech bros were doing it, so they had to. Now it's your problem because the college graduates you've been hiring are all, like worried. All the time about something or other. They're not sure what.

You presumably noticed that there was something a bit off with people who did a year or two of Zoom school during the pandemic. You probably hoped that this was a blip that would wash through the system and then your young employees would be normal again. You may have even blamed the victim when you had individual employees who couldn't seem to show up and do the jobs they had assured you when you hired them that they were ready and able to devote several years of their young lives to. The bad news is that they are all different now. It's a state change, not a blip. The brains of those who got smartphones (and then social media) as young teenagers are wired differently. They aren't going to snap out of it. Telling them to suck it up will just make things worse.

Humans, and other mammals, evolved to have a play-based childhood. Their developing brains need unstructured play, out of doors, with other children of various ages. Play needs to be self-organized and self-governed and self-policed. Children need to learn to take risks by taking risks. They need to climb trees. They need to scrape their knees and eat some dirt and run and jump and chase.... They need to get into minor spats with playmates and learn to make up so the play can continue. They need to get their feelings hurt and learn to get over it. They need to explore and get a bit lost and find their way again. They need to do all of this without direct adult supervision.

Once upon a time, dumb-ass hypnotherapists imagined that they could help people recover lost memories and perhaps quit smoking or lose weight. Some people who went to those hypnotherapists were encouraged to confabulate memories of past lives, and then when they were snapped back to awakeness those imaginings were locked in as apparently real memories. I agree that it would be cool to remember a past life as a pirate captain, but you'd better be able to prove it by telling me precisely where the booty is still buried. Less cool is ending up with a falsely-implanted memory of alien abduction. Not cool at all is hypnotizing kids and falsely causing them to recount and then remember ritual abuse by satanic cults. There was a lot of this going on just as the 24-hour cable-news insatiable maw for content was turning on. An entire generation of soon-to-be parents were understandably freaked the fuck out.

Hence, the last couple generations of American kids have grown up over-protected in real life. They weren't allowed to just go out and play as much as they should have. That's not to say that bad things don't happen to kids. "Six-year-old New Yorker Etan Patz was one of the very first children to have his image plastered on cartons of milk following his 1979 disappearance, and his case likewise went unsolved for almost four decades." It took until 2017 to get closure.[57] Stranger Danger is a literal one-in-a-million risk, though. Usually it's the scout leader or choir director or creepy uncle. Don't even get me started on Jehovah's Witnesses.

What's happening with GenZ is that they've been over-protected IRL and utterly unprotected on-line. You'd think that being always reachable/trackable via their smartphones would have enabled more operational freedom, but ubiquitous connectivity, including the ability to summon help if ever needed, didn't allow them to range further afield. It kept them quiet and occupied at home where they were presumed to be safe from predators. When asked why he robbed banks, Willie Sutton simply replied, "Because that's where the money is." Sutton's law applied to those who mean children harm means that they're all online these days. That's the opposite of keeping kids safe.

So now, you've got this cohort of young employees who are afraid to take risks and are anxious all the time. They don't really know how to figure stuff out, because the essence of that is trying what works and what doesn't work and then keeping track of the things that did. This is precisely how kids interacted with the world around them until they disappeared into their phones. Now they expect you to provide them with a detailed enough list of instructions that will get them the right answer, even though no such list exists. It would take more time for you to compile such a list than it would to just do it yourself, and that list would become obsolete almost immediately because the real world is complicated. Humans get paid money in the

---

[57] https://allthatsinteresting.com/etan-patz

workplace to manage that sort of complexity. Can I get an amen?

There's yet one more level of complexity to this problem. The prevailing culture among what some people call the laptop class is glorifying victimhood. Everybody is either oppressor or oppressed, and whoever has the most intersections of oppression gets to be the momentary winner. I happen to be an affluent, educated, middle-aged, cishet white man, so that makes me the prototypical oppressor. Affluent, educated, middle-aged, cishet white women have recently been moved from the oppressed to the oppressor side of the ledger. My high-school sweetheart, to whom I've been married since 1988, finds this rather surprising. "Welcome to my world," I say, "everything you say and do will be misconstrued to be used against you. You'll get used to it." Even young people who have grown up with a fair amount of privilege, though, can play the anxiety card to get some victim points. It's largely a learned behavior, but like memes, it spreads via social media.

Being chill and buckling down and figuring shit out at work would put someone at a disadvantage because everybody else gets to play the mental health Uno card whenever they want. If you're drinking coffee just now, swallow before you read the next sentence. At elite universities it's common for students to be granted accommodations for anxiety. For example, if ever their ever-present anxiety spikes, they get up to three days extra to turn in any assignment. That one's anxiety will tend to spike whenever there's an important assignment due seems to be lost on those who grant this sort of accommodation. Elvis Presley admitted that he had stage fright before every performance. Same for Luciano Pavarotti.

Your show must go on. You obviously can't abide employees bailing on deadlines because they get nervous. Swallow your coffee again. The students who have these deadline-effacing accommodations, don't have to announce to the professor that they're anxious and therefore are going to turn their assignment in a couple-three days late. They simply show up with the assignment two or three days late. Sometimes the professor will ask, genuinely concerned, about why the student didn't show up for the midterm only to be told that their anxiety spiked and they'd like to arrange a convenient time to take a makeup exam. That the makeup exam is always harder than the original should make their anxiety spike, of course. Professors everywhere apologize for letting such students loose upon the world. It makes us anxious.

Please do keep in mind that professors could never mention such things in a letter of recommendation. Most will simply decline to write a letter because there's no way to extrapolate from the classroom to the working world for students with such accommodations. Also, their transcripts are meaningless to you. You're going to have to screen for debilitating anxiety when you hire young people. It shouldn't be hard to do because they're, like, always worried. They may or may not have listened closely to their graduation speakers, especially if there were protesters chanting about various inequities elsewhere in the world.

Robert Parham[58] told UVA grads, "Whenever I speak with my students—I teach at the University of Virginia—they seem deeply pessimistic about the state of the world. We all know the reasons. Climate change is going to kill us all; late-stage capitalism is running amok; inequality is at an all-time high; racism and bigotry are rampant; gender-nonconforming and queer people are under unprecedented attack; economic anxiety has never been worse; AI is coming for our jobs; and on and on and on."

He then asks them which other time in history they might prefer. "If you're a woman, go back more than about 100 years and you become property (of your father and, later, your husband), with no voting rights and little protection under the law. If you're a person with above-average melanin levels, like me, the same (and worse) happens to you. Gender-nonconforming minorities would find the past just as terrible." He points out the quite surprising factoid that today the median human lives on the equivalent of $5,000 per year. "Throughout recorded history, the vast majority of humans lived in what we would today define as abject, dehumanizing poverty. Income and wealth inequality were measurably worse than they are today by orders of magnitude. Women died during childbirth at staggering rates. Most humans didn't survive childhood. And various forms of subjugation and slavery were the norm in nearly all societies. On these and a variety of other objective metrics, humanity has made breathtaking progress in the past 300 years." But here's the key bit: envy of others in one's peer group has been rebranded. It's now called fairness or equity. He tells the highly-privileged UVA business school grads, "The world is unfair. Deeply so. It's just that you're the lucky ones. You won the birth lottery." He tells them they don't have to apologize. "You are not evil. Being white/black/privileged/down-trodden/well-educated/illiterate/wealthy/poor/healthy/sickly/cisgendered/non-conforming does not make you bad (or good, for that matter). The sins of your forefathers are not your own. You did nothing wrong by being born."

On the subject of privilege Jerry Seinfeld said to 2024 Duke graduates, "My point is we're embarrassed about things we should be proud of and proud of things that we should be embarrassed about."

---

[58] https://www.thefp.com/p/to-the-class-of-2024-you-are-all-diseased

50 LRH WHO MUST NOT BE NAMED.

After college it's crazy how hard it can be to make friends. Especially if you work a lot and understand that you need to have platonic relationships outside of work in order to stay reasonably sane. Short of going back to graduate school, most of the young people who work for you are looking for something that will help them better themselves. They all know that binging reality TV while binge eating unhealthy food is not doing them any good. The dating pool is about dried up. There don't seem to be any fishes left in the sea, only sharks. Enough with the self-care. Young people are all craving some sort of old-school self-help group. They probably don't even realize that they're being chum for cults.

If one of your young employees gets sucked into a cult they are dead to you. I mean that in the sense that one of the defining characteristics of a cult is cutting off contact with any and all outside relationships. That's cult 101, BTW. It's a standard part of the indoctrination process. You can't tell them any of the really crazy things until they've stopped communicating with outsiders who might tell them how crazy this all is. Once you've invested enough time and energy into a cult member to get them to unquestioningly swallow whatever cray cray you're serving, the last thing you want them to do is leave. That would be a waste. Plus, they might tell outsiders how cray-cray you all are.

I have no idea how your HR department would respond if you alerted them to the obvious fact that one of your employees is now in a cult. Presumably the response wouldn't be, "Go ahead and hire a replacement or two right away." Certainly it wouldn't be, "Thank you so much for alerting us, we'll look into it right away and inform their parents. If that doesn't work we'll go snatch them back ourselves, de-program them and run them through new-employee orientation once again. In the meantime, here's the budget you need to cover the missing job function with temps."

From your perspective, having an employee join a cult isn't like them going out on maternity leave. It's like they just had a debilitating stroke. The kind of stroke where you get yourself an intubated, unconscious helicopter ride to the specialized hospital for immediate surgery, where the best-case scenario is you walk haltingly out of rehab under your own power six weeks later and maybe someday regain limited use of your formerly dominant hand. Your former employee is kind of still there inside, but you won't be able to tell whether you are reaching them at all and they aren't saying. There is miraculous medication for strokes these days, but you have to administer it quickly. Much of the lost brain function is going to be permanent.

I assume that you don't pay much attention to the social lives of your young employees. Generally speaking, that's none of your damn business. Unless it's an office romance that has the potential to affect job performance or create a conflict of interest, who's doing whom is irrelevant to you. You can tell when they're in the honeymoon stage of a new romance and when they are dealing with a recent breakup, of course, but it's in everybody's best interest for you to stay out of all that drama.

You will, however, notice a change in your employee when they first join a cult. If it's one of the many that purport to be simple self-improvement outfits, you may even see enough of an improvement that you note it in the regular performance review. Don't be reluctant to inquire about reading materials that they are suddenly engrossed in during every spare moment. It's a little tricky, so you generally want to frame things in terms of your organization's tuition-reimbursement program. It's a red flag if they're studying as if they're in graduate school but deny that they are in graduate school or perhaps thinking about going to graduate school.

Everybody else's church seems weird, so keep in the back of your mind that they might have just joined a church group. The primary distinction between a church and a cult is how they deal with people who leave the faith. I was raised Methodist, but my wife and I raised our kids Lutheran. For the last few years I've been driving oldster carpool to the Methodist church so my widowed mother wouldn't have to sit alone. I find the Methodist liturgy to be a bit passive and I like a challenging sight read first thing in the morning, but it's not like the Lutherans did anything to prevent me from going to the Methodist church down the block. I mentioned to the Lutheran pastor at my father's funeral (at the Methodist church) that I'd be here from now on and he understood. The Methodists are doing a schism right now, so that's entertaining for me.

Your young employee might also have joined a book club or have a new significant other who reads a lot and says, "Here's a book I liked a lot, you might want to read it." In both of those instances, your employee typically wouldn't be secretive about what it is that they're reading. Their co-workers would also know all about it. If your employees don't know what's going on, it's probably a cult. Some of them may have even attended one of the recruitment seminars and got weirded out. If you think one of your employees is getting sucked into a cult, you need to ask their co-workers. You need to do this before the cultist is dead to you.

You'll be able to easily find various resources online. Here's what I think is the key thing to watch for.[59] "New recruits are inducted into a secret language of signs and symbols. They're encouraged to identify as victims of the world outside and are promised a rebirth, a new body or identity within this life, or an afterlife. Recruits are taught to see the world as black or white, good or evil, us or them; and this creates tight group unity which is enforced by rote learning of the cult's slogans. These beliefs are often illogical as a test of 'true belief.' New recruits experience euphoria as part of a 'chosen' secretive group." The phrase you're looking for is "drinking the Kool-Ade" which is actually a misnomer.

You might also want to pick up a book by Steven Hassan or at least watch some of his videos. He has created an online course called *Understanding Cults: A Foundational Course for Clinicians*, which is helpful for former members, family, and all interested in learning more about the issues involved in authoritarian mind control cults and relationships.[60] Another important thing to keep in mind is that you spend a lot more time, day to day, with your employees than they do with their own parents. Almost certainly, the parents are the first close contacts that the cult insists on severing. Parents may have some idea that something's going on, but don't know what and aren't getting any answers from their child who was a sweet and loving eight-year-old about a minute ago. They might be offended or grateful or somewhere in between if you called them out of the blue to express your concern. Ideally, HR would make that call on your behalf, but you know that's not going to happen.

I fully understand that you don't actually want to get involved. It's obviously none of your actual business. You have no business policing your employees' social lives. You have enough to deal with in your own so-called social life. What's the worst that could happen? You might want to look into *Operation Clambake*, which is at https://www.xenu.net/. There's also the excellent *South Park* episode (S9.E12) "Trapped in the Closet" https://www.imdb.com/title/tt0761294/ which is really funny. But cults aren't funny. They're destructive. They enrich and empower a few at the expense of many. They are constantly on the prowl for young people just out of college trying to find belonging and better themselves.

59

https://www.psychologytoday.com/us/blog/word-less/202303/has-a-loved-one-fallen-into-a-dangerous-cult

[60] https://freedomofmind.com/understanding-cults-a-foundational-course-for-clinicians/

51 Remember when Myspace was cool?

Social media sites come and go. They're cool for kids until their parents, grandparents, nuns, etc. get involved and then they go through inevitable enshittification[61] which was 2023's "Digital Word of the Year." Some say there are some signals that TikTok is getting cheugy and kids are starting to move on. Some say people my age shouldn't use words like cheugy, but I'd like to point out that I had a slightly off-center center part in my 1981 senior photo. If I could go back in time and tell my young self only three words they would be, "Buy Apple Stock."

As Gen-Z gets supplanted by generation Alpha, I'll be quite curious to see what social media platforms start to dominate, become huge enough that the Gen-Zs complain about how kids' brains are being rotted by them, and then go through the inevitable enshittification curve and get supplanted by something else. Some of my wardrobe preferences have gone from fashionable to passé to retro to suddenly fashionable again. I haven't been able to do a center part for decades, though. I wear what I wear, prioritizing comfort over fashion, which leaves cap room in the family budget for my wife to stay impressively fashion forward. She tracks the development and growth of friends' grandchildren on Facebook for me.

Whatever social media platforms you happen to prefer, you can safely assume that the young people who work for you are all on something else. Leave them to it. That's where they hang. You showing up there would ruin it, sorry. Find common ground some other way. Maybe books. Probably not music. Certainly not politics or religion. Sports is often safe, unless you start going on about when you had enough hair to do a center part and were both all conference (honorable mention) in football and the state champion hurdler. On second thought, maybe stick to work.

61

https://www.versobooks.com/blogs/news/enshittification-the-2023-word-of-the-year

I once explained Twitter to my eighty-ish parents by saying it's like sending a postcard, which they understood right away. I subsequently started referring to postcards as paper tweets, which I've been routinely sending to my thirty-something children since my youngest went off to college. I sent her a few so she'd have something in her campus mailbox and she told me she liked that so I've been doing it ever since. They've each been saving them in a box or drawer, which may or may not be interesting to someone someday. Sometimes my paper tweets are funny enough that they snap pictures of them to post to social media, which obviously counts as a re-tweet.

I encourage my frosh to send postcards to their grandmothers who will post them to their social media walls with refrigerator magnets so all their friends can like them when they come over to play bridge. I provide my frosh with postcards and stamps, as well as instructions about where the stamps go. I assume they have to txt their mothers to find out their grandmothers' mailing addresses. I insist that my graduate students send postcards back to the lab when they travel, under pain of not getting their travel reimbursement approved. They've figured out that there are smartphone apps where you snap a picture, type in some text, and click submit. The actual postcard comes in the mail. I put them on a bulletin board in the lab.

In principle someone could send me a postcard with something hateful written on it. I happen to know that every piece of mail that goes through the postal system is photographed, so hate-mail postcards can get the sender into trouble. I don't know that it would hurt my feelings if someone mean (paper) tweeted at me, though. I already know that I'm bald and these unfashionable pants make my butt look big. There's a full-length mirror in my master bedroom.

Psychological bullying and intimidation and harassment and stalking via social media can be quite distressing, though. For young people these days, it's simply not realistic to expect them to swear off of social media entirely. They'll feel left out because they will be. They might think of you as their work parent, and you do care about their psychological wellbeing insofar as it affects their work and general mental health, but you don't need to get all up in their social media drama. Unless you sense that there's something really bad going on. Taking a break from social media can be healthy. Announcing IRL that you've deleted all your socials is a cry for help.

Help however you can. There might even be someone in your organization who is trained to deal with this kind of situation, and a discrete call from you could trigger a seemingly casual visit for an informal chat. I'm not a clinician so I don't presume to know, but then I'm at a university which has a counselling center and various other resources that I can engage in. I have a box of tissues available for students who need to cry about their chemistry midterm or whatever, but I tell advisees up front that I'm a mandatory reporting official so they shouldn't confide in me about anything at all serious.

It's not at all surprising that Congress began debating whether to crack down on TikTok just as it was losing its dominance. They were similarly late to the party with Facebook. Blaming social media for many and various problems in the world is just lazy governing. Don't even get me started on the Supreme Court trying to interpret the constitutionality of laws regulating social media. The justices still have their clerks' sneaker-net their draft opinions up and down the hallways. They literally do not use email. I sincerely hope none of them use Snapchat because the original point of that was to send pics of what's under your robe which would disappear from the aether shortly after the intended recipient opened the snap.

I'd like to have a cuddly robotic dog that followed me around for scritches, napped at my feet, and managed my interaction with social media specifically but the internet in general. I could tell my good boye to fetch information for me and sort through the search results to send me what I'm looking for. I don't see why my good boye couldn't be smart enough to filter social media on my behalf as well, and if someone tried to be mean to me growl menacingly back on my behalf. Social media posts that I want to see would be announced with the wag of a tail. Breaking news I need to hear could be announced with a woof.

Alternatively, you could just get an office dog as emotional support for your team. An actual good boye will know when someone is feeling sad because of mean tweets or whatever, and will helpfully distract from what the h8ters are saying by insisting on scritches and maybe even a walk out in the sunshine to smell all the smelly smells.

Social media platforms come and go. You can't possibly keep up with which ones your young employees are obsessed with. Even if you did get a good bead on that for a hot minute, they'll be on to something else before you know it or even because you know it. Just understand that this is how they hang out now, even when they are actually hanging out in real life. Do make them send a postcard to the office dog whenever they go on travel, though.

P.S. thanks to Corey Doctorow.[62] He points out that Millennials aren't leaving Tiktok. "After all, we are living through the enshittocene, the great enshittening, in which every platform gets monotonically, irreversibly worse over time, and Tiktok is no exception." His explanation is that switching costs and collective action problems make platforms too sticky.

---

[62] https://pluralistic.net/2024/03/21/involuntary-die-hards/#evacuate-the-platforms

52 IF WORDS ARE VIOLENCE, TWEETS AND MEMES ARE ACTS OF WAR.

Disinformation warfare provides a rubric for catastrophizing speech and maintaining a permanent state of fear and emergency. It's not our adversaries that are behind this, it's us. You're probably old enough to sense that something's off. The digital natives who work for you haven't ever known anything different. They don't know what life was like before the War on Terror. Pervasive surveillance seems fine to adults who grew up with an elf on the shelf as a holiday decoration. That the machinery which blossomed to counter ISIS and Al Qaeda, who demonstrated the effectiveness of social media, has now co-opted those methods and been turned self-ward is largely unappreciated.

I'm no genius. I'm high-functioning gifted across a broad spectrum, which turns out to be better for one's happiness. I'm highly-educated and widely-read. I'm highly-expert in certain things, but not a know-it-all, of course. I'm generally dismissive of bureaucrats who think they know better than me what's best for me. I tend to be socially liberal and fiscally conservative. I understand my own privilege and do my best to understand the differing lived experiences of others. I put some significant time and effort into staying up with the issues of the day. I often argue that people like me must always argue in favor of tolerance because in an intolerant society people like me are at risk. Although I teach (adults) for a living, I routinely self-censor because our formerly liberal democracy seems to be getting more and more illiberal. Like most of the Olds, I blame social media.

I assume you've figured out by now that I'm writing as a sock puppet. The logic behind that is to make it easier for readers to assess the explanations and arguments being put forward without falling back onto the crutch of assessing the believability of the author. Puppets can say things that puppeteers can't get away with. The audience might laugh or groan or get butthurt, but then the curtain drops and the puppet is put away. Jeff Dunham's puppet, Walter, happens to look quite a lot like President Biden, so his ventriloquist show now involves funny bits featuring Pres. Joe. In his recent Comedy Central special, filmed at the Warner Theatre in Washington, DC, "Dunham tackles how much time we dedicate to our devices, the ridiculous things we spend money on, and cancel culture in comedy." One of his other puppets, Achmed the Dead Terrorist, is the skeletal corpse of an incompetent suicide bomber used by Dunham to satirize the contemporary issue of terrorism. He is known for yelling, "Silence! I kill you!" to Dunham and people in the audience.[63]

In science skeptical disbelief is good manners. Whenever someone presents some novel findings, everybody is expected to respond, "Hol' up there Mr. Science. Let's all take a look at the evidence for that, shall we?" Politics doesn't work this way, which is why it's so jarring for scientists when science gets politicized. I watched with horror and fascination during the COVID-19 pandemic when Dr. Fauci tried to navigate both politics and science simultaneously. He did about as good a job as anyone could have, but ultimately failed. Miraculous, life-saving vaccines were politicized. Mask mandates became a way for politicians to demonstrate that they were doing something, whether the masks did anything or not. Questioning the dogma being issued from the podium got you a social-media death sentence. Hol' up there, said every scientist everywhere. Mostly under their breath, though. Even scientists were getting slapped down hard for having the good manners to question pseudo-political medical advice. It was a hard time for epidemiologists whose expertise was disregarded by their own extended families in favor of the rantings of somebody else's crazy Facebook uncle.

Lots of functionaries at all levels in all types of organizations got a taste of virtually-unlimited power during the pandemic. They got to tell people what to do and not do, say and not say, think and not think. It was intoxicating for them. After a few years the coronavirus pandemic transitioned to an endemic respiratory disease. The uncommon cold became just another common cold. People stopped being afraid and started to go about their business once again. Even octogenarians who get COVID don't have to worry. They do a quick video-chat with their doctor and take Paxlovid for five days. There's a bit of a metallic taste, but you can suck on Altoids for that. Some people still remember that we never even needed those hospital ships or tent-hospital in Central Park, but no bureaucrat wants to be accused of not doing all they could have done during an emergency. Emergencies can't go on forever, though, despite the TSA still touching my junk at the airport two dozen years after 9/11.

War is bad, we should stop having wars. That seems like something we could all agree upon. Nevertheless, there are a couple-three bad wars going on right about now. Bad people started them so good people have to go end them. That also seems like an axiom everybody agrees on. The problem when everybody agrees on something is that that consensus tends to shut off

---

[63] https://jeffdunham.fandom.com

questioning. It could be that what everybody thinks is wrong. Science is eventually self-correcting even about things that seemed to be settled science.

Your well-educated, scary-smart young employees probably agree with each other on most things. Some of those things that they wouldn't think to question because everybody just knows, are at odds with what about half of the population thinks. On many issues, the country is pretty evenly divided. The two sides aren't communicating, though. In many cases the division isn't political, i.e. left vs. right, it's generational. You may find yourself on the opposing side of your young employees because of this, which you'll find a little surprising because they're not teenagers anymore and it's not like you're old or anything. Teenagers all think grownups are stupid, of course, but as teenagers grow a bit older and learn a lot more, the adults around them suddenly get much smarter. Sometimes as they are coming of age, now-former teenagers have teenage siblings who take delight in telling them how stupid they are when they're home for Thanksgiving.

Back to war. The shooting kind, not the lobbing insults over turkey and stuffing kind. The War on Terror more or less wound down. It took a minute but we crushed Al Qaeda but then gave up and left the Taliban in charge once again. We might be still mopping up ISIS in Syria and elsewhere, but the Caliphate is kaput. It seems to me like we should be enjoying a peace dividend by now. Nope, the military industrial complex that Ike warned us about is not going to disarm. They have already identified new threats. Invisible threats. In our midst. Boo!

Actually the new, scary, invisible threats to everything that you hold dear are right there in your pocket and they are infecting the brains of our young and old alike. The War on Terror is now the War on Disinformation. You are hereby commanded to be very afraid. So afraid that you do not question what you are being told. Bad actors (insert scary-name here) are using disinformation to brainwash you.

I'm about to say the quiet part out loud. It's not a Q-drop, sheeple. It's from the Twitter Files, which X-owner Elon Musk let journalists dig through. The Deep State is no longer a pejorative term. It is a like-minded collaboration between government, NGOs and tech companies who group-think they know better than you. They learned from ISIS how effective social media can be to control populations, and now they've turned those tools on all of us to suppress things that we are skeptical of what they all agree to be true and therefore must not ever be questioned. Disinformation nabobs will let you natter on social media, but you must leave the real thinking to them.

53 IF JOHN GALT HAD TWITTER, HE'D GET CANCELLED.

"Do you know the hallmark of a second rater? It's resentment of another man's achievement. Those touchy mediocrities who sit trembling lest someone's work prove greater than their own—they have no inkling of the loneliness that comes when you reach the top. The loneliness for an equal—for a mind to respect and an achievement to admire. They bare their teeth at you from out of their rat holes, thinking that you take pleasure in letting your brilliance dim them—while you'd give a year of your life to see a flicker of talent anywhere among them. They envy achievement, and their dream of greatness is a world where all men have become their acknowledged inferiors. They don't know that that dream is the infallible proof of mediocrity, because that sort of world is what the man of achievement would not be able to bear. They have no way of knowing what he feels when surrounded by inferiors— hatred? no, not hatred, but boredom—the terrible, hopeless, draining, paralyzing boredom. Of what account are praise and adulation from men whom you don't respect? Have you ever felt the longing for someone you could admire? For something, not to look down at, but up to?" "I've felt it all my life," she said. — Ayn Rand, *Atlas Shrugged*

In sports we keep score. There are winners and losers. For some reason, we feel superior when the teams in our area beat the teams in your area. We wager real money on fantasy football. When it was pointed out to Babe Ruth that he earned more money than the president, the Babe responded that he had had a better year. Only in golf do we attempt equity by having different tee boxes. In bowling everybody rolls from behind the same line and everybody gets the same ten pins to try to knock down. Only kids get to put up the bumpers to prevent gutter balls. Nobody gets three or four balls per frame because they grew up in a neighborhood without equal access to smelly rental shoes. George Herman Ruth was an orphan, BTW. He then had to overcome the severe disadvantage of being sold to the Yankees, a horrible fate no Sox fan would wish on anyone. Typical fastballs were 85 MPH in those days, though.

In science there are winners and losers. We keep score via whether our research proposals get funded and whether anyone cites the papers we publish. Professors also keep score by how successful their own PhD students are, and the winners are those professors whose students are successful enough that they turn around and fund the next generation of students in their former research group. That takes sustained excellence over decades, but doesn't count in h-index.

Universities are divided into schools and each of those schools typically has several departments. Each department may have a few or several distinct academic programs. This sort of structure allows distinct schools and departments to focus on the particular things that their faculty think are most important. I have no idea whether the English department here teaches Rand, or if she has gone out of fashion. I assume our Business school at least suggests that MBA students read *Atlas Shrugged* sometime. For all I know they ask "Who is John Galt?" as a part of the application process.

This is on my mind because of plans to stand up a new school at America's oldest university. The name is still in flux but the core of the New School will be the departments of Physical Science, Computer Science, Data Science and Applied Science. The administration had previously proposed establishing an independent department of Data Science, but the faculty of Arts & Sciences voted it down. The Provost was so mad she refused to even talk to the Dean of A&S once that whole summer. A New School comes with a new Dean, of course, and as long as the departments who would nucleate the New School are on board it doesn't really matter what the A&S Dean or Faculty think about it. They don't get a vote. Also that A&S Dean promptly announced that she was planning to leave anyway because it wasn't a good fit for her. She didn't have another job lined up and she posted that she was taking a gap year. Don't worry though. Her husband had made a pile of money in a Pharma startup, so there's that.

It looks to me like a John Galt kind of moment because the departments that are leaving A&S are the ones that generate the grant funding and graduate PhDs and do other sorts of things that establish the place as a moderate-sized research university. Residual A&S will be impoverished. Their teaching load will have to be higher. There won't be money for travel or student research or even sandwiches at the Biomath journal club. The undergraduate teaching departments have perhaps gotten too used to taxing the graduate research departments to fund what they do.

But then, of course, they have no way of knowing what it feels like to be surrounded by inferiors - hatred? no, not hatred, but boredom - the terrible, hopeless, draining, paralyzing boredom. The New School is going to invite along only colleagues whose research productivity they can admire. It's going to be the opposite of boredom, especially during times when the rest of the University is empty simply because classes aren't in session.

Now that we're safely on the third page, let's discuss the actual reasons for standing up a New School. As you may have heard, there's a looming demographic cliff. That anti-wave of enrollment emptiness hits about 2026. There will be fewer and fewer college-age students, and lots of marginal institutions are going out of business. All of those that survive will have to adapt to the new demographic reality. Denial and delay will lead to institutional death. Tenured professors lose their jobs when that happens, and since it will be happening all across the country there will be fewer places hiring during the early years of the apocalypse. Zombie professors will be roaming the country in search of brains.

Some institutions will do surprisingly well, assuming they back off a tiny bit on social engineering and provide programs of study that are of interest to available applicants who are willing to pay actual money for education with credentials that help them get launched in their careers. Places that were already highly selective can also back off just a bit on their selectivity, although faculty will complain that students aren't what they used to be.

The big win, though, is to enhance the institutional competitiveness in areas that will be most of interest to potential students. We know from both the Great Recession and the COVID-19 Pandemic that students want to be positioned for practical STEM jobs with work-from-home opportunities. Those changes in student demand aren't transitory. Theatre or Religion can be a secondary major, but the primary major needs to be something that involves coding or engineering or some such thing. Many will argue in favor of digital humanities. Point taken; that high-res scan of Notre Dame was very helpful to the rebuilding effort. But to get noticed you need to signal to the outside world you understand and are serious about prospective students' futures by having a new flagship school in a shiny new building.

The New School will absorb lots of resources. It will get an unfair amount of positive publicity. The faculty will get paid a lot and they will drive more expensive cars than everybody in the English department except that colleague you're all jealous about because he wrote crass commercial fiction that got him an advance to finish the trilogy. Most of the funding for the New School will be NEW MONEY. Actual line items of base budget funding from the Commonwealth. Money for tenure-line faculty. Money for equipment. Money for new buildings. Just when everybody thought they'd never get another nickel from the State, there's lots of funding available, but only if they stand up a New School so their budget requests are taken seriously. There will also be money for related local economic development initiatives that help to cement town-and-gown relations because excellent graduates can start up companies here with their professors.

The New School will elevate the peer group. Rankings will go up. Applications will continue to flood the system. It will seem like every frosh wants to major in data-something-or-other instead of Chaucer, but some of them might want to double major. There will be pressure to reduce the breadth requirements the next time they revise the curriculum.

And then, all of a sudden the undergraduate population will have a few thousand more students than the last time you looked. That last part was deliberate. The Board of Visitors didn't ask the faculty's opinion on that. The Chief Operating Officer did a study to determine the financially-optimal size of the student body and the admissions spigots were opened to fill the pool to that depth. That's one of the most important reasons to have a New School. It can be the place where a couple-three thousand additional undergraduate students and a couple-three hundred additional PhD students can be trained and educated without badly distorting the culture and feel of the rest of the College.

Then there's the elephant in the room. The New School will pay more. A lot more. Faculty who can go make lots more money in industry get paid more than those who don't have that option. That's simply free-market capitalism.

"But you say that money is made by the strong at the expense of the weak? What strength do you mean? It is not the strength of guns or muscles. Wealth is the product of man's capacity to think. Then is money made by the man who invents a motor at the expense of those who did not invent it? Is money made by the intelligent at the expense of the fools? By the able at the expense of the incompetent? By the ambitious at the expense of the lazy? Money is made—before it can be looted or mooched—made by the effort of every honest man, each to the extent of his ability. An honest man is one who knows that he can't consume more than he has produced." – *Atlas Shrugged*

Law professors get paid twice as much as English professors because lawyers earn, on average, ten times as much as full time writers. Engineering professors make more money than math professors for exactly the same reason. Sorry, not sorry.

54 I'M TALKIN' 'BOUT EVERYBODY GETTIN' CRUNK, CRUNK.

Before the COVID-19 pandemic TikTok was the private domain of middle schoolers. Those high schoolers who used it all claimed that they only posted videos ironically. Then, during the forced togetherness of pandemic lockdown bubbles, tweens started making TikToks with their grandpas, which I find really sweet. Four years later, so many young people are on TikTok that the Olds are freaking out about how the CCP is using it to rot all of our kids' brains. Even the Supreme Court had to weigh in.[64]

Presumably you've noticed that the young people who work for you don't follow the news. What world affairs they are aware of are chosen by algorithms to show up in their feeds. Not to put too fine a point on it, it's an obvious case of mind control. Who is controlling the hive mind of American youth (and why) is perhaps the most important question of our age. Some other country weaponizing hyper-localized and individualized propaganda seems like something our government should get right on, even if the Senators' grandchildren all get mad and unfriend them.

Twenty-somethings are all on TikTok these days, although many of them will claim that they never post videos, even ironically. It's how they keep up on popular culture. They're starting to feel cheugy, which Wikipedia says is "an American neologism coined in 2013 as a pejorative description of lifestyle trends associated with the early 2010s." It means that when you hit your quarter-life crisis you've officially joined the Olds and can start complaining about kids these days who dress strangely and talk strangely and make inane TikToks.

One of the problems in dealing with a hive mind is that none of them

---

64

https://www.npr.org/2025/01/17/nx-s1-5258396/supreme-court-upholds-tiktok-ban

question their assumptions. Since everybody agrees, any evidence that contradicts commonly-held beliefs is easily discounted. Humans are naturally more skeptical of things that challenge their expectations and hive-minders take this tendency to the extreme. It's often called "drinking the Kool-Aid" but I think it's important to point out that it was grape Flavor Aid with a lethal combination of the poison potassium cyanide and several sedatives, such as Valium and chloral hydrate, which were chugged in Jonestown's mass murder. Note that I didn't say mass suicide. The cult members under the spell of Jim Jones weren't acting freely. It's not like they expected to wake up on a spaceship hiding behind the Hale Bopp comet.

What this means for you is that many of the well-educated young people who come to work for you will have a cult-like certainty about the things that they believe, having never really come into contact with people who believe differently. I've been teaching a freshman seminar on critical thinking since 1995. It's discussion based, and my goal is to have as much free-flowing discussion as possible. Due to the nature of the topics we discuss, there are a couple-three things in every class which someone could get butthurt about. This has become more and more of a problem.

Part of my pedagogical strategy is to play the part of a fictional character while I'm in class. This allows me to argue positions that don't correspond to what I actually think, and it frees the students from trying to guess what I actually believe. I explain to them the concept of kayfabe which is an old carney term adopted by professional wrestling and now common in reality TV. It means "always be fake" in pig Latin or something. Reality TV and WWE may be unscripted, but that doesn't mean they aren't highly produced, with artificial rivalries introduced to heighten the drama so you'll keep watching. Characters who are supposed to hate each other in the ring or on camera have to be careful to not be all buddy-buddy when out in public. That could destroy the illusion. I also introduce to my students the related concept of a "worked shoot" which Wikipedia says is the term for any occurrence that is scripted by the creative team to come off as unscripted and therefore appear as though it were a real-life happening but is, in fact, still part of the show.

A better definition of a worked shoot is partly true and partly fake. The work is acting. The shoot is parts that are real. What I tell my students is the reason I put on a bowtie before each class is because I'm getting into character for the work, but some of what they'll see is the shoot, i.e. the real me. I also explain to them that making bullshit appear effortless takes quite a lot of effort, and just because it looks for all the world like I'm just sitting around shooting the shit with them, that doesn't mean that I haven't planned out carefully all the directions our discussion might go off in.

A key part of the adulting process that your new hires might be missing, is practicing being exposed to—and listening to the perspectives of —people who think differently from themselves, without immediately shutting down mentally. Rational discussion involves considering others' arguments and replying with counter arguments. Unless they've had a class like mine, you're probably going to have to teach these skills. I understand that's not something you signed up for, but you can't have your employees getting butthurt and taking to social media to rant about you and your organization.

Here's a way you and your young charges can practice this when talking about the issues of the day, particularly those that revolve around social justice. At any time during such a discussion they should feel free to say "Ouch" on behalf of themselves or anyone they know. The expected response is "Oops" with a restatement and/or clarification of something that someone has just said which caused, or could have caused, hurt.

For example, consider the following: Is the term "trigger warning" itself a micro-aggression? I happen to not like guns and we can all agree that workplace shootings are bad, so when someone uses the word "trigger" I think of workplace shootings which nobody seems to know how to stop and that causes my anxiety to spike so I should get the day off, with pay.

If you don't think this is your problem, you probably haven't hired many Gen-Zers quite yet. It could also be that you've got some young Millennials running interference for you. That's what most organizations have been doing as a stopgap. As someone who has been looking deeply into the minds of nineteen year olds for almost thirty years, my advice is to get out ahead of the problem. Schedule time for discussion of the issues of the day, with pre-assigned readings. Recent college graduates will be OK-ish with this, because that's what they've been doing for the last few years. But here's the part that's going to seem so odd to you. You'll have to tell them which news sources to read because they don't read newspapers. They may not even realize that different news outlets each have their own slant, even if they claim with a straight face that they are fair and balanced or whatever.

Here's how I frame things for my frosh: Some oldsters have thought deeply about some issues for many years and we should value their insight, but if the Olds try to tell you there's one right way to think about social justice issues, that's a good time to say, Ouch! The Olds may or may not know to respond with, Oops!

If you're going to have Monday Morning Water Cooler *in lieu* of a staff meeting, perhaps once a month, you'll need to select an article from the Sunday NY Times, Washington Post, etc. that everybody is expected to read and come prepared to discuss. Getting them to talk may be a bit like pulling teeth, so they're going to have to be graded on class participation somehow. Check with HR about how to do that. You'll probably have to assign each of them structured talking turns, maybe even have each of them prepare two, or at most three, slides to talk from. You might even need to give everybody little Oops! signs on sticks which they can hold up as needed. You might think it goes without saying, but you'll have to actually say "phones off" during the meeting. Eventually they will actually talk at the water cooler.

55 Dr. John Millington: G.O.A.T. or Goat?

John Millington was born in London in 1779. After Oxford he trained as a lawyer, but only practiced for two years because he wanted to be an engineer instead so he did that. He also became a medical doctor, but didn't practice medicine because he wanted to be an engineer instead. He may have helped found the University of London, and did co-found the Mechanics Institute. He was a prominent practitioner, author and lecturer of civil engineering and practical applications of science. At age 50 he decamped for Mexico to superintend a silver mine and mint. It perhaps wasn't as lucrative as he expected, and there was a fair amount of political instability there in the 1830s so he decided to go back to England after making a tour through America. His wife stayed behind for the birth of a grandbaby, except that it was suddenly hard to get out of Mexico and she died. Millington ended up in Philadelphia, where he was affiliated with the medical school there and opened a store selling scientific and engineering apparatus, equipment and supplies. He was practically Ben Franklin.

The store didn't do well, but Millington did get remarried. He came to Virginia to run a gold mine west of Fredericksburg, and when William Barton Rogers left William and Mary for Mr. Jefferson's University in Charlottesville, John Millington joined the Faculty of Jefferson's alma mater in Williamsburg. The W&M Board of Visitors asked Prof. Millington to start up a formal program of study in Civil Engineering, and because there weren't any suitable textbooks he wrote one. His book was so widely used in its day that it's still available and I have a copy. Millington also found the scientific and engineering apparatus, equipment and supplies available at W&M to teach chemistry and physics and engineering and medicine to be entirely inadequate, so he converted a room of his century-old house on the palace green (now known as the Wythe House) into what we would call a Makerspace and fabricated everything he needed. He had brought chemistry glassware and such from his failed store in Philly. By 1848 he had spent $4,700 of his own money on this, at a time when the total annual budget of the College was $7,500. In addition to teaching his regular courses in chemistry and physics and civil engineering, Millington had both graduate students and medical students. He continued to practice engineering; his robust combination of formal academics and real-world applications may have made him unique in the world at that time.

In 1848 the Board of Visitors appointed an unqualified, 28-year-old townie to be Professor of Moral Philosophy at W&M. The faculty, students and townspeople were outraged. They knew this nepo baby well (he was the son of Dr. Peachey) and feared the damage his appointment would do. Moreover, there wasn't sufficient curriculum or budget to support a sixth professor. It's not like Archibald C. Peachy could pick up some of the teaching load for Millington. The controversy played out in the newspapers, of course, and these semi-anonymous letters to the editor(s) were reprinted in a pamphlet which is available on line. There are so many excellent quotes about administrative overreach. The result was that the entire faculty resigned (perhaps after being asked to do so) and the College closed for a year. Professor Millington left for Oxford, Mississippi where he co-founded Ole Miss. He took his ten-thousand-book personal library with him, as well as all of the scientific and engineering apparatus, equipment and supplies needed to teach his courses because he hadn't been reimbursed for those out-of-pocket expenses. Archie Peachey went to San Francisco during the gold rush and was part of a prominent law firm dealing in land claims and whatnot.

In the 1850 census for Oxford, Mississippi, John Millington is 62 years old and his second wife Sarah is 50. Their daughters Catherine (13) and Ann (9) as well as their son George (11) are living at home. They also have a 26-year-old Irish servant and ten Ole Miss students boarding with them. The associated agricultural census says the farm was 120 acres with 70 acres improved, producing grain and livestock.

Now look at the cropped portion of the 1850 Slave Schedule for Oxford and note that John Millington owned 7 slaves. While shocking, it's not too surprising. Just when you were ready to declare Millington the

G.O.A.T. you have to tentatively admit he's a goat. If there was a statue of him we'd have to take it down and put it away somewhere.

After several years at Ole Miss, Prof. Millington moved to Memphis to be Dean of the medical school there. Although he wasn't a practicing physician, per se, he was awarded an actual MD degree while in Philly and he taught pre-medical students while at W&M. Prof. Millington retired somewhere around age 80 and they still owned the house in Williamsburg, but there was concern about the looming Civil War, and for whatever reason they stayed in Tennessee. Of course the war came to them, and Federal troops occupied his house, so he went back north to Philly for the duration. After the war, Millington came to live with his daughter in Richmond, and he died in 1868. He's buried in the churchyard at Bruton Parish right where it backs up to the backyard of his old Palace Green house.

For 48 years, Millington Hall stood on William & Mary's campus—housing research facilities, classrooms, faculty offices, the biology and psychology departments, a greenhouse and much more. Millington Hall was demolished in 2017 and that site will be the future home of the fourth part of the Integrated Science Center (ISC4). I only experienced Millington towards the end of its lifespan. It was a terrible building from the outset, and then decades of skimping on maintenance took a bad toll. ISC4 is going to house the sorts of activities that Millington was so famous for, but we've been systematically removing slave holders' names from things, so it will certainly be called something else.

In 2026 there is a demographic cliff where the pool of college age students drops. Being highly selective, W&M is reasonably well positioned for this, but it's important to get to the right size and configuration before the drop-off happens. Our current numbers are: 6,543 undergraduates and 2,974 graduate students; 13:1 student-faculty ratio; 653 full-time faculty members across all undergraduate, graduate and professional programs. The Board of Visitors believes that means that W&M must grow by a couple-three thousand students, with that growth predominantly in the sorts of majors that will be included in a New School which won't be named for Millington. Establishing a New School is a way to signal to legislators, funding agencies and donors that W&M understands and is preparing for the post-2026 reality, so as to maximize the "new money" that is available for these activities. It's also important for attracting and retaining the best faculty and students going forward. Change is often scary but things change, especially at a place as old as The College. I mean the University. William and Mary, loved of old. Hark upon the gale. I'm not sure what that last part means. Go Tribe!

56 CONFESSIO AUGUSTANA.

The Augustana Seminary held its first class on Sept. 1, 1860 in Chicago, but the Norwegians and Swedes couldn't agree on whether one should put butter or cream on one's lutefisk. There may have been other issues, of course, but some schisms really can't be resolved. In this particular case the end result was two Augustanas, a Swedish one in Rock Island, IL and a Norwegian one in Sioux Falls, SD. Both are affiliated with the Evangelical Lutheran Church in America (ELCA) which is the biggest and most ecumenical of the many and various Lutheran sects.

The Sioux Falls Augie recently started calling themselves Augustana University, which I suppose helps them to distinguish themselves from that other Augustana back in the Quad Cities. Tiny little Baptist Sioux Falls College, just across town, is now the University of Sioux Falls, so Augie didn't really have much choice. Lots of little places are doing this right now because full-fare-paying foreign students assume college means secondary school while university means post-secondary. I don't know how many Norwegians (or Swedes) come to Augie these days.

I've never eaten Lutefisk and I was raised Methodist. Nevertheless, I could have attended Augie for free because my mother was a faculty member there for 24 years. My father was a varsity basketball player there. My mother is also an alum, earning both Associates and Masters degrees. I went to engineering school in Boston on an Air Force scholarship instead. My daughter was accepted to Augie, but went to High Point in North Carolina.

The day before my mother became Chair of the Education Department at Augie she got a large increase in salary and a sizable chunk of back salary. She was about to find out how much more her male colleagues in the Department of Education had been paid all those years. This is the 1980s we're talking about, not the 1950s. I remember that she used to have breakfast on Wednesdays with several of the other women faculty members and that that somehow made the men very nervous. My father used to go to Toastmasters, but that didn't seem to make anybody nervous, although I do remember that they all thought you were supposed to start your talking turn with a corny joke to break the ice.

In 2017, former SD congresswoman, Stephanie Herseth Sandlin was appointed the first woman president of Augie. Among her key accomplishments are "the implementation of a new governance model for the change in academic structure, which includes the College of Arts & Sciences, Sharon Lust School of Education and Schools of Business, Health Professions and Music" which is a long-winded way of saying a University needs to be composed of colleges, each with a dean. I should say that my mother was a highly-effective department chair, but had enough sense to not want to be a dean. Same goes for me.

The conversion of Education from department to school seemed to go fine. In Music things hit a bit of a sour note. The music department chair, Dr. Lisa Grevlos, who grew up in Sioux Falls and sang in the high school concert choir with me and my now wife, put her hat in the ring to be the new Dean of Music. She didn't get the job. She was unhappy about having not gotten the job. She had strong feelings about the process and outcome, and didn't get off on the right foot with the new Dean. He was from New Jersey, so probably had never eaten lutefisk, and was an orchestra conductor and podcaster who thought Vespers were old fashioned.

As he was getting settled in to his new job as Dean of the School of Music, Peter Folliard had a series of scheduled meetings with Russell Svenningsen to talk about restructuring and whatnot, but deliberately excluded the former music department chair, with her thirty years' experience, so they could engage in "real talk." The new man-dean thought that including her could make the meeting "emotional." Although he might be a perfectly fine conductor and opera tenor, who looks like he's eaten more than his fair share of krumkake, Svenningsen was an associate professor who had been at Augie for less than a decade at that point. FYI, if you're a n00b dean leading a restricting effort of this sort, you really want the old-timers to tell you what they think, especially if they feel strongly enough about the place to get emotional. Part of the function of tenured full professors is to say what they think especially if it's not what the administration wants to hear.

On April 6, 2021, Dr. Grevlos filed a Title IX complaint alleging discrimination and retaliation by Dr. Folliard and Dr. Svenningsen. Dr. Grevlos also told Augustana officials that her colleague, Dr. Paul Nesheim, a tenured full professor, would be a witness for her. Three days later, on April 9, 2021, Augustana removed Dr. Grevlos from the positions of Department Chair, Director of Vocal Studies, and Director of the Augustana Summer Music Camp. Augustana also reduced Dr. Grevlos's salary. Augustana used Dr. Grevlos's annual salary, based on 29 years of teaching, as a basis to change her teaching load and remove students from her courses, while younger, male colleagues' teaching loads stayed the same. Additionally, Dr. Folliard appointed Dr. Svenningsen to Dr. Grevlos's position as the Director of Vocal Studies. Augustana eliminated the Augustana Summer Music Camp previously led by Dr. Grevlos and established separate summer camps in 2022. Augustana appointed younger, male faculty to lead these new, separate summer camps. Also on April 9, 2021, Augustana removed Dr. Nesheim as Director of Choral Studies and Artistic Director of Vespers. Dr. Folliard replaced Dr. Nesheim as Artistic Director of Vespers.

In July 2021, Dr. Grevlos learned that her Title IX complaint would not proceed and that her concerns would be sent to Augustana's Provost, Colin Irvine. In September 2021, after Dr. Grevlos repeatedly requested her Title IX report, Augustana gave it to her. On November 12, 2021, during a meeting that Provost Irvine and Vice President of Human Resources Deanna Versteeg had with Dr. Grevlos, Provost Irvine threatened to dismiss Dr. Grevlos if Dr. Grevlos continued her "pattern of discontent," referring to her Title IX complaint. Dr. Grevlos was also told that her complaints were "problematic." The pending lawsuit I've extracted the above two paragraphs from doesn't say whether Provost Irvine thought Dr. Grevlos was being too "emotional." Here's a bit more.

On November 19, 2021, Dr. Grevlos filed a complaint with the U.S. Office of Civil Rights (OCR) regarding Provost Irvine's threat and the way Dr. Folliard and Dr. Svenningsen continued to treat her. On January 4, 2021, Dr. Nesheim also filed a complaint with the OCR regarding the way Dr. Folliard and Svenningsen treated him and his related support of Dr. Grevlos and participation as a witness in her Title IX complaint. A year later, in January 2022, the OCR referred Dr. Grevlos's and Dr. Nesheim's complaints to the EEOC and notified Augustana of such referrals. On February 25, 2022, Dr. Folliard removed Dr. Nesheim as conductor of the Augustana Choir and replaced Dr. Nesheim with Dr. Svenningsen. On that same day, Dr. Folliard removed Dr. Grevlos as conductor of the Angelus Choir and Director of Opera Theatre, which resulted in removing her from the choral area entirely. Dr. Folliard assigned Dr. Nesheim to conduct the Angelus Choir. I think it's important to point out that a significant part of the overall compensation package for a music faculty member is contained in the stipends associated with leading the various choirs, orchestras and such. An additional embedded benefit is funding to travel when the groups perform around the world.

On February 24, 2023, Dr. Grevlos and Dr. Nesheim requested a notice of right to sue from the EEOC. Three days later, on February 27, 2023, the EEOC notified Augustana of these requests. That same day, on February 27, 2023, President Stephanie Herseth Sandlin issued a dismissal for cause letter terminating Dr. Nesheim. A week later on March 3, 2023, President Herseth Sandlin issued a dismissal for cause letter terminating Dr. Grevlos. In terminating Dr. Grevlos and Dr. Nesheim, plaintiffs allege in their lawsuit now making its way through the courts that Augustana failed to follow several procedures set forth in Augustana's Faculty Handbook, such as failing to give them reasonable time to remedy any issues, failing to provide them a statement of reasons for termination based on evidence, failing to provide them a statement of charges, and failing to demonstrate that their termination was for cause.

Augie tried to get the case dismissed, of course, but got mostly smacked down. "In short, assuming the truth of these allegations, as the court must, Dr. Grevlos pleaded more than sufficient facts to plausibly allege that Augustana removed her from her positions, cut her pay, and ultimately terminated her because of her attempts to oppose Augustana's alleged discrimination. The court denies Augustana's motion to dismiss Dr. Grevlos's retaliation claim." The court also said that much of the analysis for Dr. Grevlos applies to Dr. Nesheim.

I spent some time listening with great interest to Dr. Grevlos about her saga in August 2023 because my wife and I were back in Sioux Falls for her 40th high school reunion. The wounds were still pretty raw at that point, of course, but she filled all of us concert-choir alums in on the discordance. I remain quite interested in how this all plays out, as does my wife who is a senior university administrator at the absolute apex/ceiling of her chosen profession but who serves at the pleasure of her dean because she doesn't have any of the usually iron-clad protection of tenure.

My mother is less interested, surprisingly, because she remembers what Augie was like in the 1970s and 80s when all the men were paid quite a lot more just because they were men and it wasn't considered unusual at all for the men to get together to have "real talk" because everybody assumed that women would be too "emotional." Objecting to this way that things had always been done would make you "problematic" of course. It's not surprising to my mother that not much seems to have changed. My daughter would likely respond something along the lines of: "WTF? The Augie President is a Woman." Personally, I'm shocked that President Herseth Sandlin didn't come down hard on her new boy-dean. If he has this kind of problem dealing with the women faculty members in his own school, I'm going to make a small generalization to conclude that he also has a problem dealing with his own #girlboss and that's simply not OK.

My wife is connected up with her classmates on social media, so I'm sure I'll get forwarded links to the eventual denouement. In the meantime, my mother and I are going to continue to never donate money to either Augustana. I'm curious to see what Dr. Grevlos does. Her husband is also Dr. Grevlos, BTW, except that he's a psychology professor and sports motivation consultant at the University of Sioux Falls. We may have played football together back in 1981. Having a spouse with a secure job provides financial stability, but to reach for that next rung in the career ladder only to be left hanging at age 58 is pretty disorienting. That's about the age when my mother retired, but that was an unusual situation. She was fed up with Augie and ready to be done. My father also took a generous early retirement package and they came to live a few blocks from their grandchildren, which worked out incredibly well for everybody. Augie may decide to settle the lawsuit. Drs. Grevlos may have to make a joint leap to some other part of their two-career jungle gym.

If you want to follow along at home, you can search for "Grevlos et al v. Augustana University" at Justia or wherever.[65] Also, lutefisk is cod that was traditionally dried for storage through the winter. Then when it was time to use it, it was soaked in a mixture of lye and water which rehydrated and softened it. The texture is like Jell-O and will fall apart easily so it needs to be handled carefully. It is an odd food for sure, fish-flavored Jell-O, so don't be too critical. Some people love it, others will hate it. Some people put cream on it, others slather it with butter. Neither sounds yummy.

---

[65] Grevlos et al v. Augustana University update: Settlement Conference held on 4/9/2024 before US Magistrate Judge Veronica L. Duffy. The parties succeeded in settling all of their claims. My wife tells me there's been nothing about it on facebook, so the terms of the settlement must be confidential.

57 GET OFF MY LAWN.

The College of William & Mary in Virginia was granted a royal charter in 1693. We celebrate that each February on Charter Day. When an institution is that old, it gets to claim a lot of firsts. And one almost first: Harvard was established first, but what's now W&M was in progress even before Pilgrims landed in Plymouth. Indeed, the Virginia Company of London was granted authority to establish a college by James I and investors set to work in May 1619. The institution was to be called "The College of Henryco" and college lands would encompass approximately 10,000 acres. It would have a specialized English community of trades people to build it, eventually coming under the direction of leading colonist, George Thorpe. The school was intended to have carefully selected Powhatan boys attend and learn literacy, trade sciences, agriculture, and, of course, Christianity. They likely would have studied alongside the sons of prominent English colonists as was done in the early years at Harvard. It was ended by the March 1622 Indian massacre, which killed a full one-third of the English colonists, and so it took seven decades to get back underway, which is why W&M is almost first.

Corporate takeovers can be scary for everyone. Even a mutually-agreed upon merger & acquisition (M&A) is very unsettling. Taking advantage of synergies is a euphemism for layoffs. You'll have to decide for yourself what's best for you and yours. The change might open up some rungs on the jungle gym for you. You might be better off seeking opportunities elsewhere. You do you.

The historical person you know as Pocahontas was actually named Matoaka. Pocahontas was her father's pet name for her, which roughly translates to little hellion. My mother has an ancestor who came to Jamestowne Colony in 1610 when she was a 10-year-old girl. As I tell the story, Cicely and Matoaka were besties, and when Cicely had a daughter, Temperance, in 1617, Matoaka's dad was Temperance's honorary grandpa.

There is no historical evidence to refute my assertions.

The English colonists thought the Powhattans were uncivilized savages, more or less like the Irish, and they were bringing them civilization and Jesus. The Powhattans thought the English smelled bad, which they did because they never bathed whereas the Powhattans bathed every day. There was also a fundamental disagreement about proper land usage and the whole concept of ownership.

Matoaka's father was chief of the Powhatan confederation. He wasn't naïve about what was happening when the English started showing up, because his brother, Opechancanough, had told him all about the Europeans. In 1561, Opechancanough had been captured by the Spanish and taken to Spain. He was gone for nine years. While in Spain he was treated as a prince and lived at court and got to know King Philip quite well. He saw the wealth and power of Spain, and got some sense of how large and populous the wider world was. He was given the title Don Luis, which somehow made the Viceroy of New Spain his godfather. After a few years he convinced King Philip to let him go home, saying that he could help convert everybody there to the one true faith. They stopped off in Mexico City for a few years, where he lived in the city center where his godfather was a BFD. He got sick from Euro-germs but converted to the one true faith so he was cured. This was 40 years or so after Cortez, so he was able to see how badly it had all gone for the Aztecs when the Conquistadors showed up. They eventually did head for home so he could help convert everybody there to the one true faith, but couldn't quite find it and went back to Spain for a few more years.

Since Opechancanough was a proper Catholic, he was eventually able to convince Jesuits to take him back home so he could help them convert everybody there to the one true faith. The stopped off in Havana for a hot minute, where Opechancanough got to see the trans-Atlantic slave trade in action, but did then make it up the river to his old neighborhood. Everybody there was all like, Opie, where have you been? It's been nine years, your mom has been so worried. So they got the mission established and the Jesuits sent the ship back to Spain. Opechancanough went off to see his relatives for a few months and then came back and slaughtered all the Jesuits with their own weapons. Thus repelling the Spanish M&A in 1570.

But then in 1607 the English showed up. Opechancanough saw what was happening, and he made three attempts to repel the invaders. The first is what was called The Starving Time in the winter of 1609/10. It almost worked. The stragglers actually had loaded up to go home and were already headed down the James River when Lord de la Ware's fleet showed up. Opechancanough's second try was in 1622. In a coordinated attack on Good Friday morning, a full one-third of the Colonists were massacred, and then at least as many died of subsequent disease. Cicely and Temperance and their extended, blended family were all spared. Nobody at Jordan's Journey was killed because Cicely was besties with Matoaka and Opechancanough knew exactly who lived where. Opechancanough made one final attempt in 1644, betting that the civil war in England would prevent reinforcements from being sent. He was captured in 1646 and held captive at Jamestowne where a soldier shot him in the back, presumably cross about various massacres and whatnot. Opechancanough was almost 100 years old.

That's all a bit different than the Disney version of things. The Powhattans knew the score when the English showed up. It was a similar situation in New England. Europeans arrived with their guns, germs and steel. Disruption and death followed. In many cases, coastal peoples were motivated to help the hapless colonists survive. Coastal populations had been decimated by disease, so there was actually plenty of room. More importantly, peoples just a bit inland were still unaffected by those diseases and keeping the Euros alive provided powerful allies against those long-standing enemies. As in Virginia, though, the colonists just kept coming.

You may have never heard of the deadliest war per capita in American history. It was exactly a century before the American Revolution. King Philip, whose father had kept the hapless Pilgrims from starving, marshalled the Native peoples of southern New England to beat back the invaders. There were atrocities committed on both sides. In a typical attack, the house would be set on fire and when people came running out they would be shot and then scalped. Both sides did that. The English didn't run out of guns and ammunition, so they prevailed. King Philip's head ended up on a pike in Plymouth and everybody else who wasn't killed ended up a slave or had to flee the region and join some other tribe. The English took full possession of New England because there weren't any native peoples left, or so they thought. Takeover complete. Two of King Philip's daughters were kept as house servants and eventually married Englishmen. One of them is my father's ancestor.

Land acknowledgement statements are fashionable right now. They are largely performative, but you should learn to perform them. Personally, I find them to be insulting. While it's true that the aboriginal peoples of the New World had no defenses against European diseases, that doesn't mean that the invaders simply came, saw and conquered. It's a much more complex interaction of three primary European powers and innumerable tribes and ever shifting confederations.

I grew up in Sioux Falls, SD but it's not quite right to call that the ancestral homelands of the Dakota who prefer to be called Lakota, so get that right in your acknowledgement statement please. The picture of the Plains Indians that we get from Hollywood is a brief snapshot in time. The Lakota were riverine people, having thrived for eons at the boundary between the eastern forests and western grasslands, more or less what we now call Minnesota. They got displaced, but then they got access to horses from the Spanish southwest and firearms from the French northeast and took to hunting Bison, being mean to other tribes settled in villages along the Missouri river, and doing their best to take advantage of European traders who all seemed to want Beaver pelts for some reason. The Lakota didn't discover the Black Hills until 1776, but then immediately claimed it as their ancestral homeland. The US military took that from them when gold was discovered and a son of Danish immigrants carved four giant white heads into a sacred mountain. The Crazy Horse memorial commemorates the final defeat of the Lakota and the final chapter of the merger & acquisition on this continent that started in 1492 when Columbus sailed the ocean blue and then ignored the obvious point that these continents were already full.

A few years ago I set out to answer two simple questions. When did my children's ancestors come to America, and how did their descendants end up in Sioux Falls, SD where my wife and I grew up and were high school sweethearts. Ten thousand names later, I have that answer. I also have compiled many of those stories into a book, along with the complete corpus of family photos going back generations, with several bound copies ready for when I eventually have grandbabies and they are interested in knowing who they came from.

It's comforting to know who you came from, and to know in detail the stories of your ancestors who overcame quite a lot of adversity. Genealogy is really easy to do these days because so many people did it when they were locked down during COVID. My wife and grown children sometimes get a little tired of hearing stories of their own ancestors, but I keep telling them anyway because I want them to have ancestors' stories to reflect upon rather than ruminating on their own troubles of that particular day. Usually it's some job-related issue. They're feeling stuck and don't know what move to make next. I don't presume to tell them what leap to make next on their personal career jungle gym, but knowing that so many of their ancestors made bold leaps can help give them confidence to do so themselves.

Cicely was 10 years old when she came to Jamestowne Colony in 1610. She didn't come with her parents, so that means she was a servant. It's a rags to riches story. When her second husband died in 1623 she was the wealthiest widow in Virginia, pregnant with his second child and with a five-year-old from her first marriage as well as a two-year-old to look after. She is said to be the original Southern Belle, running a 1,000-acre plantation which housed both indentured servants and extended family. Her third husband wasn't after her money because he was twice as rich as she was. He was a refugee from the massacre and was helping her to manage the plantation on the wild frontier, 30 miles up river from Jamestowne. BTW, Cicely's second husband is my father's ancestor, and we used to play golf with my kids quite often on that ancestral homeland except that we didn't know any of this so we never were able to acknowledge that history. I am sorry about smallpox, though.

We are a nation of immigrants. Each new wave of immigration adds flavor and richness to the American melting pot. That's a feature, not a bug. I personally think it's absurd to argue that more recent immigrants are somehow less American than those who came before. I got here on Tuesday, but you arrived on Wednesday, so I'm more American. That's as nonsensical as arguing that kelp-highway immigrants are somehow more American than those Clovis come-heres who showed up thousands of years later with their fancy stone tools and hunted the giant ground sloths to extinction and hence when Columbus sailed the ocean blue in 1492 the only germs real Americans had to fight back with was syphilis. It's profoundly sad that ninety-alot percent of the aboriginal peoples of what we now call North and South America died off in a century or so. Even American dogs all died when Europeans showed up with their germy dogs. Imagine how different the world would be if the Aztecs had had the foresight and technology to tell the conquistadors to "Get off my lawn!"

I happen to think America is the best country on earth, and I understand why lots of people would want to immigrate and be American too. The continent is fully populated, though, so not everybody who wants to come can do so. Those that have skills which are in high demand, come on down. That was easy. It gets a little tricky when employers are being tricky by using uncontrolled immigration as a way to drive down the cost of labor. We obviously can't have 99-cent bacon double cheeseburgers if we're paying union wages at the meatpacking plants in Iowa. That's kind of a sore spot for me because my father's father was a union leader in the first successful sit-down strike, which was for proper wages and working conditions at a large meat packing plant. The rank and file workers weren't out of work all that long, but the union leaders, including my grandfather who was the son of immigrants, were out of work for three years during the depths of the Depression. The conclusion that I come to is that a sensible guest-worker visa system makes good sense. Merit-based immigration makes excellent sense. Opening the floodgates to illegal immigration makes no sense, especially since those hard-working immigrants will be exploited in many different ways, starting from the moment when they put their families in debt to, and at the mercy of, criminal cartels who control that flow. Freely entering into a finite, mutually-beneficial indentured servitude is an entirely different thing than forced human trafficking, which is just a fancy modern word salad for enslavement.

I can't help but adding, that "calling dibs" shouldn't really be a thing here, even though Europeans seemed to think that sticking their flag on a beach they just "discovered" was a way of doing that. Then having their monarchs back in Europe "giving them" some of that land seems odd even to me. Pulling up in my driveway and planting your flag doesn't mean you own my house where I've lived for three decades. Get off my lawn!

Career Jungle Gym

Denouement.

Optimism and belief can be the difference between giving up after a setback and pushing through to find another opportunity. In your career, it's essential to maintain a hopeful attitude, even in challenging times.[66] Especially if you don't know anything about soccer, Ted Lasso provides a wide variety of excellent advice about both your own career and how to motivate young people who work for you. I've been in a dead-end job with no hopes of promotion for two decades, and I don't plan to retire for another two decades. I'm a tenured full professor. That's the top rung on the academic jungle gym. There are a variety of administrative positions that I know I would be brilliant at, but I also know that I would hate those jobs. Not my money, not my circus. My chosen work gives me joy and it pays me quite a lot of money. I can monkey around up here on these money bars however I wish. Mandatory retirement for university faculty was outlawed thirty years ago.

Most books that offer career advice would have a checklist for you to follow. I don't presume to know your particular jungle gym well enough to do that. Everybody's jungle gym is different, although a view from the top of my jungle gym might be useful as a general guide. I'll cave to the pressure of offering a checklist by using little checkboxes in the list below.

> ☐ Probably the most important thing to keep in mind is the importance of thinking through choices and then ultimately taking calculated risks. Most people are risk averse when it comes to career choices, and so they tend to be reactive rather than proactive. Believe in believe.

---

[66] https://www.antoinetteoglethorpe.com/leadership-and-career-development-quotes-ted-lasso/

- [ ] I find the differences in generations fascinating, and so I spend quite a lot of time talking to 18-year-olds and 81-year-olds and those in between. In most workplaces right now the key issue is helping 20-year-olds and 60-year-olds communicate with each other. Generally speaking, these two age groups communicate so differently that they might as well be speaking different languages. You can add enormous value by helping facilitate and translate, so it's worth making an effort to speak up and down the generations.

- [ ] These essays are arranged in no particular order on purpose. Words are not defined on purpose. Figure it out. No one else is going to figure it out for you. There is no syllabus. There is no roadmap. That probably didn't freak you out too much, because you're a grownup who's been out in the world for a minute. That sort of unstructured guidance will almost always freak out new-hires who are too used to getting too much guidance. You may have often found yourself trying to decide whether it's easier to give a detailed recipe for a young employee to follow or to just do it yourself. But now, if you're going to write down all the steps to accomplish the thing you want done, it's going to be easiest to just send that list to an AI chatbot who will follow your recipe without complaint. Your young charges need to add value to what AI can already do, and leverage those tools so that they continue to warrant a paycheck. You will have to explain to the Olds in your organization why it's worth paying naïve young employees while they learn this new world because they are going to be the ones to figure that out for the organization.

- [ ] The vibe shift that's underway right now is pretty harsh. You are less freaked out than your young employees because you've been through such things before. They haven't, and that doomscroll in their pockets will try to convince them that everything is terrible and getting worse. Believe in hope. It is demonstrably true that the world on average is getting better, year after year. It's also true that the world is unfair and always has been. I can't emphasize enough the importance of preaching tolerance, not just tolerance for those who are superficially different. What matters most is tolerance for differences in lived experience and world view. Those differences in any organization help to ensure success, especially in times of uncertainty. Group-think in an organization ensures that soon or later everybody will be wrong about something very important to the ongoing viability of the enterprise.

- [ ] Work is important, but so is time away from work. You and your employees need to get outside and touch grass, making sure that friends and family do the same. Being too connected is bad for everybody. You can model being appropriately disconnected and can help your young employees to learn to put their phones down and experience the actual world that's just outside.

- [ ] Knowing who you are and who you came from can help give you the courage to make your way up your career jungle gym. There's enormous value in looking back at your own ancestry to inform risk taking, ease anxiety about hardship, and be predictive and intentional about your own future. You come from people who made bold choices, some of which worked out spectacularly well and some which didn't. Collecting stories of courage from your own heritage will give you more courage than you think.

- [ ] I've been teaching college frosh to think critically for thirty years. That doesn't come naturally to most people, who have been taught to accept unquestioningly what teachers, coaches and such tell them. It's good manners to be skeptical and to ask for explanations and evidence. We're in a populist moment right now, which primes people to fall victim to cranks/charlatans/cults/demigods. There is a collective-stupidity problem which comes into play when people turn off questioning and critical thinking, and entire populations can then be manipulated by charismatic leaders with evil intent. So, question what people in authority tell you to think. Encourage your young employees to question you as well as the dictates from above that flow down through you. Tell them to leave their phones at home if they're going out to protest, though.

- [ ] One last thing. Keep going. Keep leaping. Work hard and demonstrate the value of hard work to your team. When you slide down or take a fall, pick yourself back up and get to climbing again. There's no reason to expect your career to be a straight climb up a career ladder because it's not a ladder. Be responsible for the choices that you make and be mindful of those in your wake. Success at all costs is not the goal. Making the world a better place is the goal. One more Ted Lasso quote: "I've heard folks say that if you love what you do, you'll never work a day in your life. Well, I gotta disagree. I love what I do, and I work incredibly hard."

Career Jungle Gym

ABOUT THE AUTHOR

As you are undoubtedly aware and at the risk of vastly understating his true worth, Dr. Ignatius B. Nowitall is: The most famous scholar in Oz; Professor of Interesting Stuff; Reformed Vegan, Ordained Pastafarian; Logician, Magician, Seer. His prize student is M.H. Wogglebug, P.E. who became Profoundly Educated and Magnified Highly by spending three years keeping warm in Prof. Nowitall's schoolhouse in the Winkie Country of Oz.

It is, of course, a testament to Prof. Nowitall's erudition and elocution that an actual wogglebug could literally leap off the screen and, donning a smartly tailored suit of clothes, embark upon a life of educating the finest student-athletes in the known world. Professor Nowitall's grand-students at the Wogglebug's Royal Athletic College of Oz in the Munchkin Country have no need for performance-enhancing drugs in order to run faster and jump higher and recover faster, for they have school pills enough to master any subject at the speed of digestion and can then practice their martial arts and exercise sciences with clear heads and clean urine screens. It's rather surprising that Nowitall has yet to win any Espys.

You'll, of course, find Wogglebug College clearly denoted on most good maps of Oz, presumably because all of those are based on the original map drawn by Professor Wogglebug and revised in accordance with the Royal Histories of Oz. You do need to pay attention to the windrose, though, because some maps show the blue Munchkin country on the left and the yellow Winkie Country to the right. Try not to get hung up on the western/eastern cartological conventions, and focus on the fact that Oz is surrounded by deserts on all sides, so any river will eventually get you to Lake Quad in the verdant fields immediately surrounding the Emerald City.

Perhaps the reason Professor Nowitall has yet to be awarded a MacArthur Foundation genius grant is that his famed schoolhouse doesn't show up on maps of Oz. He can be found on all the Aethers @IBNowitall and he gladly receives postcards via the US Mail (PO Box 767, Williamsburg, VA 23187-0767) but he doesn't like to talk on the telephone and will only answer if it's one of his seven contacts, because he gets so many robocalls from Sweden trying to sell him an extended warranty for his blue 1987 four-door Saab 900S that he had electrified more than fifteen years ago, just before GM killed Saab rather than selling it to the Chinese but still kept Buick going as a brand for no good reason which everybody knows voids the warranty, so some awards committees eventually give up trying to reach him and offer their prizes to less worthy but more available personages, of course.

Prof. Nowitall was touched by The Noodley Appendage late in life. He sometimes wears bacon cologne to test whether it offends dogmatic vegans. He never argues pastafarian theology with oh-so-intolerant gluten intolerants. Prof. Nowitall thinks sweet kale is a bit of a misnomer.

www.ingramcontent.com/pod-product-compliance
Lightning Source LLC
Chambersburg PA
CBHW050106170426
43198CB00014B/2476